T0377025

Thinking Media and Beyond

Media—old or new, in the cloud or underground—constitutes the very condition in which our world takes shape. Media is reshaped continuously, marked for both the profound effects it produces and the acceleration it exhibits. It is the medium through which we signal some of the most pressing issues we face in our ever-widening technologized world.

Written by authors working at the forefront of media theory today, this book charts an original and compelling path across various media forms, bringing to light the wonderful yet persistently unsettling role that media plays, and will continue to play, in the evolution of our future. It not only establishes media as a serious and interdisciplinary concept but also demonstrates how this concept can be developed beyond the current limited form and content dichotomy.

This book was originally published as a special issue of *Cultural Studies*.

Briankle G. Chang teaches Cultural Studies and Media Theory and Philosophy at the University of Massachusetts, USA. He is the author of *Deconstructing Communication: Subject, Representation, and Economies of Exchange* (1996) and coeditor of *Philosophy of Communication* (2012).

Florian Sprenger is Professor for Media and Cultural Studies at Goethe University, Germany. He is the author of *Politics of Micro-Decisions: Edward Snowden, Net Neutrality and the Architecture of the Internet* (2015). His research covers topics such as the history of artificial environments and the media of immediacy.

Thinking Media and Beyond
Perspectives from German Media Theory

Edited by
Briankle G. Chang and Florian Sprenger

LONDON AND NEW YORK

First published 2018
by Routledge
2 Park Square, Milton Park, Abingdon, Oxon, OX14 4RN, UK

and by Routledge
711 Third Avenue, New York, NY 10017, USA

Routledge is an imprint of the Taylor & Francis Group, an informa business

© 2018 Taylor & Francis

All rights reserved. No part of this book may be reprinted or reproduced or utilised in any form or by any electronic, mechanical, or other means, now known or hereafter invented, including photocopying and recording, or in any information storage or retrieval system, without permission in writing from the publishers.

Trademark notice: Product or corporate names may be trademarks or registered trademarks, and are used only for identification and explanation without intent to infringe.

British Library Cataloguing in Publication Data
A catalogue record for this book is available from the British Library

ISBN13: 978-1-138-50506-3

Typeset in Myriad Pro
by codeMantra

Publisher's Note
The publisher accepts responsibility for any inconsistencies that may have arisen during the conversion of this book from journal articles to book chapters, namely the possible inclusion of journal terminology.

Disclaimer
Every effort has been made to contact copyright holders for their permission to reprint material in this book. The publishers would be grateful to hear from any copyright holder who is not here acknowledged and will undertake to rectify any errors or omissions in future editions of this book.

Contents

	Citation information	vi
	Notes on contributors	viii
1	Of digits and things: opening remarks *Briankle G. Chang*	1
2	The agents of time and the time of the agents: the action of timepieces in Christian Marclay's *The Clock* *Lorenz Engell*	30
3	Affective mediality and its aesthetic transformation in Christian Marclay's *The Clock* *Christiane Voss*	45
4	'Can thought go on without a body?' On the relationship between machines and organisms in media philosophy *Friedrich Balke*	62
5	The metaphysics of media: Descartes' sticks, naked communication, and immediacy *Florian Sprenger*	82
6	*Meta/dia* two different approaches to the medial *Dieter Mersch*	102
7	Historical, technological and medial a priori: on the belatedness of media *Anna Tuschling*	132
8	Synthesis as mediation: inner touch and eccentric sensation *Karin Harrasser*	156
	Index	169

Citation information

The chapters in this book were originally published in *Cultural Studies*, volume 30, issue 4 (July 2016). When citing this material, please use the original page numbering for each article, as follows:

Chapter 1
Of digits and things: opening remarks
Briankle G. Chang
Cultural Studies, volume 30, issue 4 (July 2016) pp. 549–577

Chapter 2
The agents of time and the time of the agents: the action of timepieces in Christian Marclay's The Clock
Lorenz Engell
Cultural Studies, volume 30, issue 4 (July 2016) pp. 578–592

Chapter 3
Affective mediality and its aesthetic transformation in Christian Marclay's The Clock
Christiane Voss
Cultural Studies, volume 30, issue 4 (July 2016) pp. 593–609

Chapter 4
'Can thought go on without a body?' On the relationship between machines and organisms in media philosophy
Friedrich Balke
Cultural Studies, volume 30, issue 4 (July 2016) pp. 610–629

Chapter 5
The metaphysics of media: Descartes' sticks, naked communication, and immediacy
Florian Sprenger
Cultural Studies, volume 30, issue 4 (July 2016) pp. 630–649

CITATION INFORMATION

Chapter 6
Meta/dia *two different approaches to the medial*
Dieter Mersch
Cultural Studies, volume 30, issue 4 (July 2016) pp. 650–679

Chapter 7
Historical, technological and medial a priori: on the belatedness of media
Anna Tuschling
Cultural Studies, volume 30, issue 4 (July 2016) pp. 680–703

Chapter 8
Synthesis as mediation: inner touch and eccentric sensation
Karin Harrasser
Cultural Studies, volume 30, issue 4 (July 2016) pp. 704–716

For any permission-related enquiries please visit:
http://www.tandfonline.com/page/help/permissions

Notes on contributors

Friedrich Balke is Professor of Media Studies, with particular emphasis on theory, history, and aesthetics of documentary forms at the Ruhr-Universität Bochum, Germany.

Briankle G. Chang teaches Cultural Studies and Media Theory and Philosophy at the University of Massachusetts, USA. He is the author of *Deconstructing Communication: Subject, Representation, and Economies of Exchange* (1996) and coeditor of *Philosophy of Communication* (2012).

Lorenz Engell is a Bauhaus Professor in Weimar, Germany, and was the founding Dean of the Faculty of Media of the Bauhaus University. He is Director of the International Research Institute for Cultural Technologies and Media Philosophy, Germany.

Karin Harrasser is Professor for Cultural Studies (Kulturwissenschaft) at the University of Art and Design Linz, Germany.

Dieter Mersch is Director of the Institute for Theory at the Zurich University of Arts, Switzerland. His writings cover philosophy of media, philosophy of language, aesthetics, semiotics, hermeneutics, structuralism, and media theory.

Florian Sprenger is Professor for Media and Cultural Studies at Goethe University, Germany. He is the author of *Politics of Micro-Decisions: Edward Snowden, Net Neutrality and the Architecture of the Internet* (2015). His research covers topics such as the history of artificial environments and the media of immediacy.

Anna Tuschling is a Professor in the Media Studies Department at Ruhr-University Bochum, Germany.

Christiane Voss is Professor for Philosophy of (Audiovisual-)Media at the Bauhaus University in Weimar, Germany.

Of digits and things: opening remarks

Briankle G. Chang

ABSTRACT

Unlike our eyes, which bring us a world in images, our hands and fingers put us directly in touch with things in the world. Touching things directly, but also feeling themselves being touched at the same time, our hands and fingers are our first medium. But by remaining always contemporary – that is, always ready at hand – they are also our latest medium. Taking this observation as a starting point and keeping the idea of 'the digital' as a constant, this essay considers a few characteristics that establish German media theory as a distinct research project. It demonstrates, first, how artefacts 'become' media and, second, how this 'becoming media' can be formulated operationally and be studied in a manner consistent with the digital passages through which media appear as what they are. It is hoped that the discussion will shed some light on why and to what extent German media theory can be understood as 'posthermeneutical'.

The typewriter has been *unusable* since my last card … and the writing cannot be seen *at all*. If you think about it!! (Friedrich Nietzsche, letter of March 17, 1882)

The typewriter is a signless cloud … and through it the relation of Being to man is transformed. (Martin Heidegger)

… to comfortably acquire, so to speak, as many fingers as needed. (Carl Philipp Emanuel Bach, *True Art of Playing the Keyboard*, 1753)

At the centre of the small town where I live stands a scrubby store that looks out of character with its surroundings. Sandwiched between two popular restaurants, the storefront curves humbly almost a foot backward from the façades of the more prosperous-looking structures on both sides. Always dimly lit from the inside, the place appears tired of supporting the plastic banner hanging outside, a sign demurely advertising that it sells and services typewriters, computers, and the like (Figure 1). On sunny business days, passersby are likely to bump into a ragged office stand placed outside the front

Figure 1. Front view, Amherst Typewriter & Computer, Amherst, MA 2014. Photo by Author.

window, upon which rests an antique Remington clearly intended to attract everyone to stop and step inside. For almost 30 years, Amherst Typewriter & Computer has managed to keep its doors open, and the few changes made during its existence have been as unnoticeable as an old Remington is sturdy. To someone like me, who finds the Hemingwrite a truly useful (re-)invention, the storefront looks comforting and disquieting at once, as it keeps in view a slice of the world wherein evidence for the continuity between the *manual* and the digital is still visible and palpably *at hand*. The owner, I was told, can fix any computer problem. And he sells ink cartridges.

Every time I walk by the store, I stop and look in the front window; on rare occasions, the curious on the street join me (Figure 2). If looking begins with fascination, with being attracted, often unawares and unexpectedly, by what the attraction makes visible, what then is it that attracts me to look time and again, despite my knowing full well that what I am seeing is perhaps but an instance of programmed obsolescence characteristic of so many so-called useful things around us? And, being so attracted, what do I, or anyone else like me, see or wish to see? Staring at the broken telephone, used typewriters, tangled wires, sticky keyboards, discoloured shop signs, rusty cash registers, and the rest – all looking rather like castoffs more suited to a hoarder's basement or attic – I cannot help thinking that they are much less real items for sale than objects amassed here to re-collect themselves, to tell the story of how they came to be heaped together in this place and in this way. Crowded behind a glass window precisely because they have ceased to work as they once did, these junk-like items – all nonbiodegradable and thus surviving as witnesses to their becoming obsolete – are given a new life, a second life, or afterlife, that, in their new office by the sidewalk, proves to be no less deserved and telling than their ci-devant usefulness was assured. Surviving in this way, they (re-)appear no longer as simple castoffs or refuse saved by the store owner for reasons probably known only to him, but now, rather, as window-dressing artefacts embodying the comings

Figure 2. Interior view, Amherst Typewriter & Computer, Amherst, MA 2014. Photo by Author.

and goings that history has impressed upon them. Indeed, they are not merely associated or juxtaposed by chance but rather come brightly together to form what could be called a character archive, a *Kunstkammer* of sorts, to which they can be seen to belong and in which the story behind their belonging is symptomatically readable.

To see is to see more than one thing at once; it is to see each thing as it appears, but also, at the same time, to see things together. Looking through the store window, not only do I see all the items on display jostling together to staging the scene they do, but I also see, no less clearly, that they work jointly for an effect that each on its own would not be able to produce, an effect achieved not for the interpretation of their uses or values but, rather, by their forced yet simple juxtaposition. (It might be worth adding parenthetically that, as I look at the gadgets – all tools of communication of sorts from yesteryear, competing for my attention with equal success from behind the glass – not only do they, grouped tightly side by side, appear to look at, or speak to, one another, but, as if animated by the chorus of their own making, they also seem to look back and begin to speak to me as an interested onlooker, or to anyone who is 'there kinetically', to recall Aby Warburg's keen description (see Michaud 2004, p. 325). Indeed, if things of the past can speak to us from where we too once were, then things by which we used to reach out and touch someone in earlier times shall speak all the louder when we now stop to look at them again.)

So juxtaposed and forced to cohere, though momentarily, to create a tableau, these objects, as intimated earlier, are no longer viewed as mere curious 'fragments' picked by chance from we-know-not-where; rather, they invite the onlookers to regard themselves as 'details' of a bigger picture, as parts cut (*de-tailler*) from a missing or absent but nonetheless discernable whole – *exemplary* parts (*exempla*), that is to say, capable of coalescing our recollections and feelings associated with them into a story of a time and place that is rapidly receding but not yet completely lost, a story that their reappearance here and now helps to bring home afresh. As active parts returning onlookers' gaze from within the idyll they compose, these details, to use an expression few today would fail to find appropriate, 'constellate an image' – a flash of vision that, as if to keep alive a 'spark of hope in the past', reanimates *pars pro toto* what the onlookers still dimly remember and feel in 'a dialectic at a standstill' (though, I quickly add, without invoking 'a moment of danger' and carrying few traces of barbarism).[1] 'A strange weave of time and space', this image rather resembles a cubist collage, a 'force-image', as Carl Einstein, following but going beyond Benjamin, would call it, wherein things originally not for public display are redisplayed in their present configuration, à la the most basic of cubist methods of decomposition and synthesis in simultaneity, as reverberant objects-in-formation within one syntagm. And, as an immediate result, they are no longer seen 'as reinforcements of certainty or eternity – as "still lives" – but as "accents" in the ensemble of becoming' (Didi-Hubermann 2007, p. 7). Dialectical in nature because autonomous and unresolved, thematic and varied, static and transient, dynamic and ossifying all at once, this image – call it 'a crystal of crisis' – establishes an overreaching unity of its moments that, weaving punctuations of time into one shining solid as does any ionic structure disporting minerals deep underground, renders visible in one presentation all the silent forces responsible for the formation of these fossil objects in their current context. Furthermore, on the basis of their future perfect crystallization, it shows a picture of what their fate will be. In sight, therefore, is history as an image, but also an image as history and discourse, a historical image in situ, to whose 'momentary arrangement' averted eyes, such as mine, may turn as a knowing nod to our shared memories of writing and typing, of communicating with one another by means of tools that by now are fit only for window dressing in a secondhand store.

I often wonder how much longer Amherst Typewriter & Computer will remain in business. Perhaps the answer to this question lies nearby and is literally staring at us. Looking around in a place that is called a 'typewriter & computer' store, one might be surprised to find, among the stacks of items on display, fewer typewriters and computers than old telephones, cables, weather-beaten signs, transistor radios, and whatnot. So many lines of communication, so many channels to and from the past, and, were one to listen, so many noises from as many sources and into different directions, all in a small room. While it is hard to decode the message behind the cacophony, 'it does not seem to prevent', as Austin approbates in another context, 'drawing a line for our present purposes where we want one' (1962, p. 114). The line most readily drawn is the one stretching from the typewriter to the present-day computer – a line that runs through everything one can see in the store, on which the store itself is but a point, and from which the by-now-old media come back from their own future.

I

Man himself acts (*handelt*) through the hand (*Hand*); for the hand is, together with the word (μυνος, λογος) the essential distinction of man. Only a being which, like man, 'has' the word, can and must 'have' 'the Hand'. (Martin Heidegger)

The past is behind us, but images of the past may look at us from behind. Just as reality – now more than ever, thanks to digital technologies – appears as virtual so that we might see it, the so-called old media return as images from unexpected places, so that past reality may be recognized or be seen clearly anew. Keeping in view various writing instruments as telling dots along media's historical line, we can obtain a better grasp of a particular invariant – what can be called the deep-time core – across changing forms of modern communication technology by asking what exactly can be seen in the image that the store presents. If seeing is always taking in more than what is apparently visible; if, in each instance, what is seen always brings with(in) it what lies beyond the things actually in view; if seeing, to put it simply, is to make out figures against a background, receding one after another in organizing the view, what is it that one cannot fail to see in the image seen? To phrase the question differently, what in the image is so evident, so incontrovertibly visible, so blindingly clear, as it were, that one tends to overlook or become blind to it?

One cannot see a typewriter without seeing the keyboard, which one also sees when one sees a computer (at least for now and probably into the near future). At the same time, inasmuch as the keyboard is a man-made device, a mechanical means of alleviating the *manual* (*manuālis*) labour of writing with pen or pencil, seeing a keyboard is immediately to see the hand (*manu*) and the fingers (*digitus*), for which it is meant to be an extension and which, performing on it, write the user's activities as 'typing'. To see a typewriter is therefore to see the hand and its digits: a digital vision underwritten by an immediacy no less certain than the fact that when one sees the back of a hand, one also sees the palm and, by extension, the arm and the body, if not the exact colourations of the skin. In this instance, no media are involved, for nothing stands in between, not even the blinking of an eye. Like touch, vision does not infer; it reaches what is seen, the referent, *immediately*.

Looking into Amherst Typewriter & Computer – and this may be what attracted me to its window in the first place – one sees a snapshot of the digital age, a freeze-frame of the ongoing procession of our techno-medial world in which the widespread use of and dependence on media devices in our everyday lives are inextricably tied to the movements of our fingers, dialling, typing, keying, texting, tapping or clicking. Each of these seems to call to mind a specific media device, telephone, typewriter, data terminal, smart phone, tablet, much more readily than a lowborn pencil or other primitive writing tools which, we should not forget, must also be operated by hand when one writes. Anticipated by the store image's command, 'Look at me', what I call the digital vision in this context amounts to seeing the hand and fingers as the irreducible *hard core* (heart-*cor*) of modern communication – a proto-media touching all media from the very beginning – so that what we thought could only be achieved by telepathy, mesmerism, or magic is now easily performed by its own kind of magical touch on a keyboard or touchscreen.

The hand touches things, which are always and already there. But things are there for the hand only insofar as the hand is there as well; the *thereness* of things and that of the hand are equi-primordial with regard to each other and to the world in which they are found and may find themselves. Touching everything it reaches, touching every touch, indeed, touching itself touching, the hand is the first and the last medium, one that, prior to memory and in advance of thinking, brings things far and wide into the nearness of being. The hand, along with language, says Heidegger, is the essential distinction of man. This is not so much because 'word' and 'flesh' must meet in making man essentially worldly as because it is through the work of the hand as the original *tekhné* that man first comes to being himself by finding his place on earth, that the *who* of man first manifests in person through a *what* that anchors him *somewhere*, that is to say, 'by becoming exteriorized techno-logically' (Stiegler 1998, p. 141). To the extent that man and world are the *same* in that they belong together, as Heidegger makes plain, to the extent that man is inescapably (a) being-in-the-world, the work of the hand is what makes the world, is the making of the world, of which it also necessarily takes *care*. To be, to be human, is to care for things by hand, is to be *manual*. All labour is essentially digital labour.

Anthropology is fundamentally digit-ology. After all, while stars in the night sky may help give us the idea of points, we still need fingers to point at them and to draw a line; while love for the other keeps her image constantly in one's mind, one still needs a hand holing a stylus to trace the contours of her face on the wall of a cave or a finger to click the shutter before saving pictures of her in the cloud. And, closer to home, while the 'social web' can capture everything and everyone and put them in one's hand, it will be neither useful nor 'social' at all, unless one moves one's fingers to reach it. If 'man does not "have" hands, but the hand holds the essence of man', as Heidegger writes, if 'our writing tools are also working on our thoughts', as Nietzsche writes, then our fingers shall hold the key to what it means to be human and to what thinking may be like, perhaps well beyond the age of the world-pictures as Heidegger envisions it. Thinking thus of typewriters, computers, remote controls, touchscreens, and the like and recognizing how broad and deep their uses are across the long arc of time, we would do well, when taking stock of what is called 'media effects', to pay close attention to the role that our hands play as we negotiate the digital order of things, from which we can disengage only at our own peril.

II

Who *has done this?* – Not, *which* Man under which name – *but what system, neither man nor name, and by what modifications to itself, amid what conditions, did it become, for a while, detached from what it was?* (Paul Valéry)

To think about media, one can only begin in medias res. Just as Plato could question the allure of speech and inveigh against the Sophists because he had left the Homeric universe behind and wrote from within a world of literacy and relative rationality, just as Nietzsche and Heidegger could speak about the typewriter and mechanical writing the way they did only after writing had already been widely mechanized, I, too, can now write about writers' writings about typewriters and the like only by knowing how to negotiate a writing pad whose word-processing capacity is now taken for granted. The simple fact that writing about writing tools is enabled by writing tools leads quickly to the realization that writing about *writing* and about things written about it inevitably brings writing back to its own material conditions of possibility, to the persistence of writing techniques in the production of discourse on writing. To take the idea one step further, to the extent that inscriptive relays – as made abundantly clear by individuals as diverse as Marshall McLuhan, Claude Shannon, Michel Serres, and John Cage, among many others – cannot but leave traces of their own configurations in the process, that is, insofar as medium is inescapably legible in the message, betrayed as 'noise', as dysfunctions or accidents inherent, though usually kept at bay, in the transmission, discourses on media are at once *pre-mised* and *promised* by the media that also stand as the object of the critical act.[2] It is on the basis of this promise – an invitation to speak premised, in the same instance, on denying the speaker a perspective on his message free from the medium of its conveyance – that one can begin to speak critically about media, and what one therefore says is also de facto refracted by media's active procedures that enable the discourse in the first place.[3] That an object of critical reflection – media, in this case – and its discursive constraints are actively constructed in the same gesture of thought brings us back to the suggestion that any theory and criticism of media begins best with things already said of media, especially of those close to hand.

Following this suggestion, let me return to Heidegger and his remarks that the 'typewriter is a signless cloud'. Clouds forecast inclement weather and decorate the blue sky. To see clouds is to see wind and air, ambient ether becoming visible. It is to see, among other things, nature's ardor through the ethereal signs it gives. Clouds signify; their shapes and shades, like faces, speak. They are, as we say, indexical signs. By saying 'the typewriter is a signless cloud', Heidegger therefore does not and cannot possibly mean to deny the sociocultural significance of the typewriter for the individual and on society at large. Nor is he, in spite of his emphatic stance against industrial mechanization and against the blind faith in the idea of progress characteristic of the modern age, aiming to trivialize the useful writing tool by likening it to a thing of weather that blows itself away as quickly as it comes. With the invention of the typewriter, 'word-signs become type, and writing strokes disappear', and, as 'the type is "set" and the set becomes "pressed"', the triumph of the machine thereby announces itself, and a general becoming-technology of the wor(l)d begins to sweep over culture for the first time in history (Heidegger 1992, p. 80). At stake here, according to Heidegger, is nothing less than 'the modern relation (transformed by the typewriter) of the hand to writing, i.e. to the word, i.e. to the unconcealedness of Being'.[4] For 'in the typewriter', observes Heidegger, 'the machine appears, i.e. technology appears, in an almost quotidian and hence unnoticed and hence signless relation to writing, i.e. to the word, i.e. to the distinguishing essence of man'.[5] Signless, 'not showing itself as to its essence', 'the typewriter veils the essence of writing and of the script', withdrawing:

> from man the essential rank of the hand, without man's experiencing this withdrawal appropriately and recognizing that it has transformed the relation of Being to his essence. It is not accidental that modern man writes 'with' the typewriter and 'dictates' (*diktiert*) . . . 'into' a machine. This 'history' of the kinds of writing is one of the main reasons for the increasing destruction of the word. The latter no longer comes and goes by means of the writing hand, *the properly acting hand*, but by means of the mechanical forces it releases.[6]

Driven by the force of the machine age, whose levelling effects it unobtrusively helps strengthen and spread, the typewriter redefines man's connection to the world and hence to his own essence by *replacing* the hand with metal rods, by *displacing* manual or digital labour with mechanical power, more exactly, by placing the fingers across a keyboard that 'prints' and 'presses' rather than 'writes'. More potently and ominously than simply 'working on our thoughts', the typewriter usurps man as an essentially speaking and writing being, making him homeless by turning his 'properly acting' body into a 'mechanism', his fingers into precision-machined metal parts. And man, now a typist, is lost, is lost to himself, and is at a loss for wor(l)d, if not quite so 'poor in world' or 'without world', like a tick, a tree, or a stone.[7]

When one first learns to type, the hands are clumsy and the fingers are confused. In time, hands and fingers melt into the keyboard and all the moving parts, metal and flesh, begin to work together as one. As one continues to practice, the body and the machine all but disappear, fading quietly but actively into what one asks of the other, into what is taking place there and then, namely, 'typing'. And as 'typing' – an act unheard of and even unimaginable before the invention of the typewriter – becomes second nature to the typist and potentially to everyone in society, we can be certain that the inhuman writing tool has entered culture and history and is there to stay, firmly in the digital movements of its users whose reliance on it attests to the usefulness and indispensability of its tool-being. Just as all labour is fundamentally manual labour, all work essentially handiwork, all human productive works of late are forms of digital labour, if only because few things essential to our lives today are done without the help of our moving fingers.

The typewriter is a signless cloud, overcast 'in the midst of its unobtrusiveness', into which fingers and keyboard, body and machine, withdraw precisely because each, by the halo of coordinated concurrence, has also withdrawn or receded into the other. In fact, no sooner does the typewriter, having repressed and replaced handwriting, become the extension of man than man, who now types whenever he writes, is turned into the extension of this extension, subject, as it were, to the dictates of 'the prototype of digital information processing' that the typewriter is (Kittler 1999, p. 253). Tools are manmade and made to work for the maker, but in this case, as in every other where the user must work *with* the tool before it can work *for* him, the user turns out to be the result of his tool using, the product of a product, a tool for a tool, a prosthesis of a prosthesis. Digitally inclined or trained to be so, the typist belongs to and works for the typewriter as much as it belongs to and works for him, not unlike, say, a car and its driver. In this condition, man and machine in*form* each other: on the one hand, the former becomes a good 'worker', his body, in conformity with the rigour of the machine, having formed 'habits'. And on the other hand, thanks to those habits, a basic 'cultural technique' keeps the tools in circulation, now natural and necessary accompaniments to the productive being of human users in their digitalized habitus.[8] Although the typewriter is signless like a cloud, the effects it generates are unmistakably deep and far-reaching, and the imprints it leaves in our daily activities are clearly legible – perhaps, as said earlier, too visible to be noticed – not least in the digital exuberances of our everyday life, in which letter keys are *habitually* hit before the many jobs we are given are done.

The typewriter digitized the world, remaking it into a sphere as brave and vast as the keyboard can spin off it. It is in this world that one comes upon a place like Amherst Typewriter & Computer, a store that we, post-Gutenberg media consumers, can still visit and search within for supplies and in whose window display is reflected not only our own image as a customer but also the digital habits that are now perhaps more natural than 'second nature'. It is worth recalling here that, besides what Aristotle means by *hexis* (habit), 'habit', derived from the past participle of Latin *habitus*, also means 'to have or to hold' (*habére*). To have habits is to have a world; it is to inhabit the world by living in and as a relation to it – a lived relation that has already made this relation proper and made the world one's own. It is this relation, older than memory and hence beyond recall, that first exposes us to the world and that, through this ex-position, makes it familiar, intimate, and habitable – enabling us, from the beginning, to touch the world without touching it, without having to touch it, without knowing that we have already touched it and it us. Thanks to this relation, the world appears as an 'inward appearance' of what has already been appropriated and man, rooted in a world already proper, is understandably not able to break away from it. Having habits, therefore, not only shows the body to be the original site of labour and production but also makes the body happy by giving it the material proof that it existed really and first. Again, to have a habit is to have a world; it is to have a world one has already had; it is to have and to hold this *having* before anything can be had.

Touching things while feeling itself being touched, the hand – and by extension digital habits – can therefore be considered as the most primitive media: they are *media* because they *stand between* two things, man and world, mediating one by the other; they are *primitive* not only because there are no media more handy or older than them but also because they, mediated by nothing, are also without cause, are their own cause, or are caused by nothing but their own working. The hand is the first; our fingers are Number One. Anything that comes after comes from them.

What is first or primary, the primitive, is nonderivative. As such, it resists – perhaps has no need for – change, arresting itself calmly in time, staying the same. Seen in this light, the window display of Amherst Typewriter & Computer appears to stage, as hinted at earlier, what can be called the 'primal scene' of our digital age, in which 'ways of the hand', our digital habits, reveal themselves to be an active constant in the evolution of media forms, indicative of something repetitive and automatic because it is habitual, not merely ever-present but also actively productive of its persistence across multiple media embodiments.[9] This persistence of the digital, of our fingers' spreading wide over tools of all sorts, presents us the task of bringing to light the 'conditions of reality' of our experiences with media across their manifold iterations in history. I use the phrase 'conditions of reality' rather than 'conditions of possibility' because – unlike Kant's critical exemplar that posits the problem of the foundation of knowledge as 'the agreement of knowledge with its object', an agreement between our representations of objects and the conditions for experiencing anything whatsoever – what is called for in the present case is something like an 'archaeology of the digital'. It is a certain bio-archaeology that begins with the recognition that all media are *of* the hand and that the hand is both *in* and *outside* the media because each extends and observes the other. This bio- or chiro-archaeology aims at uncovering what could be called media's *historical* and *material* a priori, by virtue of which our lived experiences with, in, and through media are shaped and in turn shape the anthropogenic machine that the hand is (Kant 1999, p. A58, B82). The task, in other words, is to demonstrate how and to what extent our most handy organ takes sides and takes *after* the sides previously taken in structuring our world, an always and already mediated environment in which things ready at hand and present to hand are captured and abandoned in turn by every media-using being, human or machine.

For a quick illustration of how and in what sense the hand works as a constant vehicle in cultural production and of how the effects of its working can be brought to view *archaeologically*, let me draw briefly on a well-known study by Michel Foucault on the opposition between a particular practice of writing, the archive, and the act of seeing, the gaze, an opposition emblematic of modernity and modernism in general.[10] In *The Birth of the Clinic*, Foucault gives an eloquent description of this opposition when he relates the freedom of the medical gaze to the archive of written knowledge, suggesting that the artful practice of ancient medicine distinguished by the immediate relationship between doctor and patient began to decline when writing intervened. 'Before it became a corpus of knowledge (*un savoir*)', says Foucault:

> medicine was a universal relationship of mankind with itself. ... And the decline began when *writing* and *secrecy* were introduced, that is, the concentration of this knowledge in a privileged group and the disassociation of the immediate relationship, which had neither obstacles nor limits between Gaze and Speech (*Parole*): what was known was no longer communicated to others and put to practical use once it had passed through the *esotericism of knowledge*.[11]

With the introduction of writing, so the argument goes, vision became a function of the archive, and as a result, the immediacy of the unfettered gaze was obstructed – more exactly, mediated in both form and content – by the mechanism of archiving that, one should not forget, is always manual in nature. In other words, not only does the modern technology of writing separate the body from the person, but, on the basis of this separation, it also reconfigures the body as an object for the modern medical gaze, transforming it into a written figure, a documented body that is no longer accessible to the public, including patients themselves, and is from that moment on secretive and esoteric. When speech and diagnoses based on experiences and direct perception are no longer necessary, when a 'balance between *seeing* and *knowing*' struck earlier by the patient's bedside no longer needs protection, writing fills this clinical opening by allowing the patient's body to speak again – but only insofar as it also represses or renders silent what exceeds archival practice. *The Birth of the Clinic* is unmistakably 'about space, about language, about death; it is about the act of seeing, the gaze', as Foucault declares at the beginning, precisely because the clinic is where bodies and eyes, so separated by writing, are reunited in and by writing, thanks to which the body becomes alive on paper and speaks anew 'through the esotericism of knowledge'.[12]

Like many of Foucault's other works, *The Birth of the Clinic* makes clear that archaeology proves its worth best when it follows what actually matters before it finally assumes visible form, before it can be captured as 'fact' and formulated as an object of historical knowledge; that archaeology, in marked contrast to narratives in search of hidden meanings of the past, begins and ends by thinking *from* and *with* things rather than by thinking *about* them; and consequently, that observable events in time are junctures whereby multiple practices crisscross the social field, just like artefacts, expressive of events to which they bear witness, are overdetermined articulations of the artifices that produce them. To an archaeologist then, a blank sheet of paper means no less than a page written all over except that meaning appears to be absent. To continue reading (in) that absence of meaning, to read what nonetheless attracts one's attention, as should an archaeologist, is to adhere to what Foucault calls the rule of 'exteriority'. It is:

> *not* to burrow to the hidden core of discourse, to the heart of the thought or meaning manifested in it; instead, taking the discourse itself, its appearance and its regularity ... we should look for its *external condition of existence*, for that which gives rise to the *chance series* of these events and fixes its limits.[13]

If archaeology thinks from and with things and the practices associated with them, then it must steer itself away from thought or meaning so as to be as close as possible to 'the chance series', wherein meaning or knowledge appears a posteriori to the nonknowledge that this series is.

Reading the birth story of the clinic as told by Foucault, I cannot help playing back in my mind a few scenes I have long remembered, in which hands and fingers are busily performing tasks that are hardly considered 'digital' but that would not come to pass without them. As in an oddly edited movie, my mind's eye cuts from my doctor's office where my visits always begin with a medical assistant's fingers flipping through pages in a folio whose content comprises handwritings that only she can decode; to a temple in rural Taiwan where, as a child, I observed a Taoist healer extending the fingers of his right hand to the wrist of a sick neighbour for a divinely inspired pulse reading while raising his other hand into the air to grab an airborne elixir spared by flying spirits that only he could feel, touch, and see; to a modern laboratory on my university campus, where I watched a colleague, adroitly using only his index finger, move a small joystick on a metallic box to bring up a 3-D image of a human heart on a flat screen, an image he continued to bring into sharper focus by gently scraping a trackball attached to the monitor. (My colleague's conjuring-up of the flat-screen image may very well be the modern ocularcentric apotheosis of Dr. Nicolaes Tulp's manual prowess in parsing a dead man's limb famously captured by Rembrandt's artistic hand in the winter of 1632.) Across these three instances, the movement of the hand and the digits do their work in a way that is necessary to the task yet barely noticed in its performance. Appearing more moved by than moving the objects it touches, the hand somehow moves before everything else. Active and passive at once, the hand and digits are subjectively object-oriented, touching a thing while feeling themselves as things being touched; in this way, they remain objectively as a constant in a long digital evolution, during which the techniques of writing and record keeping displace immediate perception and touch as the sites and sources of medical knowledge, only to be displaced in turn by subsequent technologies whose invention, driven by the logic of '*seeing* the truth', appears to be a return to or distant copying of immediate perception. Returning to look at the

THINKING MEDIA AND BEYOND

Amherst Typewriter & Computer store again, I begin to realize that the scene framed by the front window is but a glimpse of a much larger picture, that its *dis-cursive*, that is, scattered, purposeless, appearance does not fail to betray an expansive and expanding digital network in which ancient healers, modern physicians, and onlookers such as myself are all caught, and finally that this scene, and the things one sees in it, looks at us as we look at them.

III

That one speaks stays forgotten behind what is said in what is heard. (Jacques Lacan, *L'étourdit, Scilicit*, 4, 1973: 5–52)

Whoever finds language interesting in itself is different from whoever only recognizes in it the means for interesting thoughts. (Friedrich Nietzsche, *Fragments sur le langage* (*note de travail pour Homère et la philoloie classique*), 1971)

At the end of *Gramophone, Film, Typewriter*, Friedrich Kittler writes that 'the good fortune of media is the negation of their hardware', suggesting that the meanings of things transmitted to us via various channels are abstractions, something extracted by these channels during their material embodiment and mooring in real space and time.[14] Kittler's observation, originally intended to remind the reader of the importance of transmission channels as the irreducible ground of communication systems, ought be taken further and applied to media in general. For while infrastructures, when working well, disappear, hidden naturally behind the service they provide, so too media, hot or cold, soft or hard, liquid or solid, appear only to disappear into their very performance we call mediation. Like Heidegger's tool, always already *at hand*, thinned out completely in the tool user's 'concern' or 'care' with regard to his environment and becoming present only when it fails to perform as expected, and like Lacan's 'fact of language', typically forgotten because of language's performativity, media exist according to the principle of immediate withdrawal, of their effective self-erasure in and as mediation. If media accomplish anything, it is always and already of and for the other, without which they would not come to be. In any event, media mediate and, in so doing, melt away; and in melting away, they make themselves actual.

That media appear to disappear, that they recede into what they do or are supposed to, affirms media's proper self-erasure. However, the self-erasure proper to media also confirms media's insistence and given charges, without which this self-erasure would not come to pass. Performing behind the scenes as they do naturally, media persist quietly in their own auto-immune transparency, active and passive at the same time, by virtue of which they maintain their absent presence in such a manner that whatever they transmit may shine forth successfully. This *known invisibility* of media – at once a fact and a principle of mediation in general – reminds us once again that reflection on media unavoidably begins in medias res and makes it clear that any approach to media best begins by facing this fact and recognizing this principle. This means that one begins by thinking *not* about what is said about the media and least about what is said in them (the content or the message), but about media's effective intensity, namely their historically specific influences in composing the relation between their users, us, and the environment, which is largely and continually shaped by our media-dependent habits. Placing pragmatics (what X can do) over ontology (what X is) – that is, focusing on formation rather than on what is formed – this thinking maps the shape of things as it is meanwhile shaped among things, not by charting the accumulation of knowledge governed by the cultural logic of archivization established by the confluences of forces not epistemic in nature, but by tracking the silent transformations in 'the mode of being of things and of the order' that produce, distribute, and regulate knowledge and experiences (Foucault 1973, p. 28). It is to trace, within specific coordinates of space and time, what arises as media fall and how this rise and this fall become indistinguishable in the experience of an individual, to whom these media are as indispensable as his habits are hard to change. This, then, would commit one's work to being *archaeological*, as one endeavours to unearth the *arché*, the origin, of media by laying bare their *logos*, their rules of change lying under unfolding time and, on that basis and for the same reason, to render intelligible the continuity as well as the ruptures of media's fortune as the material echoes of their forgotten *arché*.

Among all the standing research paradigms in media studies over the past several decades, German media theory represents a distinct tradition. Rather than taking as its starting points popularly recognized forms such as TV news, soap operas, music videos, and sci-fi films and read them as 'texts', as is done in much of the other work in the field, this approach places the formation of media and surrounding practices front and centre, all the while mindful of the fact that any reflection on media cannot be divorced from the condition in which it takes place and must therefore figure itself as a moment of the investigation.[15] To those who have long been perplexed by the sound and fury of 'textual analysis' draining energy and intelligence away from thinking about 'media' in a field called 'media studies', this school of thought not only comes as a breath of fresh air but also offers a welcome corrective to the all-too-quick reduction of 'media' to texts or messages. By holding fast the simple fact that 'message' and 'media' are two different things, that the former is not and cannot be a 'property' of the latter, it makes urgent the need to reclaim 'media' as a proper concept to be thought of on its own terms. The message, if it ever needs to be said, is loud and clear: media studies should be *media* studies; media theory and criticism should be media-centred.

'Media determine our situation', Kittler declares famously and emphatically.[16] The reverse is no less true. Moreover, media also determine how they themselves are to be thought of. Accordingly, to think about media – as consistently maintained by German media theory – is to consider them according to the principles dictated by media themselves, by the changing forms and functions of their iterations over time that, in combination or individually, constitute the corridor or frame of reference by which this thinking proceeds. Understood in this way, 'media' are decidedly separated from the message and made to stand on their own as a methodologically distinct object of inquiry. Moreover, bracketing or leaving behind 'sense', 'meaning', 'consciousness', and 'sense making', without which 'textual criticism' in media studies would not be as popular or natural as it has been, makes it possible to see how and why media, hereby set free from the message that tends to overshadow and appropriate them, are at each moment in history the function of an *Aufschreibesystem* – a 'notation or writing system' that, having been in place since before anyone could write or speak, makes possible the ever-present network of relays without which culture and history would not be (Kittler 1992). It is this system, this world, and its history that German media theory undertakes to recover and delineate, for it is in this world and this history that things first become media and media-things are then understood in functional or instrumentalist terms. From beginning to end, German media theory looks at this world and its history carefully the better to understand the media in it, recognizing that what it looks at also looks back. To the theorists in this tradition, then, what is important and fascinating is not the usual media spectacles but the world *of* media, in which a boomerang, X rays, light bulbs, the telegraph, cell phones, and the Internet are no more and no less media, and hence no more and no less interesting, than a pencil, a key, a bridge, a container, or Theo Jensen's Strandbeests. This is a world in which events and phenomena – the invention of the alphabets, maritime trade, and the Silk Road; the expansion of book production, the emergence of civic service, the organization of modern libraries, museums, and universities; the rise of an international postal service; the development of the space programme; the formation and expansion of a military-industrial-entertainment complex – connect to form one sprawling techno-cultural web, a multimedia mashup, as it were, that, regardless of individuals' intention and history's Reason, shapes and regulates in significant ways how we live on this planet as creatures of this nomos. This is also a world in which a book entitled *Aufschreibesysteme 1800/1900* can be written and be profitably read in that it shows, from a perspective it also makes sharp, that behind each medium, be it a typewriter, a stop sign, a tarot card, a drone, or a power grid, there is a *writing* programme, and that within each programme is a medium that diagrams it, all these upon a scene of inscription before meaning and sense take the stage. German media theory, we could say, begins where the field of media theory and criticism 'stops making sense', that is to say, where it begins to make sense of 'sense making' as a historically contingent and situationally bounded phenomenon or practice within the evolution of culture and technologies in general.[17]

It is fitting that German media theory has been characterized as 'post-hermeneutical' or 'post-structuralist'.[18] Blending distinct and often contentious articulations of post-structuralist thought into an 'anonymous episteme' and turning it into 'operating equipment' or 'hardware' productive of knowledge, it establishes, as one able critic remarks, 'a positive research program for a post-hermeneutical criticism' by 'eliciting from divergent elaborations of post-structuralist thought a collective epistemological apparatus'.[19] However, instead of rehearsing the ideas behind this characterization, I highlight two themes that, despite their ever-deferred convergence, will help demonstrate both the coherence of German media theory as a distinct intellectual project and this project's continued relevance and significance, which will only be made more apparent by future research on the notable topics its perspective ably comprehends.

Becoming media

Initially, not all things are media, but eventually, some things become media. And in this becoming, they also, before any change can be observed, *unbecome*, that is, become commonplace by staying in their proper place, or, as said earlier, by disappearing into their effects. Moreover, it is out of this unbecoming that they appear again in their truth, achieving a definite form, a self-definition, retroactively, that is, as the function of a function that is their raison d'etre and genesis. To illustrate this idea, consider television, a modern medium or medium of modernity par excellence. Television sees at a distance; thanks to it, we do too. However, compared to earlier optical devices and processes – such as the telescope, aerial photography, and cinematography – which also enabled viewers to see distant things in ways previously impossible, television succeeded in making true the idea of 'seeing at a distance', which earlier means of tele-seeing, however interesting at the time of their invention, did not. This can be seen in one of the most iconic of all televised events when television camera took flight to space on board *Apollo 8* in 1968 and, aided by satellite transmission, sent back to Earth the famous *Earthrise*, an image of the planet over the foreground of a lunar landscape in an infinite darkness (Figure 3). This image, seen again in a different view, *The Blue Marble*, taken by the crew of *Apollo 17* on December 7, 1972, and in a series of other views that followed, gives 'our world' the meaning of oneness, of 'one world', grasped in the image of one planet floating homelessly in the middle of nowhere (Figure 4).

Photographic representations of what normally lies unnoticed under our feet, *Earthrise* and *The Blue Marble* are not merely beautiful pictures; they are tangible proofs of what Heidegger called 'the uprooting of man'.

Figure 3. Earthrise. Photo: NASA.

> I was shocked when a short time ago I saw the picture of the earth taken from the moon. We do not need atomic bombs at all – the uprooting of man is already here. ... It is no longer upon an earth that man lives today,

Heidegger told an interviewer in 1966, just a month after the release of an even earlier *Earthrise* image, taken from the *Lunar Orbiter 1* (1981, p. 56). For the first time in history, the world and us in it were seen in and through the image of a 'globe', one among infinitely many others, from which man can dislodge or uproot himself by tele-imagining his dwelling to be both somewhere and elsewhere. Combined with the real-time broadcast of the moon landing a few years earlier, these images literally brought home the truth of television, according to which that medium itself is to be understood: not only did they give earthbound audiences 'a view from nowhere', made possible by the camera fitted to the spacecraft, but they also, through this hitherto impossible point of view, placed the audiences in an unprecedented structure of vision, by virtue of which they could see themselves seeing (themselves) at a distance, from a place where they were not and possibly would never be but were nonetheless present, palpably *hic et nunc*.

Television implies space travel, as live broadcast overcomes temporal gaps. However, unlike the stargazers in the past such as Galileo Galilei or Johannes Keppler, who could only *imagine* space flight as they looked at the stars

Figure 4. The blue marble. Photo: NASA.

through their telescopes, the audiences watching moon landings literally *saw* themselves travelling in space. In fact, endowed by satellite relays, they were even more space travellers than the astronauts themselves, who, although physically *in* space, could not really see themselves *travelling* in space while in flight. Sitting comfortably at home, audiences became both the subject and the object of this *tele-vision*, by having a view as free-flowing as it was exactingly coordinated by the most advanced of modern technologies applied to conquer the distance between man and heavens. Seeing everything the space camera saw, but also seeing that the camera was seeing on their behalf, the audience was perforce de-centred or re-placed, or as Heidegger says, 'uprooted'.[20] Their point of view doubled and was doubled by a representation not possible until the twentieth century, a visual image wherein their home, the Earth, appeared afresh as a home away from home, a home-double from which they could look back at the original one and see it anew as a brindled marble suspended in the middle of a boundless void of darkness.

As television took flight into space, the Earth was cut into the shape we now know. Thus brought into clear view was the planet as a spheroid, upon which everyone one becomes a member of one family and every point of departure turns out to be that to which one necessarily returns. Kant, the homebound cosmopolitan, once said cheerily, 'The spherical surface of the earth unites all the places on its surface' (Kant 1997, 6:262, p. 50). But what the televisual audience experienced while watching the moon landing was far more marvelous than Kant could have ever imagined in his geopolitical thinking. Indeed, as the space images bounced back and forth between the viewers and the scene viewed, in which the former could watch and even look back at themselves; as each view was reciprocated between heaven and earth on a screen, to which the viewers were quickly accustomed, tele-seeing became seeing itself as both seeing and being seen at the same time; and last but not least, as this tele-seeing was unseen as an artificial extension of our normal vision and became a wholly natural part of individuals' everyday experiences, television arrived at its own conclusion. Its logic has been materialized by the audiences it attracts and instructs as much as by the images that are instant and truly tele-visual in their presentation.

With the live broadcast of the moon landing, earlier visions of the earth can now be read as mere documents of bygone cosmographies. Television shrinks the earth, just as it enlarges our world. Indeed, when the world has become one *of* television, when television has gone above the cloud to shape our vision of the world, all the furious discourses about globalism or globalization perhaps are but ventriloquism of what might be called 'planetary television-ism'. Orbiting in the sky and watching everything on Earth, television watches us as we watch it. Television is our vision. And our world, as indicated above, is also our television's world.[21]

When it first appeared, television was not (yet) the medium it is today. It became 'television' when, working felicitously with concurrent technologies that helped assert its capacity for real-time broadcast, it reappeared to assume its current form, recognized and recognizable only against a world that it has helped to shape and in which its presence is taken for granted, its content is easily consumed, and its effects are quietly lived. If 'the principal effect of tele-technologies is to disassociate', or as I would say, to free, 'co-presence from its condition of co-localization', television gives its viewers the veritable experience of co-presence, of being with others both here and elsewhere and, as result, reconfigures the 'structure of intersubjectivity' con-stitutive of contemporary visual culture (Chamayou 2015, p. 251, 254). Common as common-sense, ever-present in its unseen presence, television stands uncontestedly as *the* medium of our epoch. The tip of the twentieth century's televisual *dispositifs*, it is also the sum and summit of all media in history. Television turns the world into a televisual world and us into a television audience, each making sense of the other because both have been televised and will continue to be televised in the medium's ongoing becoming.

Media and their conditions of actuality

To speak of media's becoming is to recognize that while the concept of media remains consistent, stable, and independent of history, conceptions of media are a function of time. Media develop in a tempo that does not correspond to that which orchestrates our experience of them; media's time is different from ours. But it is also to recognize, beyond acknowledging the historical nature of things and the possibility of their delayed effects, that media's becoming necessarily takes place under conditions that are in no small part of its own making.[22] One of the questions any theory of media must ask is how and why the becoming of media unfolds the way it does, how media constitute themselves or are constituted as such. The task is the classic project of being *critical*: beginning with the question of how it is possible that the given is given, it proceeds to lay bare what are called the 'conditions of possibility' of the given and our knowledge of the given within the limits set by these conditions.

At the same time, however, since those conditions are not given but belong to the reflection upon the given, that is, since the conditions of possibility of the given are of a different order than 'the empirical', the critical project, exemplified by Kant's architectonic, tends toward becoming 'transcendental', toward finding the foundation for knowledge and experience within reason and reason alone. This transcendental tendency, aided by the concomitant belief in the validity and transparency of reason's self-reflection, enables critical philosophies to regard themselves as *foundational*, prior to human cognition, whatever the domain to which they are applied. This tendency also makes it possible for 'the transcendental' and 'the empirical' to appear in one sentence, precisely because what one can expect to know of the latter is justifiable and justified only on the condition that one fully comprehends the former.

'To be called *critical*, a philosophy must never take *this is the way it is* for an answer but must see in such a posture the starting point of its inquiry' (Descombes 1986, p. 103). What is true of critical philosophy in general goes as well for German media theory. But German media theorists are no Kantians, certainly not in the classic sense. Instead of looking to reason and finding in it the ground of our knowledge about things – which risks being mired in circular reasoning, as in the case of Kant – German media theory casts its gaze downward to the world, toward things *made* and *found* in the environment. In this perspective, media are no longer seen as objects captured by thought or represented by our ideas about them, but as creaturely entities silently active in their practical insolubilities, as 'artifacts', that is, 'equipment(s) (*das Zeug*)', to use the word as Heidegger intends it. For it is in the fact of media as artefacts that one can begin to recapture them in their natural habitat and begin to see them as examples of themselves, to see them, that is to say, in both senses of the expression, their *making* and *becoming*. Media are artefacts, buried, forgotten, or alive; this is the starting point of German media theory as a media-centred approach, a point to which it also must return.

To media scholars mindful of the distinction between media and message, between form and content, between hardware and software, notwithstanding the occasional possibilities of contamination of one by the other, this valorization of things over concepts is not surprising, for it is the former that ultimately determines the *expressions* that the latter are and keeps these expressions in readable form. After all, just as writing requires at its practical minimum a pointed object and an impressionable surface, and just as typing requires a typing instrument, paper cut to fit it, and fingers to press its keys (not to mention all the things that must be in place before a bodily act can be understood or recognized as *writing* or *typing*, rather than some kind of behavioural miracle or accident), all media, to the extent that they are techno-cultural objects, necessarily depend for their configuration and effect on matter, their material, indeed, maternal, substrate. Just as 'lightning rods have to be grounded' and work through the mute substrate of the earth, as George Steiner says in another context, 'even the most abstract, speculative ideas must be anchored in reality, in the substance of things. (Steiner 2015, pp. 33–34).

To see media as thing so anchored is to recall them to where they naturally are, to regard them not just as points or nodes within a network of objects but as vibrant actors working together to compose the whole in which they are found and which they index by their communications. Conversely, it is also to regard them as potential media actors that bring into view what may be called the 'media archipelago', the sprawling surface of relays marked by deep-time techno-cultural changes atop historical terra firma. Upon that surface, technical objects, reverberating among themselves and animated by their human contact, and human users, always and already part machine and for that reason more or less than human, push and pull against one another and, in this commerce, finally settle and take form as 'media': old or new, emergent or convergent, they tell the story of their capture in and by the space and time that they also define and modify. The media archipelago by itself does not tell the whole truth of media's becoming, but it helps to delimit a region wherein that becoming is first legibly inscribed and can consequently be read. Mapping this region will make the truth of media known.

German media theory has been described as 'archaeological' and come to be known by the name of 'media archaeology' since its successful import into the Anglo-sphere over the past decades. Setting aside the issues of naming and translation, let me take up the idea of 'archaeology' again as a lead-in to one final observation that I hope will keep in sight the promises German media theory makes. However it is pursued in different contexts, archaeology would be nothing if it were not guided by a desire and, consequently, a search for origin (*arché*). Since any such search implies that what is being searched for must have been lost but is nonetheless recognized and recognizable in the traces it leaves behind, archaeology necessarily tracks back and forth between the present and the past: it must follow the traces back to the past so that it can understand how the present first follows its now-lost origin in the manner its traces suggest. German media theory is archaeological because it follows this principle, because it travels back and forth through spaces where the so-called media are either forgotten or yet to take shape. Such an approach proceeds with the recognition that the identity and conception of media and the search for their origin are best understood from within media's own overdetermined becoming, which is the media archaeologist's task to reconstruct and to make known in situ, that is, archaeologically. As a result, what one finds in media archaeology is not simply a past-oriented forensic exercise bent on bringing back 'what really happened' but instead a programme directed and distinguished by its concern for the present and the forces of change within it. What is revealed by this approach is not the past of media as such but their becoming visible in concrete formations, not a chronological parade of media interpreted as successive iterations of a prototype but media's buried biography apprehended here and now, that is to say, not the conditions of possibility that justify the presence of media on the basis of what lies beyond experience or beyond their world, but media's often unnoticed 'conditions of actuality', in the light of which what appears most current or contemporary is most archaeological or originary, and vice versa.

Seen from this perspective, media and the environment they establish reveal themselves as an integrated ensemble comprising artefacts, tools, their users (human as well as nonhuman), and the techniques or procedures by which the latter are tied (or not tied) to the former. Evolving with the elements it involves, this media ensemble embodies an effective com*pli*cation that, were one to follow archaeology's rule of exteriority, can be un*fold*ed or ex*pli*cated into interconnecting practices (*pli*, ply: to perform or work diligently and regularly, namely, to practice). These practices, in their regular dispersion, constitute our *Umwelt*, a world of sedimentation and heritage, in which we, as creatures of habits, coexist with others in an ambient surround that is our mediated order of things. By keeping its eyes on this *Umwelt*, German media theory maintains its 'critical' and 'post-hermeneutical' import. And it accomplishes this not only because it recognizes its own analyses in the making of its objects but also because of its pragmatist commitment to viewing media as thingly composites, as complex objects reducible, once equated by archaeological translations, only to like objects with which they form what we ordinarily mean by 'infrastructure'. If it is true that media determine our situation, it is equally true that their 'conditions of actuality' determine the situation in which this determination itself is determined and consequently grasped. Media mediate; this fact and our understanding of it are themselves mediated facts. These facts constitute the proper site of media archaeological labour. For anyone interested in exploring this site, German media theory is one of best guides available.

As I sit here trying to conclude this essay, I pause to look at the keyboard of my laptop, above and around which my hand and fingers come and go. Like the typewriters in the computer shop in town, the keyboard under my palms will soon be a thing of the past, replaced by something that probably will require no finger to operate. When that happens, when writing tools render fingers or any bodily involvement unnecessary, what will *writing* mean? Will it make sense any longer to speak of writing *tools* as tools, something useful for something or someone other than themselves? From these questions, I cannot help but see an avalanche of further questions that press us to think beyond typewriters or any writing instrument calling into question everything we used to do with our fingers. Indeed, at a time when the world is written in code and 'the globe is in our computers'; when all things that have evaporated into air can be made solid again by media; when we should 'give thanks to our computer', as Kittler reminds us, 'whenever it is summer'; when machines have become cognitive or intelligent, even meta-cognitive or meta-intelligent, while humans are fast becoming post-human; when, amidst all these, control and command are all but indistinguishable, what are we to do with our fingers by which we first touch the world that, through them, touches us as well? (Spivak 2003, p. 74, Kittler 2006) In the quaking media order now and in the near future, how do we, if there is still a 'we' to speak of, stay in touch with ourselves? How do we, without that by which we reach out and touch things, including our own body, carry on in a world into which we are digitally thrown and thrown away? As I resume typing my paper, I remind myself and say, as the younger Bach did so long ago, 'to comfortably acquire, as it were, as many fingers as needed'. For me, for now, my hand is all the earth I know!

Finally, let me say a few words about German media theory and the essays gathered under this singular, insufficient, yet inclusive name. Naming a research tradition 'German media theory' risks freezing or reifying what is in fact ongoing, lively, variable, and indeterminate. With this risk in mind, we gather the following essays in one place in the belief that they may be read with most profit in this manner. The objective is not to show how inadequate the label 'German media theory' is to the rich work done by scholars in the German-speaking world, but to invite critical reflections on and participation in the project these essays represent.

Seven essays are included in this issue, and they address as many topics, some regarding specific media forms, others bearing on questions of concept formation critical to media studies as German media theory conceives it. Taken together, they offer readers an overview of a tradition of media-centred research distinguished as much by its horizontal reach as by the vertical grafting its perspective asks of those who adopt it. The goal is not to show consensus among the contributors but to exhibit the kind of intelligence reflected in these works and invite critical examination and productive follow-ups. Written by authors in whose work German media theory continues to grow, these essays are one another's best critics and interpreters. They do not need our advertisements. It is to them we should now turn.

Notes

1. Much has been written about Walter Benjamin's idea of 'image' and its relation to politics, history, literature, theology and more. And to characterize this idea as surreal, dadaist, or cubist does not say much. Let me simply repeat what is already widely recognized: Benjamin regards images in terms of their property as writing (*Schrift*) rather than as representations. For him, image is a 'constellation of resemblances' (*Ähnlichkeitskonstellation*), a constellation 'in which the has been (*das Gewesene*) comes together in a flash (*blitzhaft*) with the Now to form a constellation' (50). See Benjamin (1989). It is clear that the word 'thought-image' (*Denkbild*) Benjamin uses lies at the heart of his work on thinking-in-images (*Bilddenken*).
2. For a discussion on how the ideas of 'promise' and 'premise' relate to the concept of communication, see Chang (2012).
3. The interplay of medium and message is widely explored in literature and modern arts. See, for example, Dworkin (2013).
4. Ibid., 81.
5. Ibid.
6. Ibid., 80, emphasis mine.
7. It is well-known that Heidegger thinks poorly of animals in relation to man. According to him, while the stone is worldless and the human is 'world-forming', animals are 'poor in world' or 'without world'. His view on the animal, as expressed in *The Fundamental Concepts of Metaphysics*, has been the subject of much critique recently, most notably by Giorgio Agamben and Jacques Derrida. See, for example, Agamben (2002) and Derrida (2004).
8. For a brief description of cultural techniques, Geoffrey Winthrop-Young's remarks regarding Bernhard Siegert are as good as anyone can find:

   What theorists like Bernhard have in mind when they speak of *Kulturtechniken* are operational sequences involving actors, things and practices that, coming together, give rise to established cultural practices. Out of these operations emerge those entities we subsequently tend to view as the foundations of culture. Actors will turn into subjects, things will turn into objects, and practices will be seen as either emanations of careful, deliberate planning toward a predetermined goal or the natural results of essential human traits.

See his 'More Things in Theory Than Heaven and Earth are Dreaming Of'. A Conversation with Winthrop-Young (2014)

9. One can freely speculate on the similarity of typing and playing the piano in free jazz as discussed by Sudnow (1983).

10. For a good example of an archaeological approach to media, see Vismann (2008).

11. Foucault (1978, p. 55). Emphases mine.

12. For comparative historical reasons, it is worth mentioning that the critical relationship between manual labour and a productive and harmonious society was not lost on the emperors and government officials of China's classic period, as reflected in the historical documents, such as *Discourses on Salt and Iron* (鹽鐵論), produced in 81 BCE. Reflecting on the relationship between technological developments, moral economy, politics, and bodily discipline in Chinese history, Francesca Bray observes:

> For late imperial officials, agriculture and [the] textile industry were a symbolic pair, inseparably bound together as 'correct' male and female work. From this perspective, farming and weaving were the activities that constituted at once the moral and material foundation of a proper social order; they were technologies that produced subjects as well as material goods. (p. 168)

See Bray (1999).

13. Foucault (1972, p. 229). Emphases mine.

14. Kittler, *Gramophone, Film, Typewriter*, p. 221.

15. I recognize that the label 'German media theory' is quite vague and cannot capture within clear boundaries all the works that share at best 'family resemblances'. Given the precedent, however, I hope I can be excused for adopting it anyway. For a quick survey of the literature, see, for example, the special issue on new German media theory in *Grey Room*, edited by Eva Horn (2007) and the special issue on cultural techniques in *Theory, Culture & Society*, edited by Geoffrey Winthrop-Young et al. (2013).

16. Kittler, *Gramophone, Typewriter, Film*, p. xxxix.

17. Wellbery (1992), 'Post-Hermeneutical Criticism', p. iv.

18. Ibid., i–xxii.

19. pp., ii–iv.

20. That seeing and being seen are inseparable in tele-vision is one of the ideas explored by many artists, such as Trevor Paglen and Ted Molczan. Discussing their well-known project *The Other Night Sky*, in which the viewers are invited to watch the Keyhole satellite as it arcs over North America, Paglen remarked that 'truth is something like a point of light reflected in the evening sky, able to be seen by anyone who bothers looking through a telescope'. But what is the truth in this case, a truth that comes only through a telescope pointed to the night sky? Perhaps nothing but the affirmation that in television seeing and being seen constitute one act, that seeing is at once seeing oneself being seen in return, that seeing is, in a word, counterseeing. This becomes unmistakably clearer when one realizes that by design the Keyhole satellite 'looks down back to earth rather than to space'. The truth referred to by Paglen is then not so much what is made visible to the viewers as the very logic of visualization at a distance. See Happé (2009). For a discussion on the sovereign power of digital

visualization, which *The Other Night Sky* attempts to speak back to but remains complicit with in the end, see Hu (2015, esp., Chpt. 4).

21. An observation contrasting cinema and television can be made here. In *Apocalypse-Cinema: 2012 and Other Ends of the World*, Peter Szendy discusses a cluster of popular films and draws on the concept of *cineworld*, borrowed from Jean-Luc Nancy (Cinéfile et cinémonde, *Trafic*, no. 50 [Paris: P.O.L, May 2004]):

> The cineworld is a world, our world, whose experience is given its schema – in the Kantian sense of the word, meaning made possible in its configuration – through film. This does not mean our world answers only to this schematism, but it counts it among its conditions of possibility. When we look at a landscape from a train, plane, or car, or else when we suddenly stare at an object, a detail on a face, or else an insect with a certain movement of our gaze, when we discover a street's perspective, when we appreciate an incredible, strange, surprising or worrisome situation but also while we drink a coffee or go down a staircase – these are all occasions that lead us to think or to say, 'This is out of a movie'. Nancy even goes so far as to say that the cinema is nothing less than an 'existential' in Heidegger's sense of the term … (p. 143)

Like cinema, television too configures the world as we experience it. However, while we certainly find ourselves reacting to things or experiences like those mentioned above by saying, 'This is out of a movie', we rarely say, 'It is out of (a) television' or 'It is just like on television', when we undergo similar experiences. This suggests that television, inserted as it is in our environment like a piece of furniture or home appliance, is much more potent and conclusive than cinema in determining our view and sense of the world, precisely because of its inconspicuous presence. Seamlessly integrated into our 'ontic' existence – and hence more tool-like, in Heidegger's sense of the term – television is more an 'existential' than cinema.

22. I do not mean to suggest the idea of 'deep time' as it has been used in the already sizable literature in media studies and beyond but only to highlight the fact that nominal attribution of 'media' to things or objects is the combined function of the environment in which these objects are found and the unspoken conception of communication that helps pick out certain objects therein and call them media. For example, few of us are likely to think of shoes, fire extinguishers, cargo containers, keys, or doors as media unless we are cued to do so. See, for example, Siegert (2012).

Acknowledgements

The editors would like to thank Leuphana University Lüneburg and the Ministry for Sciences and Culture of Lower Saxony, Germany, and the Department of Communication, University of Massachusetts, Amherst, for their support in the preparation of the essays. Thanks also go to Samantha Gupta, Tina Ebner, Ina Dubberke, and Randi Heinrichs, who provided help for this project from the institutional side.

Disclosure statement

No potential conflict of interest was reported by the author.

Notes on contributor

Briankle G. Chang teaches Cultural Studies and Media Theory and Philosophy at the University of Massachusetts, USA. He is the author of *Deconstructing Communication: Subject, Representation, and Economies of Exchange* (1996) and co-editor of *Philosophy of Communication* (2012).

References

Agamben, G., 2002. *The open*, trans., Kevin Attell, Stanford, CA: Stanford University Press.

Austin, J.L., 1962. *How to do things with words*. Cambridge, MA: Harvard University Press.

Benjamin, W., 1989. N (Re The theory of knowledge, theory of progress). trans., Leigh Hafrey and Richard Sieburth, In Gary Smith, ed. Benjamin: philosophy, history, aesthetics, Chicago, University of Chicago Press, 38–83.

Bray, F., 1999. Toward a critical history of non-western technology. In T. Brook and G. Blue, eds. *China and historical imperialism: genealogy of sinological knowledge*. Cambridge: Cambridge University Press, 158–209.

Chamayou, G., 2015. *A theory of the drone*. New York: New Press.

Chang, B., 2012. Of 'this' communication. In B. G. Chang and G. C. Butchart, eds. *Philosophy of communication*. Cambridge, MA: MIT Press, 3–32.

Derrida, J., 2004. *The animal that therefor I am*. trans., David Wills, New York: Fordham University Press.

Descombes, V., 1986. *Objects of all sorts*. trans., Lorna Scott-Fox and Jeremy Harding, Chicago: University of Chicago Press.

Didi-Hubermann, G., 2007. Picture = rupture: visual experience, form and symptom according to Carl Einstein. trans., C.F.B. Miller, *Papers of surrealism: the use-value of documents*, (7), 1–25.

Dworkin, C., 2013. *No medium*. Cambridge, MA: MIT Press.

Foucault, M., 1972. *The archaeology of knowledge*. trans., A.M. Sheridan Smith, New York: Harper & Row.

Foucault, M., 1973. *The order of things*. New York: Vintage Books.

Foucault, M., 1978. *The birth of the clinic*. trans., Alan Sheridan, New York: Vintage Books.

Happé, A., 2009. A night sky of mystery and wonder. *Totorontoist*, August 17, 10:00 PM.

Heidegger, M., 1981. 'Only a god can save us': the *Spiegal* interview (1966). In T. Sheehan, ed. *Heidegger: the man and the thinker*. Chicago: Precedent Publishing, 45–67.

Heidegger, M., 1992. *Parmenides*. trans., Andre Schuwer and Richard Rojcewicz, Bloomington: Indiana University Press.

Horn, E., 2007. Special issue on "New German media theory," ed., Eva Horn, *Grey room*, (29).

Hu, H., 2015. *A prehistory of the cloud*. Cambridge, MA: MIT Press.

Kant, I., 1997. *Groundwork of the metaphysics of morals*. Cambridge: Cambridge University Press.

Kant, I., 1999. *Critique of pure reason*. Cambridge: Cambridge University Press.

Kittler, F., 1992. *Discourse networks 1800/1900*. trans., Michael Metteer with Chris Cullens, Stanford, CA: Stanford University Press.

Kittler, F., 1999. *Gramophone, film, typewriter*. trans., Geoffrey Winthrop-Young and Michael Wutz, Stanford, CA: Stanford University Press.

Kittler, F., 2006. Lightning and series – event and thunder. *Theory, culture & society*, 23 (7–8), 63–74.

Michaud, P.-A., 2004. *Aby Warburg and the image in motion*. trans., Sophie Hawkes, New York: Zone Books.

Siegert, B., 2012. *Doors: on the materiality of the symbolic. Grey room*, (47), 6–23.

Spivak, G. C., 2003. *Death of a discipline*. New York: Columbia University Press.

Steiner, G., 2015. *The idea of Europe*. New York: The Overlook Press.

Stiegler, B., 1998. *Time and technics, 1: the fault of Epimetheus*, trans. Richard Beardsworth and George Collins, Stanford, CA: Stanford University Press.

Sudnow, D., 1983. *Ways of the hand*. Cambridge, MA: MIT Press.

Szendy, P., 2015. *Apocalyptic cinema: 2012 and other ends of the world*. New York: Fordham University Press.

Vismann, C., 2008. *Files: law and media technology*. trans., Geoffrey Winthrop-Young, Stanford, CA: Stanford University Press.

Wellbery, D., 1992. Foreword: post-hermeneutical criticism. In Kittler's, ed. *Discourse networks 1800/1900*, trans., Michael Metteer with Chris Cullens, Stanford, CA: Stanford University Press, vii-xxxii.

Winthrop-Young, G., 2014. Interview with Geoffrey Winthrop-Young by Melle Kromhout and Peter McMurray. Digitalpassage.wordpress.com [Accessed 14 December].

Winthrop-Young, G. Iurascu, I., and Parikka, J., 2013. Cultural techniques. *Theory, culture & society*, 30 November (6), 3–172.

The agents of time and the time of the agents: the action of timepieces in Christian Marclay's *The Clock*[†]

Lorenz Engell

ABSTRACT

In the first part, the paper introduces and unfolds the concept of the 'agent' as contrasting the concept of the 'actor'. The figure of the secret agent, for example, in TV series and feature films, serves as a starting point for the analysis of the concept. Agents, efficient only if they work independently and under command at the same time, having agency only within networks of both persons and artefacts, cross the border between the active and the passive. Even objects can be addressed as agents, an example of which is the clock. As an agent of timemaking, the clock has an intricate relation to intentionality; it hence deals with the problem of how and under which conditions it is possible to qualify certain operations, such as the functioning of a clock, as actions without actor. In the second part, the concept of the clock as agent of time and the time it produces is re-examined against the backdrop of Christian Marclay's video installation *The Clock*. It shows that, according to Marclay's work, the intersection of two operations of timing, namely the punctuating rhythmic measurement on the one hand, and the opening of undefined duration, creates moments of continuous presence in which an operation can change its course, take another direction or be affected by another. The overlapping of time measurement and duration thus opens up the necessary possibility for intentionality to inscribe itself into the chain of operations which then can be ascribed the quality of action, however, infiltrated with passivity at the same time.

Introduction

The following discussion, in conjunction with Christiane Voss' contribution to this volume, is concerned with Christian Marclay's film installation *The Clock* and the media-philosophical perspectives that it unleashes. The problem of the mediality of affects and the affectivity of media was discussed by Christiane Voss in her contribution to this volume. There, the primary approach

---

[†]This article was translated by Peter Kuras.

to the phenomena of media concerned passivity, concerned enduring, concerned suffering. Here we will proceed from a complementary position and observe the moving image's cluster of medial relationships from a perspective that treats it as a generally active and effectual phenomenon. We are concerned here with the question of action, and especially with the strangely configured and mediated, externally controlled action of agents (as distinguished from autonomous, self-centred actors, and also a network of actors).[1] We ask: how does a configured and relationed field, 'agency', handle, in a single process, that which is addressable as 'action', and how are purportedly passive and purportedly active moments related thereby?

In order to investigate this question, one need only take Marclay's work literally, and with superficial seriousness. *The Clock* is actually nothing other than a secret agent film, not only because it contains a surprising number of clips from this genre of film and even pieces from secret agents' television series, but also because it has a main character, a protagonist, who rapidly reappears, changed into different disguises and functions, in always changing contexts. She seems to guide, directly or indirectly, the figures who appear in a single scene, to influence them or manipulate them. She also seems to be under foreign orders on a mission from outside, and even gets us, the viewers, wrapped up in her mission, which we can only gradually guess at or deduce. It is finally revealed that these orders are at once given by, carried out by, and aim to serve the agent herself. This need not impress us all that much. In the final analysis, there are lots of secret-agent films. *The Clock* is nevertheless extraordinarily relevant as a secret agent film because the agent the film is about is the clock. And this poses a three-part challenge to consider. The first consideration is whether, and how, an object like a timepiece can be an agent; the second is what it means to be an agent, to act as an agent and be treated as one. Finally, the function of time in the action of agents, in the action of film, and in acting through film is naturally an especially important consideration in this case.

These challenges present important and fundamental media-philosophical questions. The contours of media philosophy, as they have been developed to date, have been shaped by two main tendencies, in addition to the continuous work towards defining the term 'medium'. The first tendency is directed towards the materiality and the materials of media. Initially this might include specific materials such as glass, air, electricity, celluloid, paper, or silicone, but can also be directed to compact and complex objects, artefacts, and material-technical things and arrays, such as projection apparatuses, buildings, keyboards, optical instruments, instruments of measure, tools, and writing implements. They do not shape meaning (*sinnförmig*) in and of themselves, but they have a stake in the experiences through which meaning and reflection are accomplished, and which are made possible and rendered by media. This interests media philosophy.[2] So much for the first tendency. The other tendency of media philosophy by contrast is characterized by the conception of media as relative and relational, and therefore constituting operatively effective measures: media are relative and relational, they enter into relational structures and are themselves only addressable as relational structures. Media make interventions into already existing relations possible or actual, and are therefore demarcated from the referentiality and changes that are performed within those relations.[3] Media only become media when they establish the relationships that they themselves will eventually embody.

It is exactly this process that Christiane Voss has described using various concepts of affective flow of events – the affectual capacities and capacities of binding, which media embody, and which she explicated with the help of the concept of the 'loaned body' and of 'anthropo-medial relations' (Voss 2006, 2010, 2013). In her contribution to this volume, she placed special emphasis on the temporality of medial relationships and demonstrated their importance with regard to *The Clock*. The affective field, as she demonstrated, is composed in a genuinely dynamic and temporal manner, and exactly this reciprocal moulding of time and affect through film is explored in *The Clock*. The material assembly, on the one hand, and the relational and operative capacities, on the other, which media compile, render, and constitute in and of themselves, cannot merely be terminologically and conceptually described and understood. They are, rather, themselves embodied, observed, and represented (*Darstellung*) by and in media.[4] As in Voss' considerations in this volume, the following remarks assume that this clearly takes place in the film.[5] The film fosters at least an implicit knowledge of the relationship between materiality and operativity, including of the transformation (*Umschlag*) of the one into the other, which media – in various ways – recognize and distinguish. This filmic knowledge of the operativity of a definite (*bestimmten*) material apparatus, namely that of the timepiece, is made available to us by Christian Marclay's installation *The Clock*.[6] And it accomplishes this in a filmic form, as a film and through the progression of a cluster of unique filmic operations. And for these filmic operations, the timepiece, whose operativity *The Clock* reveals, has a central function, from this point on as the timepiece in the image and the timepiece as image in the film.

The thesis that undergirds the following considerations is, however that, from the point of view of the film, it is not only relationality and operativity, as an always already ordered flow of events, that are under discussion. Instead, even the agency and the execution of actions are called into question. Affects, as Voss has shown, are always already directed and do always give direction, and as such they are in no way purely passive or pacifying. They are always already effectual: they expand and have a transformative power.[7] Under certain conditions this transformation can assume the form of action, and it is exactly this transition – from affect to agent – that we can observe in *The Clock*. The distinction made directly in this thesis between the mere discharge (*Ablauf*) of an operation on the one hand, and the intentional performance of an operation on the other, is naturally highly problematic and contentious. It has been negated or retracted by many theorists of media because it seems to contradict the most fundamental concern of media philosophy, namely, the strict insistence on materiality.[8] Action always seems to refer back to difficult measures such as intention or even the will, consciousness, or subjectivity, which always themselves require a foundation in an organized materiality.

On the other hand, one can distinguish a conception of action using the term 'social action', as employed by Hannah Arendt, for example, that seems to avoid making recourse to these problematic residues by avoiding the moment of intentionality of action.[9] The systems theory of Niklas Luhmann works in exactly the same way, even if it places the concept of action far behind that of communication by explicitly imputing an assumption of causation, defining action and experience in contradistinction to one another (Luhmann 1984). In addition, it takes consciousness, more or less in Husserl's usage, to be the fundamental medium of psychic systems – that is to say, it is a measure explicitly based on intentionality (pp. 60–63). In Latour's conception of a sociology expanded through materiality, which deviates substantially from systems theory, even intentionality must be comprehensible as an effect of material operations, such as in Voss' reading of affects.[10] It is, in adherence to the creed of media theory, the product of complex mediations, for example, of subjectification, or also, at once straightforwardly and with difficulty, of mere imputation.

Actions can be differentiated from mere operations when intention can be ascribed to them (Davidson 1980). It is possible that there are conceptions of action, such as Arendt's, which largely manage without the motivation of intentionality. But once a purpose has been ascribed or imputed, it is clear that an operation has become an action. Operations – complexly distributed, as always, across diverse relations – proceed from multiple relations of causation, and are describable as the unwilled effects of material or medial orderings (*Anordnungen*). Actions, by contrast, are marked, and can be qualified as actions through the minimal condition of the attribution of some kind of authorial intention to them. More precisely: actions are only observable under certain conditions, namely, that an authorial intention has been attributed to them, an intention that, naturally, need not come to fruition, but can and will in such cases be read as failed, latent, confused, or broken. Actions are operations that are observable as a consequence of constantly changing intentions, intentions realized or frustrated, effective or inconsequential, accomplished or failed, completed or aborted. In the investigation of the turning of mere operations into actions, our aim will therefore be to determine the conditions under which intentionality can be observed in materially effectual operations (Mersch 2010).

It is exactly this observation of the emerging of intentionality and hence of agency from non-intentional and non-active conditions that seems to be the special function of the medium of film. Film, perhaps especially the feature film, observes and describes material and concrete assemblies – the scenery and necessarily also gesture, costuming, and acting, even extending as far as lighting, framing, mise en scène, and montage. Yet it also refers to actions, to operations with imputed intent (Engell 2011). When talking about film, as a rule we talk first and foremost about the action of characters, but also we frequently refer to the intentions of the film's producers or the film industry, if not about the intentions of the filmmaker. For film as a medium, and in individual films, and especially in the constant transition between the two, what concerns us is the constant back and forth between material operations and intentional actions. This transition necessitates, according to the following thesis, an arbiter – the figure of the agent. And concerning the film medium, the question arises to which extent and under which conditions we accord agency to the moving image itself.

In this transition from object to action and from causality to intention, the timepiece plays a prominent and exemplary role as an agent in film. The timepiece is operative in and of itself, simply because it functions. But beyond itself, it has the function of at least triggering (*auslösend*) other operations, and possibly even of prompting action. This is particularly true [, therefore] for the filmic images of timepieces. Gilles Deleuze has described the filmic image of timepieces as not only preceding all action, but also enabling it and serving as the condition of possibility for the transmission of the functions of human consciousness. This occurs through close-ups of faces, of things, especially of the timepiece, and of the filmic image itself (Deleuze 1989). The timepiece, furthermore, has the function of triggering (*auslösend*) action.[11] It allows me as a viewer, for example, to assume a fictive simultaneity between two sequential scenes. The timepiece is also capable of acting on foreign orders, those of the narration or those of the narrator. Finally, film even ascribes the timepiece a kind of quasi-action of its own, something that Marclay's film offers every occasion to investigate more closely.[12] The timepiece wakes figures in film, for example, or lets them stay awake. It drives them forward, it sends them off, lets them linger or wait, it reminds them of something. The clearest case is probably that of the alarm clock. It converts mere operativity into the aforementioned quasi-action. This is true even when it encounters a point of resistance, of indolence, when it countermands the cherished intention of a character in the film – namely, the wish to sleep further. The alarm has its order, an order that sometimes means turning against figures in film. The order can make a character into the object of a mission – whoever sets an alarm anticipates exactly this deviation between a current order and possible later resistance, whether in the world or in a film.

To this extent, I sometimes encounter my own expressed intentions when the alarm goes off, in the same way that a figure in a film does: as a delayed external effect, which the alarm exerts on figures in film as it does on viewers or on real people. The relationship between mechanical causality and the intentionality of an order is stretched through the act of projection, but it is certainly not completely severed. One can treat the alarm as though it had its own intention, can trust it, curse it, or even attack it physically. The alarm can even make its own additions to, or wrench something from (*abgewinnen*), this order. In the case of a well-regulated dispatch of an order, this would be the alarm's unique ability to preserve, expand, and transmit the order through time. The alarm can carry out its own share better or worse, or not at all. Timepieces can be imprecise, they can malfunction, or they can be reset by a third party. It is amazing how imprecisely the timepieces in Marclay's compilation sometimes run, and how difficult they frequently are to read. I will return to this point.

In various ways, all of this is true for not only alarms, but also other uses of timepieces. Although it is an object, a timepiece nevertheless simultaneously embodies both an order and the intention to which it is set, the intention of its user. Naturally, I, or any person, can either reject or accept the orders received or read from a timepiece, just as the timepiece itself can fail or be imprecise. This is true all the more so because a timepiece does not simply assume my own orders and transmit them through time, but instead becomes available to a diverse and complexly distributed group of commanders – to employers as well as to subordinates, and to partners of all kinds, some of whom we already refer to as 'dates'. Highly complex organizations belong on this list too, for instance, systems of travel or information, whom we refer to as [if they were] actors: not only 'the train', 'the airline', 'the university', but also 'the television' and 'the film' ('the film starts at seven'). My timepiece tells me: 'I have to hurry.' All of these mixed, and then defunct, givers of orders, sometimes including myself as Other, at an earlier or later time, all exercise their effect on me through the same agent, the clock. And this is also exactly the way in which I subordinate myself to the directives and decrees of the timepiece. The same holds true for the action of watching a film. Very much like the characters in a feature film, I, as a spectator, let myself guide through (diegetic) time by (film) time, for example, by ordering time along with actions qualified as prior to other ones, as simultaneous or as subsequent.

It is exactly this condensed and reified, then deferred and erased set of orders, which constitutes the particular figure of the agent. We can confirm this wonderfully with reference to the personal agent, the secret agents of film and television series. Although it is not the theme of this essay, a diversion will be instructive. In the somewhat older secret agent series *Mission: Impossible*, which I will briefly introduce as a representative example here, each episode begins with the now legendary opening ritual (White 1991).

Someone – after a few repetitions we know that it is a member, and usually the head, of a troop of secret agents – finds or receives a tape or tape player along with a file under conspiratorial circumstances. When the tape is played, the voice that gives the agent the orders offers a few explanations and then indicates that the mission can be rejected. If it is accepted, however, then it never existed: the commander (*Auftraggeber*) has no identity, and all institutions that might be responsible for giving such orders will deny that it ever existed. Once the message has been played, the tape, clearly acting automatically, catches fire, so that the transmission of the orders is untraceably deleted. Agents are thus not autonomous and self-centred actors. They are instruments that proceed according to the intentions of another under foreign orders, characteristically even under multiple orders simultaneously, which might even exclude one another (Mersch 2010). But they tend to destroy the giver of orders in the process. They become, when they accept the assignment, the bearer of a foreign purpose that has no bearer. To this extent, that which they do remains an operation which, however, is simultaneously a quasi-action or a weak, deferred action.

The agents in the series can only carry out the orders by breaking them down into numerous smaller assignments, and distributing the single operational steps. The original intention of the total plan is no longer recognizable in these individual steps. The purpose of the individual actions often remains concealed from the viewers, and even from the filmic agents, and is only revealed through a montaged interaction of sequences across the whole of the episode. The carrying out of the mission therefore requires the absolutely perfect adjustment of the individual actions of the team, which always consists of multiple operators. This coordination requires a timeline above all else, and the most precise synchronization of the individual actions and their scrupulously preserved succession. The whole operation has to run like clockwork. The coordination of the individual actions required for the completion of the orders is achieved especially through the relationing and distribution of time, and this, once again, takes place mostly through timepieces. Timepieces and shots of timepieces are naturally required for this. Close-up shots of Timex watches, or snappy zooms to wall clocks or clocks in towers – images that can be integrated directly into the repertoire of *The Clock* – therefore belong to the standard vocabulary of *Mission: Impossible*.

The agents encounter the display of time through time pieces in various forms as they set about bringing the orders, or the foreign intentions, to completion. Technical means of communication, such as radios, apparatuses of surveillance, video links, or televisions, however, are also frequently employed. These devices can help achieve simultaneity, but can also be manipulated to give false information. It is again surprising how often in *The Clock* telephones, radio apparatuses, or television screens appear alongside, and simultaneously with, timepieces in order to support this synchronization.

The timepiece functions in yet another capacity as a model of a reified agent. In no small part, the agents distribute their orders, they transmit the individual steps by delegating them to all manner of sophisticated devices and unique apparatuses, just as we saw in the case of the alarm clock above (Latour 2002). This is related to yet a further capacity of the agent. On one hand, they use these devices; on the other, the devices use them. Devices and people tolerate and deal with one another. Their reciprocal mastery is absolutely indispensable for the completion of the mission. This places significant demands, however, first on the suitability of the instruments, and second on the agent's dexterity, control of their own bodies, their skill. What makes for a good agent is less abstract intelligence and purely representative knowledge than skill and cleverness – that is to say, situational, contextual, and network-specific gifts. The agent is, therefore, to use Bruno Latour's terminology, a figure of Odysseus' type: not wise and educated, but rather a clever and tricky 'polymetic' (from the Greek 'polymetis') figure (p. 212).

Deception is the most important form of cleverness which agents must master. Agents are constantly employed as figures of some sort – as the very figures they are (cause themselves to be) in their iconic, self-presenting quality, or 'in disguise' as other figures, which they occasionally cause themselves to operate as. For this purpose, they once again employ material aids, not only masks and uniforms, but also all kinds of apparatuses for projection and illusion. The manipulation of timepieces belongs once again, and with surprising frequency, to the deceptive operations of the agents in *Mission: Impossible*. Finally, however, a highly developed capacity to deviate from the original script of the entire plan and to improvise is needed if the original plan must be changed due to adverse circumstances or other unforeseeable difficulties – that is, if everything does not run like clockwork. The demand for improvisation occurs in all cases, and repeatedly through the malfunctioning of the devices employed. Something like the self-will (*Eigensinn*) of the object is made evident through this resistance of the material.[13]

An important characteristic of the agent as a figure of agency remains undeveloped in *Mission: Impossible*: the agent's capacity for treachery, or at least to subvert the mission. The agents' relative passivity which we have stated above is in its core ensured by their fundamental approachability, their receptivity to command, qualities presumably due to the ideological and didactic context of the Cold War. Being prepared to subordinate themselves to unknown orderings, agents have to be available not simply to one, but rather to multiple commanders. Just like public timepieces, they can be employed in the most diverse quasi-actions by many people at the same time, which they then carry out, pass on, or pass back (*weiter- oder zurückspielen*).[14] One example from *The Clock* is an alarm that has been alienated from its purpose and made to serve as the time fuse for a bomb next to the hero of the film. A misappropriation of the timepiece takes place in the fragments of *The Clock*, exactly as happened in the original film. Images of clocks are separated from the purposes that they assumed in the original film and are given new orders. They produce new contexts, but above all else, they coordinate filmic time with real time. It is [completely] essential that agents are able to act either on their own account, taking only their own interests into account, or in the interests of a third party. And they need not betray the original order to do so. It is enough for them to carry out their orders with different methods, for example, with indirect methods. Most importantly, however, they can only subvert their orders when they are subordinated to them. Only as the instrument of a foreign, delegated intention can they register their own intentions. But it is only as unreliable instruments that they can act in accordance with their orders, can produce the necessary illusions, can demonstrate their skill, and can improvise.

If, then, Marclay's installation is itself the timepiece that the installation is about, how is it about agents? To what extent do they transcend their operative function as timepieces, in order not only to create elbowroom for the depicted and montaged timepieces, but also to create the space in which they themselves can contribute to the mixed intentionality of the action of agents?

In the light of day, the timing that Marclay seems to undertake is in no way as precise or unrelenting as it might appear.[15] The moments of imprecision in the succession of time might appear to be minimal, being under a minute, but they are still striking and noticeable. To begin with, not every cut actually manages to generate the progression of time. The second hand's tick to noon, 12:00 pm exactly, is very noticeably divided into numerous, if short, shots of timepieces and therefore last notably longer than the second that is being displayed: the hand's advance to 12 o'clock is shown exactly 12 times; but these 12 displays interrupt the principal of absolute succession. They are simultaneous. The sounding of the bell at 12 o'clock exactly is also repeated 12 times.

Another example of this kind of imprecision can be found at minute 15:29 hours (3:29 pm). The time '15:29:35' is displayed for precisely 50 real seconds before the hand of the timepiece jumps to '15:30', and exactly 8 seconds after that another timepiece makes the jump to '15:30'. There is a duration of 70 real seconds between the first and the last displays of the filmic time '15:30', and the following minute is correspondingly shorter. An hour later, at '16:30', the display of the exact time, that is to say the jump to 4:30 exactly, is also shown 3 times, with 40 seconds between them. Additionally, there are countless shots of analog clocks that are not clearly legibly, and can therefore be cut into the film at various points in order to obtain the desired simultaneity between filmic and real time. A surprising number of images occur in which timepieces might be visible, or in which figures in the film look at a timepiece, but which in no way make the time available to the viewer. They can therefore also be deployed anywhere without consequence for the time. The clip from *M* showing the children's counting song provides an excellent example: the arm of the counting girl rotates in steps over the heads of the standing children, just like the hand of a clock over the numerals – but there is neither a time displayed, nor a precise visual metonym, as there are not 12 children in the circle.

Naturally the point here cannot be to accuse Marclay's installation of imprecision. Exactly the opposite, these macroscopic, clearly visible overlaps, hesitations, accelerations, condensations, and dilations, even the brief reversals of clock time (*Taktzeit*), have their own method that we can consider as potential intention, without asking to whom this intentionality might belong. These imprecisions as symptoms indicate a principal factor that they display, but which they do not cause. Even if the installation were accurate to the minute in all of its transitions and coordinated to real time with the same precision, even if it were correct down to the second, there would still invariably be a progression of time between two points of measurement that would not have been punctuated and in which time, seen metrically, would remain unobserved. The present, as an exactly precise meeting of the unlike, and as a pure difference, without distortion or corporealization, between past and present (as in the filmic cut), will always require a second present. This second present can be conceptualized, according to the circumstances, as a coextension of the variance, and as the persistence of an operation. It can also be conceptualized as that temporal space in which a condition is (still) capable of changing, in which a progression or an act (*Handlung*) can be carried out, and within which a new direction can be adopted (Bergson 1896/1982, pp. 131–135, 1920/1989, pp. 60–106) for a conception of presence as difference (see Luhmann 1984). In film, this would manifest in the continual flow of new shots (Bazin 1985).

The remarkable thing about Marclay's installation is, then, that this polarity between the two different concepts of present time as difference and as duration is not exhausted in the tension between the inflexibility of systemic time, understood as a number, that is, as a measure of movement on the one hand, and the flowing internal time of the shots on the other hand. According to a theory of agency, this polarization would therefore proceed in order to likewise polarize the prescribed function of coordinating images of a clocks' agency in film with their strong-willed resistance (*Eigensinnigkeit*) to external control. But this is exactly not the case here: the determination of time in Marclay is itself never exact, it never designates a point in time formally. It is, rather, always already a specific progression of time, which can be empty or full. It is not, then, as though there were a series of interlaced exact points in time, which were then all synchronized and made to take place in exact succession. The display of time is fundamentally a series of interconnected, interwoven overlaps and superimpositions. A minute for Marclay is not a numerical value or a particular point in time. Instead, it is, at best, a duration, during which change can take place, and which is provided with, or delineated through, a numerical value – though even that is not necessary (Luhmann 1999, pp. 51–56).

These imprecisions demonstrate that even the cuts between the same image of a timepiece reveal their own temporal durations, that is to say that they themselves have the ability to generate progression and change, that they have tactile, gesticulatory, action-like characteristics. They reveal that, for Marclay, even the display of time is either an apparative-mechanistic or human gesture is, which itself makes use of time and is therefore in no way a disembodied or, above all else, timeless operation (Flusser 1994). Even time, insofar as it is the result of an operation, is timely and within time. Beyond this linkage between intention, indexicality, and time, it is also the case that without the determination of a point in time, that is to say without temporal, itself inflexible punctuation, the present can be neither understood nor articulated as either a gesture or as a transmission. Without these survey marks of time (*Zeitmesspunkte*) in Marclays installation, these violations of the strict cadence of time would be impossible. There would be no point of reference for presence as persistence, nowhere for it to erect itself (*sich aufspannen*). Changes or changes of direction, in the sense of deviations from the script, would not be possible.

The operations of the exacting and condensing measure and display of time in *The Clock* produces, then, through its necessarily unfaithful agent, the timepiece, a flexible openness that is perceptible through its imprecision. This is the condition for the imputation of an agent-ruptured intentionality in the technical operations of the production of timing in or through film. Precision and blurriness are not fundamentally different, as they continually allow themselves to be translated and transmitted into one another. As with the apparent errors in Marclay's timing, each specific point in time is at once a way of condensing a flexible and flowing present, which is itself the dilated version of a more or less dense chain of indexical points of synchronization. In and through Marclay's work, time becomes both an essential medium of the agent and a product of that same agent. The implicit thesis of the clock can be described in the following manner: film itself, functioning as an agent, produces, through its regimentation of time, the preconditions for the blurriness of its operations and the addressability of its objects and figures as personal and material agents. It becomes capable, thereby, of becoming the agent that it itself finally represents.

Following the assumptions that are inherent to, and implied by, *The Clock*, and allowing them to be generalized for a moment, we can reach three conclusions regarding *The Clock* with reference to our initial questions. The first concerns the dichotomy between tolerating and effectuating, between acting and suffering, active and passive. Through the figure of the timepiece and its status as an agent, it becomes clear that these polarized categories are not mutually exclusive, nor are they convertible into one another, nor do they require one another, because they are only recognizable through the contrast between them. This all correct, but the crux of the aforementioned argument implied in Marclay's work is that they constantly push one another forward and establish one another: only insofar as the agent is capable of acting under its own power, can it be passive, and vice versa.

The second conclusion concerns the relationship between materiality and intentionality. Similar to passivity and activity, the two are in no way reducible to one another, nor do they replace one another. They do not contradict each other; instead, they overlap with one another. Appearing only in already mixed configurations, they are inscribed on one another. Each imputation of the one must return to the other. Outside of its complex and interrupted structure of intentionality, which we have observed in detail above, the very material artefact of the alarm or of the timepiece does not even appear as an object of observation or description or subjected to actions. And this is exactly the claim that *The Clock* makes for *The Clock*, and for the moving image as such. As a material field, the moving image is always already a field of action and only as such it is possible, respectively observable, and effectual. To impute materiality to the field is necessarily to make reference to its intentionality, and vice versa. In this respect – as Marclay's installation claims – there is no materiality that can be distinguished from and set against materiality, and therefore also no simply effective operativity, which could be stably opposed to intentionality, and thereby to the characteristics of action.

The third and most specific conclusion, finally, distinguishes synchronization, and time along with it, as the decisive operation or action that serves to generate the initial recursive organization of interpenetrating materiality and intentionality, as well as of passivity and activity. An operative, precise punctuation of time is not to be had, *The Clock* assumes, without the simultaneous generation of an open, action-enabling present, neither can this present be observed or imputed on its own. At least in the medium of the moving picture, and possibly far beyond, both operations and actions require time, because it is exactly through the foundation of time that they always produce operations and actions. The timepiece, and the image of a timepiece that is the film, are also the very agents that are constantly creating the preconditions that are required for their own action, and to which they are constantly, doubly synchronized.

Notes

1. For a critique of the concept of 'actors' in actor-network theory, see Latour (2006; see also Cuntz 2012).

2. Friedrich Kittler remains a primary media-historical paradigm for this kind of investigation (Kittler 1999). For a media-philosophical approach, see Engell (2003).
3. For the characterization of film as an intervention into reality, see Pasolini (1972). On the relationality of media, see, for example, Vogl (2009).
4. The term 'represented' here and below translates the German *Darstellung*, which has a wide range of meanings in German, all of which are employed here. It means 'representation' (in the sense of an image or scene that depicts a particular event), but also exposure (in the sense that an anatomist exposes one of the body's organs), it also means 'to produce' or 'to supply' (in the sense that a housekeeper 'produces' or 'supplies' a necessary sum).
5. The term 'film' is not reserved especially for celluloid images here, rather it applies – surely without media-theoretical consequences – simply and without distinction to all moving images notwithstanding the means of their delivery.
6. Regarding The Clock, see, for example (Leader 2010, Velasco 2012, Zalewski 2012).
7. See Voss (2014).
8. See, for example, John Law, *Machinic pleasures and interpellations*, 2001.
9. Sigrid Weigel made reference to Hannah Arendt's conception of action in contrast to that of Bruno Latour in her unpublished lecture during the lecture series on media theory at the Bauhaus Universität Weimar in 2012 (see Arend 1994, Greven 2003).
10. Voss (2014).
11. And to that extent would be thematizable as a motif (Engell and Wendler 2009).
12. The term quasi-action is used here in analogy to Michel Serres concept of quasi-object (Serres 1981).
13. On the malice of objects, see Vischer (1996).
14. On the ontologically relevant connection between time and the public sphere (*Öffentlichkeit*), see Heidegger (1979).
15. This is in contradistinction to Hartmut Böhme's claim, which precedes from the assumption of mechanistically precise timing in Marclay's work (Böhme 2011).

Disclosure statement

No potential conflict of interest was reported by the author.

Notes on contributor

Lorenz Engell is a Bauhaus Professor in Weimar, Germany, and was the founding Dean of the Faculty of Media of the Bauhaus University. He is director of the International Research Institute for Cultural Technologies and Media Philosophy, Germany.

References

Arendt, H., 1994. *Vita activa*. Munich: Piper.

Bazin, A., 1985. Montage interdit. *In*: A. Bazin, ed. *Qu'est-ce que le cinema*. Paris: Cerf, 48–63.

Bergson, H., 1896/1982. *Materie und Gedächtnis*. Berlin: Ullstein.

Bergson, H., 1920/1989. *Zeit und Freiheit*. Frankfurt am Main: Athenäum.

Böhme, H., 2011. Wollen wir in einem posthumanen Zeitalter leben? Geschwindigkeit und Verlangsamung in unserer Kultur. *In*: M. Brüderlin, ed. *Die Kunst der Entschleunigung. Bewegung und Ruhe in der Kunst von Caspar David Friedrich bis Ai Weiwei*. Wolfsburg, Germany: Kunstmuseum Wolfsburg, S. 2–8.

Cuntz, M., 2012. Agency. *In*: C. Bartz, ed. *Handbuch der Mediologie. Signaturen des Medialen*. Munich: Fink, 28–40.

Davidson, D., 1980. *Essays on actions and events*. Oxford: Oxford University Press.

Deleuze, G., 1989. *Das Bewegungsbild, Kino 1*. Frankfurt am Main: Suhrkamp.

Engell, L., 2003. Tasten Wählen Denken: Genese und Funktion einer philosophischen Apparatur. *In*: S. Münker, ed. *Medienphilosophie. Beiträge zur Klärung eines Begriffs*. Frankfurt am Main: Suhrkamp, 53–77.

Engell, L., 2011. Macht der die Dinge? Regie und Requisite in Federico Fellini's "8 ½". *In*: F. Balke, ed. *Die Wiederkehr der Dinge*. Berlin: Kadmos, 298–311.

Engell, L. and Wendler, A., 2009. Medienwissenschaft der Motive. *Zeitschrift für Medienwissenschaft*, 1 (1), 38–49.

Flusser, V., 1994. *Gesten*. Frankfurt am Main: Fischer.

Greven, M.T., 2003. Hannah Arendts Handlungsbegriff zwischen Max Webers Idealtypus und Martin Heideggers Existenzialontologie. *In*: W. Thaa and L. Probst, eds. *Die Entdeckung der Freiheit*. Berlin: Philo, 118–142.

Heidegger, M., 1979. *Sein und Zeit*. Tübingen, Germany: Niemeyer.

Kittler, F., 1999. *Gramophon film typewriter*. Redwood City, CA: Stanford University Press.

Latour, B., 2002. *Die Hoffnung der Pandora*. Frankfurt am Main: Suhrkamp.

Latour, B., 2006. Über den Rückruf der ANT. *In*: A. Belliger and D.J. Krieger, eds. *ANThology. Ein einführendes Handbuch zur Akteur-Netzwerk-Theorie*. Bielefeld, Germany: Transcript, 561–572.

Law, J., 2001. *Machinic pleasures and interpellations* [online]. Available from: http://www.lancs.ac.uk/fass/sociology/research/resalph.htm [Accessed 14 October 2014].

Leader, D., 2010. *C. Marclay's the clock*. London: White Cube.

Luhmann, N., 1984. *Soziale Systeme*. Frankfurt am Main: Suhrkamp.

Luhmann, N., 1999. *Die Gesellschaft der Gesellschaft*. Frankfurt am Main: Suhrkamp.

Mersch, D., 2010. Meta/Dia. Zwei unterschiedliche Zugänge zum Medialen. *Zeitschrift für Medien- und Kulturforschung*, 2 (1), 185–208.

Pasolini, P., 1972. La lingua scritta della realtà. *In*: P. Pasolini, ed. *Empirismo eretico*. Milan: Garzanti Libri, 198–226.

Serres, M., 1981. *The parasite*. Minneapolis: University of Minnesota Press.

Velasco, D., 2012. Borrowed time. Christian Marclay's "The Clock". *Artforum international*, 8 (2), 200–201.

Vischer, F.T., 1996. *Auch einer*. Frankfurt am Main: Insel.

Vogl, J., 2009. Becoming media: Galileo's telescope. *Grey room*, 27, 14–25.

Voss, C., 2006. Filmerfahrung und Illusionsbildung. Der Zuschauer als Leihkörper des Kinos. *In*: G. Koch and C. Voss, eds. *… kraft der Illusion*. Munich: Fink, 71–86.

Voss, C., 2010. Auf dem Weg zu einer Medienphilosophie anthropomedialer Relationen. *Zeitschrift für Medien- und Kulturforschung (ZMK)*, 2 (1), 169–184.

Voss, C., 2013. *Der Leihkörper. Erkenntnis und Ästhetik der Illusion*. Munich: Fink.

Voss, C., 2014. Affektive Medialität und ihre filmmediale Relflexion in 'The Clock'. In: L. Engell, F. Hartmann, C. Voss, eds. *Körper des Denkens. Neue Positionen in der Medienphilosophie*. München: Fink, 289–304.

White, P.J., 1991. *The complete mission: impossible dossier*. New York: Avon Press.

Zalewski, D., 2012. The hours. How Christian Marclay created "The Clock". *The New Yorker* [online]. Available from: http//www.newyorker.com/reporting/2012/03/12/120312fa_fact_zalewski [Accessed 26 June 2012].

Affective mediality and its aesthetic transformation in Christian Marclay's *The Clock**

Christiane Voss

ABSTRACT

This essay brings together a traditional philosophical theory of affect with mediaphilosophical considerations about the various non-anthropocentric roles that affects may play in aesthetics and especially in film-aesthetic regimes. In a first part it deals with the logics and functions of affect as they are made explicit by the philosopher William James. With this theoretical tool at hand the second part tries to overcome the anthropocentric implications of the introduced definitions of affect by confronting them with aesthetic transformations as they are technically evoked by filmic artworks. To be able to describe those transformations adequately, the philosophical conceptualization of 'affect' has to be critically complemented and enlarged in the light of mediaphilosophical reflections. In applying some aspects of James' affect-theory to what is triggered, imposed and negotiated as affective effects by the film-installation *The clock* (2010 by Christian Marclay), different kinds of hybridizations of technical and organic elements can be identified. They lead to the introduction of the neologistic term and concept of 'Anthropomediality'. The latter is supposed to figure as a new substitute concept for 'the man', while merging 'anthropos' and 'mediality'. It describes a hybrid mode of existence that may be analysed as a nonreducible form of being in future endeavours within the (still young field of research) of Media Anthropology and Philosophy of Techniques.

Introduction

The main focus of this essay is to reflect, with a special reference to film-aesthetics, on the processes and functions of affective operations from a media-philosophical point of view. In the widest sense of the word 'affective' every form of perceivable movement can be called an affective operation that brings about a change in a state of affairs, whether this change is due to causal, intentional, or otherwise functional powers. Whereas cognitive and volitive modes of gaining access to the world (and therefore also to art) are widely analysed in their functions and processes in the context of

---

*This essay was translated by Peter Kuras.

philosophical aesthetics and epistemology, affective modes are rarely, if at all, analysed with respect to their influence on understanding and/or epistemic perception. Although most aesthetic theories rely at least implicitly on concepts of affect-arousal and aesthetically elicited forms of affectivity, they rarely elaborate on this, or make their concepts explicit. Therefore, the main questions to be dealt with here are: what are affective operations, what can affective modes and functions contribute to the nature of an aesthetically arranged audiovisual artwork, and how do they shape (aesthetic) perceptions?

When it comes to questions of the aesthetics of audiovisual artworks, such as movies or film-installations, it becomes of utmost interest to figure out in more detail *how* the implied organic and technical elements get intertwined in the medium of affect-arousal. This last question is set out concretely in regard to the aesthetic experience of the film-installation *The clock* (2010) by Christian Marclay.[1] The focus of analysis lies especially on the combinatory/connecting and the separating/distinguishing functions of affective procedures. These affective functions can be further diversified, so that functions of amalgamation, of cross-fading, of penetration, of contrasting, of affirmation and negation, of increasing and decreasing, etc. may count as such as well. From a media-philosophical point of view, it is not to be considered to be a categorical mistake if affective functions are not solely ascribed towards organic systems but also to technical systems. In their material instantiations, figurations and appearances, even entities such as pictures and sounds, can be equipped with the power 'to act out' in affective ways. Therefore even audiovisual arrangements of pictures and sounds can be identified as *affective/affecting agents*. The pictorial and/or acoustical manners of 'acting-out affectively', so to speak, consist, among other things, in the repelling and/or attracting effects they (the pictures and sounds) may exert on other entities and organisms. Affective qualities, operations and devices do therefore belong to human *and* non-human entities and systems as well and can migrate between things, programmes, spaces and/or situations. Because, for example, in cinema the affective powers figure as conjunctions of and for heterogeneous elements, simply by vibrating between of-screen and on-screen, the heterogeneous technical and organic elements get aesthetically transformed by the same token. This aesthetic transformations of the technical and organic elements that are implied in the process of cinematographic experience give rise to the emergence of something else, a third entity. That emergent entity is the ephemeral aesthetic body of the whole cinematographic scenario and embraces both the bodies of the spectators and the technical-material aspects of the cinematographic apparatus, as shall be pointed out in more detail below.

Because the terms 'affect', 'affective powers' and 'affective operations' are key concepts in my argument, they require an explanation. Theories of affect, as they are developed in the fields of philosophy, neurophysiology, and psychology, have debated the ontological qualities of affective phenomena exclusively from the point of view of their evolutionary and culturally orienting function for human organisms, associations, and interactions. The more technological and aesthetic aspects of affective organizations, as well as the dependence of the latter on technical media and mediations of different kinds, have been widely neglected. Moreover those theories of affect do normally not take into account that affective procedures are able to generate mediating effects by themselves, for example, by *combining or separating, by strengthening or weakening* the states and conditions of organisms and other entities. The fact that affects and affective qualities can figure as mediating forces in aesthetic and non-aesthetic scenarios as pointed out before is something that should be kept in mind while we lead over to more general ontological questions of affect and to the affect-theory of William James in particular. Although James' focus is anthropocentric too, the relevant characteristic phenomenological functions and features of affects and affectivity may be gleaned from his conception nevertheless. Subsequently, these phenomenological characterizations of affects will be reflected in the light of the aesthetic construction s of the 24-four-hour film-installation *The clock*, by Christian Marclay. The media-philosophical framing in this essay aims at a twofold-perspective on its main topic: (1) a more thoroughly *technically grounded* and less anthropocentrically grounded understanding of 'affect' and 'affectivity' (2) a more *affectively* grounded understanding of cinematographic technique, and of aesthetics in general.

The activist facets of affects

Before discussing James' affect-theory, it may be instructive to reflect on some common uses of the terms 'affect', 'feelings', and 'affectivity'. First, the Latinate term 'affect' (from *affectus*) is in most cases used interchangeably with the English word 'feeling' and the German word 'Gefühl': they do function as interchangeable designators of the entire spectrum of affective phenomena. This spectrum extends from phenomena of low-threshold and subliminal kinaesthesis to language-dependent, judgment-based emotions, moods, and even to generalized affective dispositions towards life as a whole.[2]

When we start talking about *feelings* or *affects* in an everyday-live context, an association with purely passive phenomena related to suffering is quickly established. As presumably passive phenomena that serve to make those who experience them passive as well, feelings/affects appear to be distinguished, *per se*, from volitional impulses and cognitive operations of knowledge. And in most cases only the latter are considered to be *active* forms of processing perceptual impression and information. This presumption leads to a 'division of the mind' into two more or less disconnected and even incompatible systemic functions. This dualistic theory of the mind can not only be traced back historically to Plato and Descartes. Dualistic theories of the mind dominated the traditional eighteenth century, and reverberate up to the present (Mendelssohn 2006, Kant 1790/2000, Baumgarten 1750/2007). Only the capacities of thought and volition, according to this dualistic tradition, shall grant us freedom because they are supposed to be self-produced and boot-strapping, rather than arising from environmental factors, or from the corporeal demands and drives of an organism, as feelings are supposed to be. Emotionally transmitted perceptions are meant to operate pre-predicatively and a-conceptually. They are therefore traditionally made into phenomena that weaken the will, as in the thought of the Stoics and in Plato, and are held to account for all other arrational and irrational human action and thought.

Yet this mental divide consigns feelings/affects all too firmly to the category of physical reflexes, passive impulses, and reactions. This reduction however serves to obscure their productive functions in mapping reality, as well as it hides their genuine rationality and their epistemic functioning.

Etymology alone already indicates that 'affect' contains the verb 'afficere', which means something like 'to stimulate', 'to add or enrich', or 'to operate'. In the same vein: 'facere' also belongs to the verbal constellation of 'affect', and literally means 'to make', 'to do', or 'to add'. And also the etymology of 'feelings', derived from the old English 'félan', and with its roots in the Old High German 'fuolen', meaning 'to grope' or 'to fumble', hints at the fact that affects operate beyond the antagonistic differentiation of active and passive forms of movement. Where affective powers come into play, the passive *and* active facets of movements seem to be more interlocked than contrasted. This phenomenological interlocking of the active and passive qualities of movements, or ways of being-moved, may be rendered a function of the *tactile* – and less of the *symbolic* – order set up by affects. And in fact, the broader denotation of 'to grope' or 'to fumble' brings a searching and tentative form of touch into view. Perhaps it is this tactile basis of affective movements that allow us to get in close contact with matter and (even with our own) materiality, and perhaps it helps orient ourselves as corporeally constituted beings existing in time and space.

William James' feedback-theory of affects

It is especially the corporeally orienting function of affects that leads James (1884) to emphatically include them in what he called the 'aesthetic sphere of the mind'. In his essay 'What is an Emotion?' – the founding text of the philosophy of affects – James identifies affects with the perception of physiological changes. Where no physically discernible arousal is perceptible, according to James, there is also no affect. But affect is not only identified with a physical quality, but also with an embodied way of looking at the world in an evaluative manner. The fact that affects are accompanied by sensory self-perceptions should be reflected in their neurophysiological instantiation, as James makes clear in the following passage:

> The purpose of the following pages is to show that [...] emotional brain-processes not only resemble the ordinary sensorial brain-processes, but in very truth *are* nothing but such processes variously combined. (1884, pp. 188–189)

While the ordinary intuition dictates that affects initially arise, as it were, from 'inner' states of the mind, and only express themselves visibly in the body afterwards, James presents an opposing thesis:

> My thesis on the contrary is that the bodily changes follow directly the PERCEP-TION of the exciting fact, and that our feeling of the same changes as they occur IS the emotion. [...] one mental state is not immediately induced by the other, [...] the bodily manifestations must first be interposed between, and that the more rational statement is that we feel sorry because we cry, angry because we strike, afraid because we tremble, and not that we cry, strike, or tremble, because we are sorry, angry, or fearful, as the case may be. Without the bodily states following on the perception, the latter would be purely cognitive in form, pale, colourless, destitute of emotional warmth. (James 1884, pp. 189–190)

James considers the nervous system, which dictates the entirety of our behaviour, to be a network of dispositions that makes an organism capable of an adapting to its environment. Affects, too, are among such dispositions, and are unique, according to James, only in that they are capable of being triggered by the *direct* perception of environmental influences. The circulatory system is seen as functioning as a kind of resonance space capable of provoking a reaction from organic and chemical shifts and eliciting at least subliminal perceptions of change (kinaesthesia). In James' opinion even cases of weak stimuli lead to measurable physiological differences, and therefore to a change of a feeling-quality (this is why affectivity is a kind of movement).

The emphasis on the directness of affect-arousing impulses may suggest that James holds a deterministic position. But James counters this suggestion with the following argument: a certain tendency towards nervous emotional discharge can be elicited by all possible objects as soon as this tendency has been learned. There might be an affective memory that enables us to learn from experience generally. That should not, however, be taken to imply that our affective reactions are tied to certain inputs. And it certainly does not imply that our affective range is strictly determined by the influence of external impulses only. Imagination, too, has the capacity to provoke emotional reactions. Even imagining emotional states can produce an emotional state, such as when we feel fear of fear.

To complete this thought, let me point out that the experience of fear is certainly not limited to contexts of our everyday life; we also experience it in aesthetic fields and spaces, as in the cinema or museum, for example. Confronted with fiction we frequently enjoy the sensation of thrill, suspense and pleasurable fear. In these cases we produce so-called 'second-order' emotions: we enjoy our fears, for example. Aesthetically produced affects are somewhat different from otherwise produced affects. First of all, to be able to react with fear to a fictionally depicted threatening scenario, the precondition has to be met that we recognize this depiction as appropriately falling under the category of (what is stored structurally as) a cause of fear. However, it is only because we know that we are in a safe space like a cinema that the cinema-related fear is less intense than when we are in a situation of actual life-threatening danger. Because we are conscience of our security in the cinema, the sensomotoric system is only latently impelled to flight, though the subjectively experienced physiological changes, specific to fear in general, remain distinct enough. Fear experienced in the cinema is therefore always weaker than in situations of actual danger because the sensomotoric system is stimulated more weakly. And this is due to the automatic *and* yet reflexive realization of the aesthetic character of the situation.

James' emphasis on the measurable physiological signature of affectual stimulation and perception leads to a demystified understanding of feelings, as they no longer are seen as radical, subjective, and locked-in-phenomena, accessible only from a first-person-perspective. Feelings/affects become, instead, tangible as phenomena identifiable from a third-person perspective as well. To sum up: In James' conception, feelings/affects are understood as measurable changes and movements that are both perceptible subjectively and observable objectively, and as both physical and imaginative (implying cognitive).

Moreover, he offers a dynamic conception of the causality involved in affective arousal by pointing out its special feedback-mechanism. This is the reason why his theory is also known as the *feedback-theory of affect*. The *causes* of affective movements, as James put it, could only *analytically* and *post festum* be differentiated from the affective *effects* on the organism. In fact the causes and the effects of the affective changes and movements are bound together inseparably *in the medium of their experience*.

Yet another aspect of James' conceptualization of affect is important here. According to his conceptualization, affective reactions bring with them a sort of pre-conceptual schematization, insofar as they translate their inputs into a sensory resonance capable of distinction. When feelings are triggering, their inputs or stimuli get instantaneously translated and categorized in affective terms. Though this is not, as it were, identical with explicitly predicative forms of identification and (re-)categorization, it is nevertheless a means of generating distinctions that has immediate effects on the identity of the perceived. This epistemic aspect of the distinct qualification of the affectively perceived leads James to a radical reversal of the standard conception. He chooses an example to illustrate this: When we encounter an object, such as a bear approaching while we are wandering through the woods, this would not cause us to fear because the bear would be inherently threatening. Rather, as James puts it, the bear would be categorized *as* threatening because we respond to him that way. The supposedly affective *reaction* to the bear – that of fear – becomes the *cause* of an affective categorization of the bear *as* a scary object.

With reference to James' feedback-theory and the etymological indications as to the meaning of 'affect' and 'feeling' provided above, an initial claim can be made: where affective perceptions or movements are activated, our responses to and views of the world get tinted. These colouring effects of affective arousal correlate with varying qualities of sensation. One affect can be distinguished from another merely by its different feeling-qualities. But whatever is perceived or encountered in an affective mode is per se endowed with a positive or negative value according to whether pleasurable or unpleasurable reactions are elicited as well. Affectively perceived reality is then presented to consciousness as always already evaluated on a scale ranging from the joyously positive to the unpleasant negative. Therefore an affectively schematized objectivity is not simply given as an unchangeable primordial nature or world. It is much more a changeable effect of the affective transformation in a given situation.

The spectrum of affectual phenomena

Affective phenomena differ in regards to their modes and intensities of progression, their effects, the conditions of their transmission, and their immanent 'logic', that is, their intentional objects, their feeling-tones, and their evaluations. The five central subclasses of affects, which I will introduce here without making any claim to comprehensiveness, are: (a) hedonic feelings (ranking from pleasure to unpleasure), (b) cognitive/narrative emotions (e.g. infatuation, guilt, shame, jealousy, etc.), (c) corporeally diffuse or localizable sensations (such as: stitches, queasy feelings, rapid heartbeat, etc.), (d) moods (e.g. sadness, euphoria, etc.) and (e) atmospheres (stiff or erotic atmospheres or even suspense, etc.).

James himself did not differentiate, say, between sensations and hedonic feelings. But there are phenomenological differences between, for example, a stomachache and a diffuse negative feeling. And it is important to note that *hedonic feelings* in particular serve a special function for other affects as well. Hedonic feelings as pleasure and unpleasure (or better: positive and negative feelings) equip the diverse affects (like emotions, moods, and atmospheres) with a positive or negative affective value. This means they are always part of affect-arousal, no matter what. It is *hedonistic colouring*, that is, colouring through concomitant positive or negative feelings, that first makes a perceivable (bodily) change or movement into something affective.[3]

The subclass of *emotions* constitutes a special type of affect. They are cognitively/narratively structured and based on judgments that can be made explicit in propositional form. Anger, happiness, feelings of guilt, gratitude, and infatuation are all directed towards a special narrative scenario in a situation, and require, furthermore, a certain amount of time before their experiential, cognitive, and behavioural components are fully evolved. Emotions progress in a dramaturgical vein, passing different phases of development: a rising activation initially, followed by an increased level of intensity and focus, and finally a declining phase before they have dissipated again. In regard to their involved judgments, emotions offer more or less rational motives and reasons for action. Annoyance at an insulting gesture may lead, for example, to a gesture of retribution; a reaction of joy at a gift may lead to a demonstration of gratitude directed at the giver, and so on. Furthermore, emotions are developed and learned in and through processes of cultural and linguistic socialization. Historical as well as cultural changes in the causes and evaluations of emotions like shame, guilt, and pride, among others, confirm the cultural dependency of emotional scripts and emotional understandings in general.

In contrast to emotions, *sensations* such as hunger, being thrilled, and goosebumps belong to the non-cognitive subclass of affects. Sensations are more or less corporeally localizable and correspondingly overtake the function of physical signals for an organism. Hunger, for example, is a direct demonstration of a need for nourishment; being thrilled can indicate a tensed preparedness for concentration or activity; goosebumps can be a reaction to cold. In contrast to emotions, these sensations do not have any representational content, and are also observable in beings that are incapable of speech, like babies and animals.

Moods (such as euphoria, sadness, boredom, etc.) also constitute an affective subclass of a unique type. They must be differentiated from emotions as well as from purely physical arousal and sensations. Moods are a matter of comprehensive psychophysical changes, which are usually not corporeally locatable, frequently extend longer than emotions, and employ a diffuse or global intentionality. In their intentional diffusion and tendency towards universality, moods tint the more global relations and modes of reference to the world and also go along with positive or negative feelings. From the perspective of boredom, everything seems uninteresting and tough, whereas euphoria makes everything seem rosy and accessible. The mood-specific function of colouring the world-views in positive or negative ways can also be transferred to others who are around and keep in touch with whatever is moved by the atmosphere at hand. This effect of instantaneous transference mirrors again the basic tactile mode of affective functioning.

Atmospheres constitute another unique affective subclass. They are less distinct in their capability of altering perspectives than are moods, though they are more encompassing than the aspectualizing emotions. Atmospheres have a centrifugal power, and they form whole situations by disseminating their perceptible and hedonic frameworks. The affective qualities of atmospheres can differ. An atmosphere may be more strict or tense, stiff or relaxed, inspiring, erotic, threatening, etc. Entering physically into such a hedonic framing of an atmosphere makes one an ephemeral habitant of it. A special light in a room, or the texture of any material or thing may be responsible for an atmospheric change and quality. Also any form of behaviour, facial expression, or even the mere sound of a word or speech-act may also be responsible for disseminating an atmospheric quality. But generally, the origins of atmospheres can never be conclusively determined. Atmospheres, too, demonstrate a perceptible positive-negative valence, and this is exactly what makes them affective phenomena. Additionally, atmospheres are also capable of uniting, and even merging, human and non-human spaces and/or entities in their course.

Between the pole of non-cognitive affects (such as sensations and atmospheres) and cognitive affects (such as emotions), there exists, from a phenomenological perspective, a twilight zone of fluid transition. The transition between a mood and an emotion, for example, may sometimes only be a question of the intensity of their feeling-components. Different affective states frequently merge with one another and alternate between strengthening or neutralizing one another. This is the case, for example, when a sad impulse meets an already existing depressive mood and serves to strengthen the latter, or when a cheerful message neutralizes a threatening mood. These functional modes of mutual superimposition, diminishment, or enhancement are all characteristic affective modes of operation and processing. And, as was said before, these affective modes supervene among human and non-human-systems in equal measure. Where an operational logic of affectivity is at stake, there is always a possible gradation in the intensity of energy levels at stake as well. A tension-filled situation or mood can be elevated or diminished, a fear of something specific can be diminished and diffused into a generalized mood of mere attentiveness, or it may, on the contrary, lead to a blind panic-attack. This also means that the question of the intentionality of affects is not an easily determinable all-or-nothing issue. It is rather a question of the gradations of energy-levels underlying the respective affective occurrences in a given situation.

While an affective access to the world of any sort is always, as James suggested, a matter of an *amalgamation* of causes with effects – signs with their meanings, subjects with objects – an affective access differs from a purely cognitive access to the world in some respects: the latter aims primarily to enable clear-cut conceptual distinctions, and a semiotic or symbolic representation of something otherwise absent. In non-affective forms of cognitive operations, a categorical gap is opened up between the corpus of representational signs and that which is being designated by them. It is exactly this representational gap of non-affective cognitive operations that the affective modes of reference bridge and subvert at the same time. The affective modes of mapping and/or perceiving the world transport the world into the presentist positivity of their own hedonic-somatic-logic. Whenever a 'logic of affect' becomes the dominating principle of perception in a given situation, an evaluative reality that is *intuitively* accessible simultaneously is brought into a presence. Four aspects of affective forms of access to the world may be distinguished analytically, even when they operate in conjunction normally or overlap:

(1) The *cybernetic-amalgamating* aspect of the affective access. (This aspect mirrors James' bio-cybernetic subject-object-feedback-loop in affective forms of being-moved.)
(2) The *contagious* aspect of the affective access. (This aspect covers the more or less instantaneous migration of perceptible qualities of affects and their dissemination in time and space among human *and* non-human entities.)
(3) The *haptic-tactile* aspect of affective access. (This third aspect designates all forms of affective mediations serving to connect a perception of something with (self-)perception in direct physical contact and touch.)
(4) The *evaluative-presentative* aspect of the affective access and perception. (This fourth aspect designates the more narrowly representational content of affective modes, and especially their power to endow reality with a positive or negative value.)

Because of their cybernetic-amalgamating functioning, affective interventions lead to short circuits, mixtures of states of affair, and situational embedded entities. They thereby generate new phenomena (e.g. as value-laden states of affair). The contagious modes of affective interventions allows moods and atmospheres to arise all of a sudden, and to change a whole situation by merely setting it temporarily under the condition of a special mood-quality. The haptic-tactile aspect of affects allows affective qualities of different subjects and/or objects to communicate with and determine each other simply by getting literally *in touch* with one another. And the evaluative-presentative aspect of affective operations, finally, lead to the charging of an object with affective value, in a semiotic sense, that also can be even made linguistically explicit in some cases. Affective operations work within human bodies, for example, by moving the organic, endocrine, peripheral, and cognitive functional areas. And they also take place within non-human entities, such as in movies, where affective operations also serve to combine or separate relevant acoustical and visual elements. As could be demonstrated with the help of the well-known Kuleschow-experiment, one shot of a movie may shape and determine the atmospheric quality of the next shot, and vice versa. This can be interpreted as an example of the contagious aspect of affective operations, being responsible for the transformation of parts, or of whole conditions of, organic and non-organic systems in their meanings or expressions. Although films are obviously lacking the processing of organic resources, they are nevertheless machines of affect-production, affect-transformation and affect-transmission. Therefore it is interesting to figure out in more detail how a technical and organic system may interact affectively and aesthetically, when it comes to their encounter in cinematographic settings.

The clock as a reflexive medium of affect-transformation

A reflexive treatment of the aforementioned affective modulations in and of filmic interventions and cinematographic settings can be found in Christian Marclays artistic work *The clock* (2010). The work in question is a 24-hour film-installation, for which Marclay edited thousands of clips from across the range of genres and from 70 years of film history, with the aim of finding sequences in which clocks appear. The remarkable point of the installation, which is going on around the clock, is a performative one. That is because the installation does not merely point out what various kinds of dramaturgic, semantic or symbolic functions clocks may inhabit in a movie and in the history of movies. Much more than that, the film-installation *is* also a chronometric device by itself, or, briefly stated: this film-installation *is* also a clock. Whether in New York (Paula Cooper Gallery), Paris (Centre Georges Pompidou), or Venice (2011 Biennale), its own 24-hour rhythm is always precisely tied to the local time at its place of presentation. The presented time in *The clock* both depicts and exemplifies the local time, down to exact changes in minutes and seconds.

Once a spectator enters the installation's space, he/she sees images flying by on the screen, snapshots and fragments of well-known scenes and dialogues of different movies, spots of faces and actions of famous, and not so famous, actors; scraps of music pass in succession and overlap in an apparent enigmatic order. We know and remember some of these very well, while others, much less, or even not at all. Without any clear orientation about what exactly it is what we are looking at and for, we follow these moving audiovisual impulses and 'cues' in a kind of flow. Only after a while we recognize something nearly unbelievable: suddenly (and of course only if we were not informed before about it already) we discover the strict chronometric character of the installation itself. At this moment a shockingly new perspective is accessible and another imaginative route of association opens up: the exploitation of a strict chronometric tact and rhythm of a clock seems to determine the montage of the film-clips, which initially seemed to obey another, much more poetic or aesthetic, order. The scenes, shots and jump-cuts that seemed to be wildly and associatively edited initially, suddenly expose themselves as being arranged in a strictly mechanical and logical way: the repetition of a clock-rhythm and its 24-hour progression reveals itself as the aesthetically ruling principle. This 'discovery' changes the role of things, and especially those of the clocks seen in the series of clips onscreen. Instead of playing the role of a mere prop any longer, the clock is 'promoted', one almost wants to say, just by being variously repeated, to become the main signifier of the film-installation. Another way to put it is to say: A mere prop – which is what clocks in movies normally are – figures as something completely different, namely as the polymorphous star of the whole filmic scenario. This trans-valuation of the prop and the new position it takes in the hierarchy of the constitutive network of the filmic elements in general (embracing other props, figures, speech, persons, camera-movements, furniture, rooms, places, light, sound, etc.) is mediated in *The clock* by the affectively changed perception of the beholder. And the resulting interference with the established hierarchy of filmic elements in relation to each other, which *The clock* is pushing forward, corresponds to the well-known Brechtian aesthetic of the 'alienation-effect' (Verfremdungseffekt).

Affect-formation thereby adopts a simultaneously motivational and epistemic task in the aesthetic reception and appearance of the *The clock*. The aforementioned shock-effect of the 'eureka-experience' does soon bring about an even more far-reaching irritation, which is also epistemically relevant. The commonly known function of a clock is to guarantee some orientation in time and space. However, the installation-specific way of staging *and* depicting the chronometer leads to a deviating result: by synchronizing real and fictitious time, two ontologically incompatible and isolated spheres and realms of reality get paradoxically merged: the realities on-and off-screen suddenly share a common rhythm of being, in the aesthetic perception and appearance of *The clock*. But precisely this merging effect on the originally separated regimes of reality and fiction counteracts any possibility of coherent orientation for the spectator. The resulting uncertainty towards what is perceived exactly can therefore also not be acted out in any straightforward way. The nevertheless concomitant energy of this affective arousal is somehow locked-in and cannot be dissipated. This affective energy needs therefore another exit-option. It may be invested, for example, in further curiosity towards the progress of *The clock*, whereby the installation attracts attention and stimulates immersive behaviour towards itself. This immersive effect can be prompted although, in its additive and incoherent style of montage, the installation seems to push forward one disturbance of the cinematographic illusion after another. The latter is normally taken to be a hindrance for the rising of immersive behaviour. Nevertheless, in this respect again *The clock* reverses the conventional methods of narrative cinema. And in refiguring the affects it absorbs, *The clock* interferes aesthetically also with the normal adaptive functions of the affect-arousal-system. Affect-arousal normally functions to judge a situation quickly, motivate an adaptive behaviour; and ensure, finally, the dissipation of tensions through action.

All of this is simultaneously invoked and circumvented by the way *The clock* brings about affect-formation. While the film-installation triggers *and* disorients affects and affectivity at the same time, without offering a release for its feeling-components, what remains to be done for a body, resonating this double-binding-input, is to 'give-in', so to speak, and enjoy at least the increased excitement and aesthetically forced passivity. Because in aesthetic contexts we do not have to cope with serious existential challenges, we can only in such contexts enjoy a form of active passivity as circumscribed. The motivational force of affect-arousal is limited, in an aesthetic context, to the ludic and quite active (self-)awareness of the recipient. In aesthetic spheres, such as in the context of the reception of *The clock,* affective arousal serves no further functions anymore, including self-protection. Instead, it gains an intrinsic value in its own right. One can conclude, in line with Kant, that aesthetic formations of affect differ from other formations of affect in that they decouple affective changes from any subjectivist and instrumental forms of (self-)reference. And this decoupling is a necessary condition for any form of prompting aesthetic disinterestedness and open-mindedness. That an artificially elevated intensity of affectivity remains enjoyable, is, then, both a fundamental task and balancing act for what has to be performed by art in general. *The clock,* in its affect-(trans-)formations, is dealing and playing with these tasks by pushing them to the limits. Put paradoxically, therefore, the work *The clock* both *is* a clock, yet *is not* (only) a clock.

The contagious aspect of affect-formation can also be observed on multiple levels in *The clock.* In many moving images, the installation shows us, for example, people looking at their watches, while obviously waiting for something or someone. Without recognizing what exactly it is they are waiting for, this waiting-scenes instantaneously incorporate an emotional atmosphere of nervousness and impatience, or of suspense – even when the persons do not at all seem to be stressed or afraid themselves. The impression of the somewhat nervous atmospheres of the moving images is reinforced by the character of the places in which the waiting-people are located. These are mostly inhospitable places of passage that seem to be more or less only there to depart from with greater or lesser haste: train, bus, and taxi stations, hotel rooms, roofs, street corners, waiting rooms in hospitals, cafes, etc. are the most depicted ones. While on one hand these waiting-scenes could be taken as spatial ciphers of an urban mobility, Marclay's way of dealing with them in *The clock* – by adding and looping them in hundreds of sequences – seems on the other much more to retard movement and mobility. But despite this rhythmical acceleration, no real action takes place, and no narrative development is being advanced. By this aesthetic strategy *The clock* repeatedly plays with the register of frustrated narrative anticipation. Narrative and acoustic traces and cues are constantly laid out – while the search for an overall meaning of the installation must constantly fail. Thus this dramaturgy of affect-formation of *The clock* leads to a constant toppling between tense-expectation, boredom, and a perplexed contemplation of the installation on the side of the beholder. Thereby the film-installation triggers mixed feelings of immersive and distancing moments in its ongoing movement.

The tactile aspect of affect-formation and affective transmission can be observed in *The clock* with particular clarity in the way it relates sound with image in its montage. In one clip that correlates to the time 12:05, for example, we see a man leaving a house as we hear extra-diegetic music rising dramatically. The protagonist is suddenly made aware of a hidden corpse by an intra-diegetic bellowing of a dog. This corpse is presented to the viewer in a subsequent shot showing the corpse with eyes wide open in a close-up. The extra-diegetic music continues and overlaps into the next scene and shot, which belongs clearly to a completely different movie. Whereas the previous scene was in black-and-white, we now see a woman approaching a window in a colour-film. She opens the window and looks out. We observe this from a low-angle shot from outside the house. That this jump-cut is not taken as such, but much more as a continuous flow, leading us smoothly from the first frame to the one with the woman at the window, is due to a moment of what Slavoj Žižek calls 'suture'. This term describes a special act of reception, whereby shots and cuts that follow immediately one after another are logically, as well as temporally and spatially, bound to one another in the imagination of the beholder. What the woman sees from her point of view while looking out of the window can only be inferred from the previous sequence or shot. We must take the image of the corpse as that which *she* is supposed to watch at this moment. Although this may be a valid inference, this is not all that is going on. Something additional occurs here, which I would like to refer to as an 'affective suture'. The imaginative completion also includes an immediate new interpretation of the mimic expression of the woman. Because we attribute to her vision the dramatic reference to the corpse, her way of looking itself is now charged with the expressive qualities of the suspect, even of the guilty, or at least of the conspirator. What we perceive in the register of the horrid, now *becomes* horrid exactly because of that perception. This is exactly the feedback-effect of all affectivity that was emphasized by James. Through affective schematization the mood or atmosphere of a filmic element or situation gets entirely transformed: robbed of its neutrality, the aforementioned scene at the window is carried, through the medium of an affective suture, into the register of the thriller.

The moving images of *The clock* reach out into our space, that of the spectator, as do their bodies via sound-qualities as well as via optical arrangements. These visual and acoustic-qualities literally get incorporated simply by being heard and seen. Here again it is useful to speak of a tactile mode for the film installation's affective qualities, and not only because they do literally touch our senses. The sound, say, of an image of a huge empty train-station that we hear and see in one clip, is also modifying the aesthetic effects of the subsequent or previous clips. Therefore we can also talk of an intra- and inter-pictorial, as well as of an intra- and inter-acoustical, contact of sounds and images – finding a place on a horizontal line of the montage of the filmic clips.

While these tactile translations of, and transmissions between, images and sounds may even dominate the aesthetic of *The clock*, the original narrative contexts of the selected moving images are more or less suppressed. So, within and between the cuts of the heterogeneous scenes and shots, the recipient's emotional memory of the movies has to fill the gaps. The interweaving of these idiosyncratic emotional memories also has a feedback-effect on the installation. The audio-visual structure of *The clock* assumes affective qualities of gradation and intensity, and these vary according to the strength or weakness, positivity or negativity, of the interwoven memories.

After the affective suture progresses for a while, the memory-triggering effect of it, and therefore that of the installation, becomes ambivalent and inconsistent again. The latter happens because every trace of filmic memory is followed by a new scene of reference, which eclipses the previous trace of memory and is, in turn, pushed aside by a new scene and memory. In this manner ever more emotionally marked memories and half-memories of films and their narratives, as well biographical situations of film-reception in certain cases, are piled on top of one another. In the intervals between digressive associations and the reentry into the trance-like tact of the flow of the film-installation, which moves forward day and night, *The clock* displaces us into a kind of *time-battle*. As was said at the beginning: that *The clock* is also a *clock*, remains always ready to be newly discovered and remembered, while we are displaced by the flow of its progression in time. The unpredictable temporal development of the installation as a whole, as well as its incoherent splitting of layers of temporality and affect, seem to share only one function: that this all – every cognitive and affective suture involved as well – is repeatedly leading to dead ends, without reaching a final ending of the whole time-flow.

Anthropomediality as the aesthetic reality

As we saw in the context of the aesthetic experience of *The clock*, and its implied affect-transformation, aesthetic reception leads in great parts away from the normal affectual logic and functioning. The latter primarily consists in the detection and evaluative distinction of the useful and harmful for our psychosomatic organism. On the basis of the bracketing of the reference to an empirical self and well-being, it becomes possible, in the aesthetic context, to place our affectivity in the service of an aesthetic playfulness and game.

Through its collage-like arrangement of moving-images and sounds *The clock* elicits a corresponding polymorphous formation of affect and affectivity. This polymorphous affect-formation also has a feedback-effect on the whole aesthetic experience in question. The main feedback-effect is that it works as a productive medium of transforming the interacting technical and organic elements involved in that process. The affect-formation (such as its operations of amalgamating, merging, translating, and distinguishing) is bringing about a *third form or level of reality*, that supervenes on the cinematographic techniques, as well as on the organic processing involved in the progression of the aesthetic reception. Therefore the installation awakens, in cooperation with its recipients, the actions and passions on- and off-screen to what can be called, with a neologism, an *anthropomedial life* of its own. And exclusively, in relation to this third ontological sphere of pure aesthetic appearance, it may be true that it is only intuitively accessible, if at all.

Notes

1. Marie Luise Angerer indicates that there has been an especially strong interest in the theory of affects among scholars of dance, and supposedly among media theorists such as Mark Hansen and Brian Massumi (2013). She does not, however, mention the fact that a systematic discussion of the term affect, such as has taken place within the discourse of analytical philosophy, remains a desiderata in current media theory. My impression to date is that the few theoretical models that refer to affect that have been generated within media studies have continued to refer to it predominantly as a regime of non-intentional phenomena. My efforts in this field, at least, aim to add the integration of the intentional forms of affect to the picture, and to reflect on affectivity in general beyond any body-mind-dualism.
2. Compare the elaborated affect theory of Agnes Heller, who expounded her position in the monograph *Theorie der Gefühle* (1981). See also the summary of philosophical theories of affect provided by Sabine Döring in her edited volume *Philosophie der Gefühle* (2009).
3. I develop this argument in my monograph *Narrative Emotionen. Möglichkeiten und Grenzen philosophischer Emotionstheorien* (2003).

Disclosure statement

No potential conflict of interest was reported by the author.

Notes on contributor

Christiane Voss is Professor for Philosophy of (Audiovisual-)Media at the Bauhaus-University in Weimar, Germany.

References

Baumgarten, G., 1750/2007. *Ästhetik*. Hamburg: Meiner.

Hansen, M. and Massumi, B., 2013. Die biomediale Schwelle. Medientechnologien und Affekt. In: A. Deuber-Mankowsky and C.F.E. Holzhey, eds. *Situiertes Wissen und regionale Epistemologie. Zur Aktualität Georges Canguilhems und Donna J. Haraway*. Vienna: Turia und Kant, 203–223.

James, W., 1884. What is an emotion? *Mind* 9 (34) 188–205.

Kant, I., 1790/2000. *Critique of the power of judgement*, ed. Paul Guyer, trans. Paul Guyer and Eric Mathews. Cambridge: Cambridge University Press.

Mendelssohn, M., 2006. Rhapsodie, oder Zusätze zu den Briefen über die Empfindung. *In*: Anne Pollok, ed. *Ästhetische Schriften*. Hamburg: Meiner, 142–188.

'Can thought go on without a body?' On the relationship between machines and organisms in media philosophy[†]

Friedrich Balke

ABSTRACT

All philosophy of media has its origin in the Cartesian distinction between *res cogitans* and *res extensa* – a distinction that poses the question of whether thinking is detachable from its bodily carrier and presents the possibility of outsourcing cognitive operations to apparatuses or machines. In the Cartesian elimination of the body, Jean-Francois Lyotard identified the philosophical force of current technoscientific culture, which is in the process of freeing thinking from its forced coupling with the human body. The speculative *tabula rasa* brought about by the Cartesian 'demolition' takes the form of a technological wager in the twentieth century. Technology is an attempt to respond to the extreme challenge that cosmic development poses for human beings: to guarantee that thought remains possible even after the ultimate catastrophe of a solar explosion, which threatens all planetary life a few billion years from now. The technological utopia of an ultra-stable infrastructure that would enable the continuation of thought even after the demise of its hitherto ecological conditions perpetuates, on the one hand, the politico-theological notion of a second body, one equipped with mysterious forces that guarantee invincibility. On the other hand, the naturalism and the rhetoric of crisis with regard to the history of mankind at stake in this utopia of human self-assertion ignore the complex interplay of thought and the body, whose parallel relationship Spinoza first pointed out against Descartes' dualism. Rather than confine thought to the body, as in a vessel, Spinoza demonstrates that thought exists only because it is, in a certain way, affected and disposed by the body, in a physical as well as cultural sense (i.e. through objects, signs, institutions, and apparatuses).

[†]The essay was written for a lecture series entitled 'Der Körper des Denkens', organized by Lorenz Engell, Frank Hartmann, and Christiane Voss which took place at the Bauhaus-Universität in Weimer during the winter semester of 2011/2012.

This work was translated by Valentine Pakis and Nathan Taylor.

Descartes's exclusion of the body and the dislocation of thought

'Can thought go on without a body?' This question seems to give us good reason to doubt the sanity of the person posing it. Only philosophers can ask such questions. To be without a body certainly means to exist no longer or not at all. Yet who is able to think without existing? For René Descartes, however, the answer to this question can only be the following: we cannot only think without a body, but that is precisely what we must do, because everything that we perceive with our five senses is highly dubitable, and thus requires the utmost reservation with respect to its truth and certainty. Peculiarly enough, I am that which doubts, and yet if I place everything into doubt, I am incapable of doubting. Deception is impossible in this case, even by a wicked god (*deus malignus*). According to Descartes, everything can be separated without forfeiting the self-certainty of the thinking being: in Descartes's (1996, p. 18) philosophy, the 'ego' is a function, not a corporeal figuration, not a human, not a 'structure of limbs', and this is because the form, shape, and size of all bodies can be modified – by means of thermal processes, for instance – in such a way that I would no longer recognize them as the same bodies. Thus, the thinking being cannot rely on its body. For cultural and media theorists, what is striking about this radical doubt of the body is that it is not simply due to a mere cognitive operation, but rather implies a complex setting; it implies a particular spatial arrangement of things, signs, and a reflective person that the text, in which Descartes charts his doubtful path, expressly elevates into a major theme. Regarding the genesis of this new philosophy, the 'ego cogito' is by no means the point of departure; it is not the first or foremost matter that had long been overlooked but rather the result of a complex 'meditation' that presents the meditating subject in a certain situation, namely a situation of having 'a clear stretch of free time' (1996, p. 17) of sitting in a winter coat by the fireplace and taking note of his reflections – and all of this with the intention of effecting 'the general demolition' (p. 17) of his opinions, and thus of discovering 'what can be called into doubt', which is the very title of the first 'Meditation'. In order to gain access to the truth, Descartes helps himself to the arsenal of those classical body techniques and ritual practices that alter the subject's mode of being.[1] Like a recluse, the subject of Cartesian meditation must withdraw into himself, be alone with himself (the spiritual technique of *anachoresis*), and no longer squander his intellect on the colourful temptations of bodily things (the technique of concentrating the soul) in order to make progress with the very *cogito* that can ultimately be promulgated as the kernel of every truth that is immediately accessible to mankind.

'Can Thought Go On Without a Body?' is also the title of a lecture that was held in 1988 by the French philosopher Jean-François Lyotard (1991). The purpose of the lecture was to bring us, in a single bound, face to face with the modernity of the Cartesian strategy, a modernity that is itself unaffected by the (then much-discussed) transition of our culture into so-called postmodernity, of which Lyotard was the most significant philosophical proponent. Published in 1982, Lyotard's book *Le condition postmoderne* remains even today a key text in the field of media philosophy, because its theme is the situation of knowledge in the most highly developed societies – and because it analyses the situation of this knowledge as an effect of that which he describes as its technological transformation (1984, pp. 3–4). The technological transformation is defined more precisely as that of a computerization of knowledge and thus as the implementation of a new performance, which Lyotard describes as a 'thorough exteriorization of knowledge with respect to the "knower"'. He adds: 'The old principle that the acquisition of knowledge is indissociable from the training (*Bildung*) of minds, or even of individuals, is becoming obsolete and will become ever more so' (p. 4). However, is this exteriorization of knowledge with respect to the knower really a genuinely postmodern experience? Or did it not manifest itself already at the moment in which Descartes reduced pure thinking to the function of the mere operative basis of all potential cognitive content, and thus, in his way, fundamentally separated this potential cognitive content from the act of thinking itself?

With this in mind I can return to Lyotard's 1988 lecture, from which I have borrowed the main title of my article. The text consists of a thought experiment, at the heart of which is an effort to translate the Cartesian exclusion of the body into a grand sociological project. Descartes's *Meditations on first philosophy* (1641) begins indeed with nothing less than the announcement of a catastrophe: he demands that the thinking being call into doubt everything that he had previously believed to know and thus create the situation of a *tabula rasa*, upon which the world and our knowledge are to be reconstructed. At the very onset of this modern philosophical meditation is thus an act of destruction, an act of destruction – one might presume – that would also include the undoing of our capacity to act. On which certainties are we able to rely, that is, if we are truly to take seriously the Cartesian commandment to doubt? To destroy everything in order to construct it anew is the calculus at the foundation of this gesture of thinking, which, since its establishment by Descartes, has undergone a variety of theoretical and political revivals.[2] In his seminar on psychoses (1955/1956), the psychoanalyst Jacques Lacan stated the following about the certainty with which Descartes is concerned: 'Surely, certainty is the rarest of things for the normal subject.' In fact, we do not even desire it. It is rather typical of the normal subject to acknowledge a certain number of realities that are highly uncomfortable or even threatening, but he or she never takes them 'fully seriously'. Lacan then addresses his audience directly:

> [F]or you think, along with Paul Claudel's subtitle, that *the worst is not always certain*, and maintain yourselves in an average, basic – in the sense of relating

to the base – state of blissful uncertainty, which makes possible for you a sufficiently relaxed existence. (1993, p. 74)

It is precisely about this life in 'blissful uncertainty' that Descartes wishes to know nothing at all, for which reason he expects of thinking nothing less than the catastrophic dismantling of all his previously cultivated opinions and convictions about reality and its reliability. However, Descartes embarks upon this experiment without any urgency – at a self-chosen point in time and in a state of solitary leisure – so that, even though a shiver might be running down the reader's spine, the same reader is simultaneously aware that he is dealing with the thought experiment of a philosopher for whom the project must have had no practical consequences whatsoever. The Cartesian exclusion of the body is implemented in the medium of thinking; in itself, it certainly has no 'sociological' repercussions. It does nothing to intervene with daily life, which can just as well carry on along its normal path without any disturbance from such speculations.

Is it not perhaps possible, however, that things might be completely different? With the seemingly idyllic framework of his radical doubt, has Descartes perhaps led us down the wrong path, one that has obscured from us the fact that our present socio-technical culture has long been in the process of liberating thinking from its once compulsory connection to the body, if perhaps not from its every bodily association? Since Descartes, the suspicion has prevailed that all epochal upheavals have already been experienced and that nothing more can be made of the world; since Descartes, a sense of mistrust has crept into our heads against all attempts to understand thinking as an exclusive attribute of man, as a feature of humanity that is impossible to separate from its 'natural' bearer and extend or transfer to other bodies, organisms, apparatuses, or machines. The human, as Aristotle once defined with admirable philosophical clarity, is that being which possesses the *logos*; in the case of Descartes, a fissure has opened up in this definition, one in which a so-called scientific-technical civilization has been able to establish itself. It is not only the case that this fissure has allowed for the disassociation of thinking from the human body or from those certain exclusive places in which thinking is supposed to take place; I suspect that the scientific disquiet that is compelling us to think about media, without ever being able to provide an adequate definition of the term, has in this fissure the very condition of its possibility. This condition arises from a deeply felt uncertainty about *where* thinking takes place, about *what* its 'natural' milieu is, and about *who* its privileged or exclusive agents are.

The radicalization of the Cartesian exclusion of the body, or Lyotard's technological wager

Already in Descartes – it must be remembered – the gesture of regression was related to the certainty of the thinking self, the *res cogitans*. The critical trajectory of this gesture moved from the insufficiency of the thinking self towards all philosophical and theological ('scholastic') knowledge, which mankind had allegedly not advanced throughout the civilizing process, a process that consisted of the emancipation of mankind, from its subordinate position with respect to nature and its installation into a dominant role. However speculative or unworldly the Cartesian foundation of modern philosophy might seem, its application was eminently practical. In an effort to construct, scientifically and thus on the basis of true causes, apparatuses, and machines as well as mechanical interpretations and simulations of organisms, its ultimate goal was to enable a comprehensive manipulation of natural processes. All of knowledge was meant to serve the improvement of the human condition; the practical leitmotifs of this philosophy, which is ostensibly so speculative, are in fact the improvement of technology and medicine, the deliverance of humans from hard labour, and the prolongation of human life (Canguilhem 2006, pp. 7–21, esp. pp. 10–13).[3] I make a point to mention the connection between the theoretical radicalism and practical orientation of Descartes's endeavour because this connection is also at the foundation of the thought experiment with which Lyotard confronts his audience. Lyotard's text, to which I would now like to devote closer attention, consists of two main sections. The respective titles of these sections are 'He' and 'She', and thus it is immediately apparent that the philosophical question at hand will be addressed in terms of the problematic of gender.[4]

As becomes clear over the course of the dialogue, it is not *He* but rather *She* who speaks in the name of philosophy (and in the name of Lyotard). The philosopher is female and, as it turns out, this is not contingently the case. The body discussed in Lyotard's text, which he argues is inessential to thinking, does not simply appear as such in the case of humans (and other life forms) but rather as one that is marked as male or female. This also means, however, that in Lyotard's text *She* acts as the advocate for the body in terms of a problem that immediately poses the question of 'whether one can think without a body'. This in turn leads to the question whether thinking can occur outside of the delimitations that are prescribed by a certain 'gender affiliation', even if this affiliation is understood as an effect of the cultural technique of classification, and thus as a notion devoid of all natural constancy. It would nevertheless be too rudimentary simply to understand the confrontation between *Him* and *Her* as that between non-philosophers and philosophers, even though the text goes out of its way to make this very suggestion. Even *He* is a philosopher, though one who feigns to lack a particularly high opinion of the typically philosophical passion for aimless, open-ended inquiry and inconsequential speculation. That said, it is *His* response to the initial question of whether one can think without a body that is formulated along the lines of the foundational scene depicted by Descartes. *He* does this by freeing the question from this speculative foundation and attributing to it an unexpected performative value, by reformulating it as the question of the 'technical minimum' of thinking under extremely inhospitable living conditions – or, more precisely, under the conditions of a 'natural state' that, for the first time in the history of philosophy, is worthy of the name, insofar as this 'nature', as regards humans and life in general, reveals the highest degree of hostility.

In his book *The legitimacy of the modern age*, Hans Blumenberg explicated Descartes's problem as a question of human self-assertion that requires one to step outside of the anthropocentric illusion, an illusion that consists in believing that the world is configured according to the will of mankind, to which it is fundamentally 'amenable'. Blumenberg demonstrates that the temporality – and thus the loss of faith that tomorrow and next year will approximately be the same as today – of Descartes's era becomes the 'crucial handicap' of the human spirit:

> This affects not only the identity of the subject, the presence of which at any given moment does not guarantee it any future, but also the persistence of the world, whose radical contingency can transform it, from one moment to the next, from existence into mere appearance, from reality into nothingness. (Blumenberg 1983, pp. 161–162)

According to Blumenberg, this temporalization of human and social existence, that is, the experience of the dismantling of all historical constants – and the resulting 'insecurity' of human existence and of the social and cultural structures in which this existence takes place – is motivated and justified by the Cartesian mistrust of the world and by the consequent 'great separation', which objectified the totality of non-human entities as so-called nature and gave them leave to be dominated by mankind. Descartes endowed this modern ontology, which has admittedly never been without competition in modern philosophy, with his identification of nature as a *res extensa* determined by the laws of physics and mechanics and also with the quite distinct notion that unextended thought is self-referential or reflexive. According to Blumenberg, however, this ontology is not merely a philosophical error – it is not a speculative eccentricity of modernity or a Lacanian 'psychotic phenomenon' – but can rather be legitimized by its preventive function with respect to an overpowering nature against which humans, if they care to survive, must react by means of technological mobilization. Technology, for Blumenberg, is an expression of human self-defence in the face of a natural world that makes palpable our physical impotence and the perilousness of our existence.

We have thus arrived at the starting point of the accusation that *He*, the Cartesian revenant in Lyotard's thought experiment, raises once more against the philosophers of the old school and their boundless trust in the world: there are pressing questions that cannot afford to be left unanswered. Descartes was right that one cannot trust the world, and yet matters are far worse than he supposed, for his ultimate concern was to strengthen the position of mankind against the overwhelming power of nature and the damage that it causes. Descartes understood apparatuses and machines as artificial prostheses with which, like armour, weak and exposed humans could equip themselves to increase their chances of survival. Yet there was something that Descartes was not yet able to know: humans will never succeed in making any arrangement with the hostile nature that forever guarantees their perpetuation as beings with two innate attributes, one corporeal and the other intellectual. The time will come in which the constitution of humans as living beings with two natures will prove to be incompatible with their further reproduction. The issue here is not the nature of gardens and parks, not that of primeval forests and deserts and seas, but rather the material monster of modern physics: this nature will tolerate mankind and its environment, the biosphere, for a few billion years to come, but then things will come to a definitive end:

> While we talk, the sun is getting older. It will explode in 4.5 billion years. It's just a little beyond the halfway point of its expected lifetime. It's like a man in his early forties with a life expectancy of eighty. (Lyotard 1991, p. 8)

As *He* portends, with this end, one that for once is not the consequence of human war, the true ending will have been reached; no one will remain to inaugurate a fresh new beginning. In four and a half billion years, Descartes's hypothetical separation of the mind and body will no longer be a philosophical possibility; it rather describes a problem whose technical solution will exact nothing less than the physical reality of human beings:

> But in what remains after the solar explosion, there won't be any humanness, there won't be living creatures, there won't be intelligent, sensitive, sentient earthlings to bear witness to it, since they and their earthly horizon will have been consumed. (Lyotard 1991, p. 10)

The earth will be consumed in heat and clouds of matter; its familiar ecology, which has furnished all the necessary provisions for human survival, will no longer exist; and the condition that will replace it will no longer be compatible with the existence of organisms. This new condition, moreover, will also no longer be compatible with thinking, *so long as* (it must be added) this thinking is still inextricably associated with neuronal infrastructure of organisms. The physics of the body is advancing ineluctably towards this apocalyptic state, and yet this condition is still so far removed from us in the future that we can quickly set our minds at ease in order to philosophize, as did philosophers from Epicurus to Husserl, 'in the cozy lap of the complicity between man and nature' (Lyotard 1991, p. 11).

THINKING MEDIA AND BEYOND

There is, however, an alternative to jaded philosophical musings and to the consoling promises of religion, and this alternative happens to be *His* response to the question of whether it is possible to think without a body. In a fundamental way, the question has been poorly formulated, for the drama of secular temporality is such that thinking *must* be able to take place without a body, if thinking is not to come to a definitive end along with the end of all corporeal organizations of life. For Descartes, the exclusion of the body was still the free choice of a speculating philosopher, one who decided to 'withdraw from the world into solitude' and yet could comfort himself with the knowledge that this same world would go on existing beyond his solitary seclusion. The catastrophic scenario addressed by Lyotard's text, on the contrary, elevates the exclusion of the body into an imperative of self-preservation according to which this self can only be preserved if it is completely liberated from its corporeal foundation. It is thus required of humans to react to the challenge of this impending disaster 'with means belonging to that category' (p. 11). What does it mean, however, to 'anticipate the disaster' and to accept the 'challenge'? According to *Him*, the task ahead is as follows:

> And then the only job left you – it's been underway for some time – the job of simulating conditions of life and thought to make thinking remain materially possible after the change in the condition of matter that's the disaster. This and this alone is what's at stake today in technical and scientific research. (pp. 11–12)

And then *He* adds a sentence that can be understood as the methodological *a priori* of all research concerned with cultural techniques and the philosophy of media:

> You know – technology wasn't invented by us humans. Rather the other way around. As anthropologists and biologists admit, even the simplest life forms, infusoria (tiny algae synthesized by light at the edges of tide pools a few million years ago) are already technical devices. (1996, p. 12)

He understands technology in much the same terms as the media theorists of today:

> Any material system is technological if it filters information useful to its survival, if it memorizes and processes that information and makes inferences based on the regulating effect of behaviour, that is, if it intervenes on and impacts its environment so as to assure its perpetuation at least. A human being isn't different in nature from an object of this type. (p. 12)

The titular question of this thought experiment – 'Can thought go on without a body?' – appears at first glance to be 'anti-body' and unmaterialistic, as though its goal is to render thinking into an *actus purus* and to disassociate it from *all* corporeal infrastructure. The 'topicality and urgency' of media philosophy derives from a situation,

> in which machines are made more and more capable of acts of consciousness, in which thought itself can be described as a neurological process and represented with visual images, and in which moral problems, for instance, can be treated pharmacologically.[5]

Whatever media might be, the presence and obtrusiveness of these entities and the operations enabling them clearly depend on the diagnosis of an increasing 'extension' of capabilities, that is, an increasing delegation or transference of such capabilities to non-human agents. Although this process may be intensifying in our present age, it has always been underway, for human beings, and living beings in general, are compelled by the weakness of their constitution, which anthropologists of all stripes are quick to underscore, to seek as many 'mediators' (Latour 2005, p. 39) and 'associations' (p. 7) among other (human and non-human) bodies.

Thus, when *He* recognizes that our scientific-technical meta-objective is to develop, for the 'software' that is human thinking, 'hardware' that is no longer dependent upon terrestrial conditions, then the anthropological difference concomitantly inscribes itself into the difference between 'hard' and 'soft', namely, that peculiar privilege of humans (those 'reeds shaken by the wind'), the standards of which are set in their infirmity and illnesses, their propensity for error, and their capacity to suffer. Thinking without a body is not at all body-free thinking; the link between thinking and bodies has proven to be inevitable. This is not likewise the case, however, with the link between thinking and *a particular* body, something like the bodily equipment that lies at our disposal today. In short, the experiment that *He* outlines is concerned with manufacturing 'hardware capable of "nurturing" software at least as complex [...] as the present-day human brain, but in non-terrestrial conditions' (Lyotard 1991, p. 14). To borrow a term from the historian Ernst Kantorowicz, all of media theory is the study of two bodies. Even lawyers in the Middle Ages were faced with the problem that Lyotard's *He* expresses: How can one guarantee the continuity of a political or social order that is embodied in the figure of a prince or king if the representative of this order shares with all of his subjects the 'frailty' and dispensability of the body, if he can fall sick, age, and is generally susceptible to all the threats presented by inimical forces (be it by nature or political opponents)? Kings, as the lawyers argued with the help of theological arguments and tropes, are privileged to the extent that, in addition to their weak body (the body natural), they also possess a second, immortal body (the body politic), which is invisible and intangible and therefore impervious to whatever deficiencies and defects might plague the first body. The second body of the king is in possession of 'mysterious forces' (Kantorwicz 1957, p. 9). 'For as to this Body the King never dies' (p. 13) because it can free itself from the first body and be transferred, for instance, to the king's successor, and thus it is ensured that the death of its former 'bearer' does not entail the end of the corporation that the king publically represents or even 'embodies'. To think without a body means the following: thinking under the condition of generating an independent second body that is 'maintained and supported only by sources of energy available in the cosmos generally' (Lyotard 1991, p. 14). In light of Lyotard's computational distinction between hardware and software, both the definition of the problem and its solution are situated on the horizon of a particular epistemic configuration that, among other things, is concerned with so-called artificial intelligence. This is a field of knowledge that *He* clearly regards as being already sufficiently predestined and consolidated, such that *He* waits until the end of his speech to consider the question of its possibilities and the problems and limitations of computer-simulated cognitive capabilities. A reference is made at this point to the objections of the philosopher Richard Dreyfus, but *He* fails to draw any conclusions from them regarding his technological vision (Lyotard 1991, pp. 15–16).

Such conclusions are left for *Her* to draw. In her rejoinder, *She* is clever enough not to doubt the fundamental feasibility of the project (nor to doubt its existence, as looming as it is today, as a field of practical research); *She* is rather doubtful of the Cartesian implications of such a project, which proceeds by assuming that the familiar synthesis of thinking and the body can be undone so unproblematically, as though the body that 'bears' thinking (at least as we know it) is somehow not part of the form and operational mode of thinking itself. At first glance it seems as though *She* wishes to contradict *Him* in the name of those 'warm' and 'soft' values that have come to categorize soothing thought as 'feminine'. What will become of intuition and the power of analogy, which are inherent to thinking? Thinking does not subsume matters under concepts; it never comes to an end with its conceptual provisions; without any conceptual safeguard, as Kant already knew, it can reflect more or less aimlessly and derive its pleasure from that alone. What thinking shares in common with the corporeally bound experience of perception is the ability to focus on a particular event without entirely overlooking the shadows and contours that surround every object or process. Its strength, to a certain extent, is that it is somewhat blurry and thus inexhaustible; it is never able to satisfy the demand of producing a complete description of any state of affairs, but it does not want this satisfaction. In fact, it is with the utmost mistrust that thinking encounters any such claims of complete description. Perhaps more importantly, thinking depends upon something given, something that it does not itself create; we have to proceed from the fact that, in *Her* formulation, 'thinking and suffering overlap' (put philosophically: spontaneity and receptivity or, in more current terms, 'agency' and 'patienthood') (Lyotard 1991, p. 18). Like any other power to act, the power of thinking is never without the reverse side of passivity, never without one surface or another upon which something 'inscribes' or manifests itself that can, in turn, be thought about.

It is no coincidence that media theory attributes such great significance to writing and projection surfaces, canvasses, stages, pages, and screens, because they allow for the question of data (literally 'given things') to be reflected upon as a problem of modes of givenness (*Gegebenheitsweisen*) and points of access: 'It is not the given but that by which the given is given' (Deleuze 2004, p. 176). That, to a modest extent, such 'scenic' surfaces can also serve as the storage spaces of bygone 'inscriptions' lends to representational media, upon which thinking relies, a dimension of the historical deposits of thought, deposits from which no act of thinking can entirely release itself. Philosophers, according to Gilles Deleuze, enclose thinking in a self-reflective loop; they are fascinated by the reflexes and escalations of thought thinking about itself. In doing so, Deleuze notes, they ignore the exterior forces, the affections of the body and their forms of expression, and the cues that compel one to think: 'Thought is primarily trespass and violence, the enemy, and nothing presupposes philosophy: everything begins with misosophy' (2004, pp. 175–176). In order to think, a reason is needed to do so that lies outside of thought itself. If Deleuze is to be believed, thinking is at its most intensive when one pursues and attempts to master a thought in vain. Thinking does not occur unbound to a body, like an object on a table that can be removed at any time, but it is nevertheless not integrated with any particular body. It is much rather the case that bodies can serve as 'vessels' for the thoughts of others, a phenomenon subsumed by media technology under the term 'spirit media' (*Geistmedien*), a concept that no longer obeys the close Cartesian association of *cogitare* and *ego*:

> Spirit possession is a discourse of the non-ego that introduces the paradox of a person simultaneously being and not being that which he or she affects to be. It is a manner of speaking without being the subject of speech and a manner of knowing without being the subject of knowledge. (Behrend 2012, p. 114)

Descartes only acknowledges the possibility of a 'person simultaneously being and not being that which or she affects to be' in the speech of insane people, and speech of this sort is expressly excluded from the doubtful course of meditation (see Foucault 1976, pp. 9–28, Balke 2009, pp. 197–202).

Thinking is always reliant on the *highly various* 'bodies' that provide its operational contexts and operational resources. According to *Her*, 'we think in a world of inscriptions already there. Call this culture if you like' (Lyotard 1991, p. 20). 'Finally', *She* adds, 'the human body has a gender' (p. 20) and the symbolism of this gender, which neither coincides with biological gender nor can be read from it, is responsible for the fact that our visible and tangible body is always supplemented by a second, unconscious body whose effects manifest themselves only as symptoms in the first. Whereas it might conceivably be possible, *She* concludes, to simulate bodiless intelligence in a technologically perfect manner, this thinking, which will outlive the explosion of the sun, will have already been deprived of the features that comprise the complexity of thought itself.

The body as a form of ultimate self-assertion or as a power to be affected

Descartes vs. Spinoza

If it is correct to keep in mind that 'technology wasn't invented by us humans – rather the other way around', the question arises of whether our conception of technology is sufficiently aware of the problem, that is, whether it comprehends technology as an information system whose sole function is to ensure 'survival'. Quite surprisingly, *He* and *She* are in agreement on one point: *sub specie aeternitatis*, everything depends on rescuing the human, the 'crown of creation' that resulted from a more or less contingent evolutionary process, from the moment of its destruction. This human, however, will have forsaken all of the phenomenal characteristics that we associate with human beings, but will finally have entrusted its 'essence', which is understood here as the epistemic function of the subject, to a suitable body that is no less 'firm' and 'immortal' than the function itself. As Descartes demonstrated, this function is invulnerable to all of the deformations that are typical of the bodies familiar to us. As far as thinking is concerned, the solar explosion will provide the singular opportunity of finally being bound to an ultra-stable body that is 'worthy' of it. For *Him*, the salvation of mankind beyond the thermonuclear catastrophe is associated with the Cartesian condition of separating, completely, the *res cogitans* from its previous bodily infrastructure and with 'grafting' this 'pure intellectual capacity' onto a sort of hardware that is truly deserving of the name. Against this notion, *She* insists upon the perdurable intimacy between the human and 'his' body, in which the 'spirit' ('Geist') to some extent resides and from which it can only be removed at the expense of its complete alienation. For this reason, *She* places all of her hope in the development of a type of software that is able to accommodate and perpetuate the cumulative formational history of the human spirit (*Geist*).

There is no reason, however, for a phenomenological nostalgia for the body that attempts to preserve it by means of constructing an adequately complex type of software, considering that at no time has the body itself been sufficient. In fact, it has always relied on a great variety of supplements from and alliances with other bodies, so much so that the body has never been able to be regarded entirely as 'one's own' body. This body – as Spinoza, Descartes's great opponent, observed – is always already a body of bodies, an intricately assembled structure composed of various systems with relative autonomy, so that it has never been possible to conceive of it as being identical to the wholeness or form whose image is reflected back at us in the mirror. 'The human body', writes Spinoza in his *Ethics* (1675/1677), 'needs for its preservation many other bodies from which it is, so to speak, regenerated' (1963, p. 52). 'The human mind', on the other hand, 'is apt to perceive many things, and more so according as its body can be disposed (*disponi potest*) in more ways' (p. 52). Thinking, according to Spinoza's non-reductive and parallelistic materialism,[6] requires for its reproduction much more than simply the 'platform' of the body in which it takes place; thinking only exists because this body operates in the function of a medium, and the complexity of the mind or of mental operations depends on the availability of this medium.

Had this concept been known to him, Spinoza would have defined it in media-operational terms, namely as a power to affect and be affected. In Spinoza's work, the position of the medial is subsumed by the concept of the sign, which is understood as an effect or trace (*vestigium*) that one body leaves on another and that leads to an alteration (*mutatio*) in the affected body. This occurs in such a way, moreover, that the effect does not need to be accompanied by an adequate understanding of its cause. For this reason, however, signs provide an endless amount to think about, because the ideas, impressions, and images evoked by them are stubbornly opposed to being resolved into concepts (see Deleuze 1998). The greater the variety of conditions that this body can assume, the more able thinking is 'to perceive many things'. That Spinoza regards the affection (*Affizierung*) of the body and mind in the sense of *being disposed* is indicative of the role of artificial impulses or dispositions that are construed specifically to bring about changes in the state of the body. It is not a coincidence that Deleuze (1989), an enthusiastic reader of Spinoza, privileged the type of cinema that afforded its utmost attention to the affections of the body and to the ideas that arise from them – not a cinema of cleverly calculated diegesis and breezy dialogue, but rather one of intervals, abbreviated action, and affection images; in other words: a cinema of stagnation, of time standing still, of purely optical or acoustic situations to which one is uncertain how to respond or react.

The ability to be affected represents the most extreme opposite to the conception of the body that finds its reflection in the metaphor of hardware. That which medieval lawyers could only attest in the figure of the sovereign, namely his possession of a second, immortal body that never suffers from corporeal infirmity or poor judgment, will be implemented technologically by hardware engineers from now until doomsday. Lacan commented extensively on the conception of the body as a total form that has overcome bodily defects (with which we will have to be content for the time being) in its ability to imagine and misrecognize its constitution. This should be kept in mind, because the answer to the question of whether thinking can occur without a body depends on whether the body assumes the role of a medium (according to Spinoza) or that of a form or *Gestalt* (according to Descartes and subsequent defenders of 'human self-assertion'). Lyotard's thought experiment turns out to be an extreme variant of the logic of the mirror stage, for here the body is conceived from the outset as being characteristically divided. The body, without which we will be forced to think at the end of times, is that fragile and vulnerable and mortal body – the human *physis* – with which even a small child indicates his discontent when he jubilantly confronts in the mirror 'the total form of his body', and, as Lacan (2002, p. 4) writes, 'by which the subject anticipates the maturation of his power in a mirage'. The ultimate maturation of human power, however, will come about at the historical moment in which, on the basis of its own constitution, it can demonstrate its readiness to cope with the destructive forces of nature at their most extreme. Because the unification of the body, which is suggested by the identification with one's mirror image, is never fully complete, this 'aggressive tension', Lacan (1993, p. 95) notes, 'is entirely integrated into every kind of imaginary functioning in man'. As long as he is capable of doing so, the subject attempts to identify himself so completely with his mirror image that he is never again afflicted by the experience of there being an original division between the two. The more completely the subject devotes himself to this imaginary body image, the more delusional these efforts become, efforts that will ultimately 'mark his entire mental development with its rigid structure'. Lacan (2002, p. 6) also refers to this '"orthopedic" form', the imaginary and simultaneously technical compensation for 'insufficiency', as 'armour' – and it is precisely this quality of armour-like self-reinforcement with which the thought experiment was ultimately concerned, except that Lyotard replaced the metaphor of armour with the more timely metaphor of hardware.

Less finality, more potentiality

The life of machines

If one takes Lacan's advice to heart and thus avoids being completely overtaken by the latent and paranoid logic of the imaginary, if one dismisses the utopia of a 'total form of the body', which denies any experience of organic insufficiency, then one must also challenge the role of technology within the Cartesian apparatus. As in all current anthropological theories, this role consists in compensating for the organic deficiencies of humans. The Cartesian thought experiment concerning the technological perpetuation of life after death, however faithful it might be in technological development, is in fact inspired by a deep mistrust in technology, given that it associates technology with an ultimate finality, with a rigid and unambiguous purposiveness that denies technological objects their own evolutionary dynamic. As far as the relationship between machines and organisms is concerned, no major shifts are expected to take place over the course of the next four billion years, for machines will always fulfil only those functions that scientists and engineers assign to them. Cartesianism does not allow for any event that might affect the thinking enclosed in the *res cogitans* because the radical interiority and self-referentiality of this 'thing' ('Sache') safeguard it from the danger of being 'de-natured' or mixed with other bodies. It was Spinoza, again, who confronted the Cartesian idea of the mind's superiority over the body; he observes, first of all, 'that no one has yet had a sufficiently accurate knowledge of the construction of the human body as to explain all its functions', and he adds:

> [T]he body can do many things by the laws of its nature alone at which the mind is amazed. Again, no one knows in what manner, or by what means, the mind moves the body, nor how many degrees of motion it can give to the body, nor with what speed it can move it. (Spinoza 1963, p. 87)

For Descartes, on the contrary, the dominion of the mind over the body is beyond doubt, above all the dominion of the mind over its own body, which can be set in motion by the merest inkling of thought. What is more, this dominion extends over the many technical objects that the mind has created and whose sole function is to fulfil as well as possible the purposes assigned to them.

At certain points, however, Descartes seems to doubt his conception of the relationship between theory and technology, according to which technology always occupies a subordinate position. For instance, he feels compelled to admit that, without the invention of the telescope, 'many good thinkers' would have had to think a great deal longer; they would not have been able to make more discoveries in the field of optics simply on the basis of their theoretical considerations (Canguilhem 2006, p. 18). The telescope is not simply a technological entity – it is not a materialized theorem – but rather an event, a machine that affects thinking, that forces thought in a new direction, and that creates new opportunities for formulating physical and optical theories. The telescope is one of those bodies that Spinoza had in mind when he wrote that the human mind 'is apt to perceive many things, and more so according as its body can be disposed' – or affected – 'in more ways'. In this light, however, bodies can no longer be disqualified as potential sources of disruption and deception that must be eliminated in order for us to reach any epistemic certainties. Bodies produce effects according to their own set of laws and they depend on whatever other bodies might happen to be in their area of effect. Technology, which produces these effects by constructing special apparatus-bodies, is thus not fully derivable from science. From the perspective of effects – and no other perspective matters here – the distinction between natural and artificial (technical and social) bodies plays no role whatsoever. In order to think about the body beyond the distinction between naturalness and artificiality, Gilles Deleuze and Félix Guattari revived the classical usage of the term 'machine', which precludes the Cartesian dualism of nature and culture. Today it is somewhat difficult for us to set aside the notion of the machine as a technical apparatus constructed for purposes of industrial production. However, philosophers such as the Roman materialist Lucretius spoke of a *machina mundi*, a 'world machine', which is neither a divine creation nor a world in itself but rather 'a contrivance that is both complex and purposeful, without that purpose being immediately apparent to the untrained eye' and thus something like 'a cunning maneuver or "machination", a deceitful trick, a startling effect'. The term *machina* (at least in the strict sense reserved for the transportation or storage of goods), it should be remembered, 'has accrued so much of its history in the theater' (Blumenberg 2010, p. 63) where its central function was to produce effects on the audience (think of the famous *deus ex machina*, for instance).

What distinguishes machines from tools is the impossibility of thinking about them in terms of a strict instrumentalism that seeks to transform them into fully and theoretically describable and controllable objects. Thus understood, the machine designates a technical object that possesses a higher degree of freedom than the tool, the intended purpose of which is conspicuously inscribed. The technical complexity, heterogeneity, and openness of machines, at least with respect to their interfaces and their enhancement or integration of new elements, constitute their contingency, that is, their ability to act in different and surprising manners, and their ability to be used for applications unanticipated by their inventors. In this sense, machines are not trivial; rather, they have the potential to create – along with other entities, such as human beings – emergent orders and socio-technical connections that would not be possible without their contribution. The life of machines is no less preconditioned than that of other living beings. An enormous amount of effort is required to ensure their ability to exist and survive: designs must be made, knowledge and capital mobilized, and 'contexts' or interfaces – complex and extensive infrastructures – need to be made available, into which the machine-object has to be integrated in order for its operations to commence and for its life to persist. What distinguishes machines from mere mechanisms is the very characteristic that they share with organisms. They are less and less associated with finality and thus more and more with potentiality and operational freedom. At the same time, their susceptibility to falter and their need to be repaired are thereby increasing, and from this reality not even a universal discrete machine is exempt. It is this sort of machine that, in Lyotard's scenario, or at least in that of his Cartesian ventriloquists, is supposed to bear the burden of the survival of thought and perpetuate its function. It can be stated with 'the empiricism of engineers' that, over the course of the future development of hardware, the codes controlled by machines will quickly lose their former 'mathematical transparence' and come to approximate, of all things, 'the opacity of everyday language', something to which such codes should have no resemblance (Kittler 1997, p. 167). Machines, which hold the promise of a 'finite state', will all too soon take the shape of a Babylonian tower 'in which the ruins of towers that have already been demolished remain built-in' (p. 167) and they will do so in order to guarantee the compatibility and historical nexus between various generations of computers.

According to Guattari (1995, p. 9), who has a different conception of the relationship between technology and machines, the latter should no longer be regarded as 'secondary to a more general system – that of *techne* and technique', but rather this point of view should be reversed, 'to the extent that the problem of technique would now only be a subsidiary part of a much wider machine problematic'. In addition to its technological component, this problematic also contains institutional and individual elements: 'Thus the machine's environment forms part of *machinic agencements*' (p. 9, emphasis by the author). With this I can return once more to the question posed by Lyotard's *Him*, namely, of whether thought can go on without a body. At the heart of the thought experiment lies a future event that is supposed to prove the truth of naturalism. What is meant by this naturalism, for its part, is that nature can be distinguished entirely from culture, that one is incapable of speaking or negotiating with it, and that it will prove to be uncontainable and ultimately untameable; The only way in which this naturalism, which has prevailed for a long time, will lose legitimacy is by means of *a future event of the greatest possible threat*, by a sort of final 'state of nature', in anticipation of which the development of our civilization has already begun to orient itself. In the end, the truth of a certain concept of nature should indeed emerge, a concept that we have always half-heartedly (and against our better judgment) opposed with the multifarious exchanges and alliances by which human beings have established tolerable relations with the various agents and bodies in their environment.

In order to survive, the subject, which was brought into the world by Descartes, will have to rely on an extreme objectification of the world, on the creation of that which we have come to refer to as NATURE (with capital letters). This is entirely different from any man-made constitution and history; it is, in Rheinberger's (2005, p. 39) words, 'the limit against which civilization can only assert itself by driving back, excluding, and dominating nature'. The enormous expansion and transcendental escalation of this nature corresponds to the extreme confinement of the human to that of his particular subject, which is itself absolute. Under these apocalyptic conditions, salvation will depend exclusively on the residual and solipsistic thinking that Descartes achieved by fundamentally separating it from any bodily relation, above all from the body to which it is bound, and by compensating for this separation with the *res cogitans*, an independent substance of its own. The function of a salvation scene of this sort consists in securing the absolute separation of nature and culture *today*, and in discrediting their factual hybridization as a distraction from the 'actual' objective of preserving ourselves under the severest of hostile living conditions. The technical body, which Lyotard designates with the term 'hardware', would then indeed be the irreducible and imaginary materiality that is able to serve as a depository or receptacle for a type of thinking that will no longer interact with other bodies, no longer be affected or disposed by them, and will thus truly be able to persevere 'in itself' ('in sich selbst').

Notes

1. On this notion, see Foucault (2005, pp. 47–51).
2. On (Carnap's) neo-empirical project of achieving a 'logical construction of the world', on its scientific-utopian assertions, and on its context within the 'life-reform' movement, see Galison (1993).
3. For the original French version of this article, see 'Descartes et la technique', in *Travaux du IXe Congrès international de philosophie, Etudes cartésiennes, IIe partie* (Paris: Hermann, 1937), 2:77–85, which was reprinted in *Cahiers philosophiques* 69 (1996), 93–100.
4. In the text, 'He' and 'She' are not simply used as personal pronouns; they rather designate personae, marked by gender, who represent the foundational philosophical conceptions for which the author has provided a stage. Here I have treated them as proper names and, for the sake of their recognizability, placed them in italics.
5. This quotation is from the advertisement for a lecture series entitled 'Der Körper des Denkens', which took place at the Bauhaus-Universität in Weimer during the winter semester of 2011/2012. The text was co-written by Lorenz Engell, Frank Hartmann, and Christiane Voss.
6. On the ontological parallelism in Spinoza (a concept to which Spinoza is indebted, though he never uses the term itself) as an alternative to all types of reductionism and exceptionalism, see Deleuze (2005, p. 109):

   Spinoza's doctrine is rightly named 'parallelism', but this is because it refuses any analogy, any eminence, any kind of superiority of one series. Parallelism, strictly speaking, is to be understood neither from the viewpoint of occasional causes, nor from the viewpoint of ideal causality, but only from the viewpoint of an immanent God and immanent causality.

Disclosure statement

No potential conflict of interest was reported by the author.

Notes on contributor

Friedrich Balke is Professor of Media Studies with particular emphasis on theory, history, and aesthetics of documentary forms at the Ruhr-Universität Bochum, Germany.

References

Balke, F., 2009. *Figuren der Souveränität*. Munich: Wilhelm Fink.

Behrend, H., 2012. Geistmedien. *In*: C. Bartz *et al.*, eds. *Handbuch der Mediologie. Signaturen des Medialen*. Munich: Wilhelm Fink, 113–117.

Blumenberg, H., 1983. *The legitimacy of the modern age*. R.M. Wallace, trans. Cambridge: MIT Press.

Blumenberg, H., 2010. *Paradigms for a metaphorology*. R. Savage, trans. Ithaca, NY: Cornell University Press.

Canguilhem, G., 2006. Descartes und die Technik. *In*: H. Schmidgen, ed. *Wissenschaft, Technik, Leben. Beiträge zur historischen Epistemologie*. Berlin: Merve, 7–21.

Deleuze, G., 1989. Beyond the movement-image. *In*: *Cinema 2: the time-image*, H. Tomlinson and R. Galeta, trans. London: Athlone, 1–23.

Deleuze, G., 1998. Spinoza and the three "ethics". *In*: *Essays critical and clinical*, D.W. Smith and M.A. Greco, trans. New York: Verso, 138–151.

Deleuze, G., 2004. *Difference and repetition*. P. Patton, trans. London: Continuum.

Deleuze, G., 2005. *Expressionism in philosophy: Spinoza*. New York: Zone Books.

Descartes, R., 1996. *Meditations on first philosophy: with selections from the objections and replies*. J.J. Cottingham, ed. Cambridge: Cambridge University Press.

Foucault, M., 1976. My body, this paper, this fire. *Oxford Literary Review*, 4.

Foucault, M., 2005. *Hermeneutics of the subject: lectures at the Collège de France 1981–1982*. F. Gros, ed. New York: Palgrave-Macmillan.

Galison, P., 1993. The cultural meaning of *Aufbau*. *In*: F. Stadler, ed. *Scientific philosophy: origins and developments*. Dordrecht, The Netherlands: Kluwer, 75–94.

Guattari, F., 1995. On machines. V. Constantinopoulos, trans. *Journal of philosophy and the visual arts*, (6), 8–12.

Kantorowicz, E.H., 1957. *The king's two bodies: a study in medieval political theology*. Princeton, NJ: Princeton University Press.

Kittler, F., 1997. Protected mode. *In*: J. Johnston, ed. *Media, literature, information systems: essays*. Amsterdam: OPA, 156–168.

Lacan, J., 1993. *The psychoses 1955–1956: the seminar of Jacques Lacan, Book III*. Jacques-Alain Miller, ed. New York: W.W. Norton.

Lacan, J., 2002. The mirror stage as formative of the *I* function as revealed in psychoanalytic experience. *In*: *Écrits: a selection*, B. Fink, trans. New York: W.W. Norton, 3–9.

Latour, B., 2005. *Reassembling the social: an introduction to actor-network-theory*. New York: Oxford University Press.

Lyotard, J.-F., 1984. *The postmodern condition: a report on knowledge*. G. Bennington and B. Massumi, trans. Minneapolis: University of Minnesota Press.

Lyotard, J.-F., 1991. Can thought go on without a body? *In*: *The inhuman: reflections on time*. Redwood City, CA: Stanford University Press, 8–23.

Rheinberger, H.-J., 2005. Natur, NATUR. *In*: *Iterationen*. Berlin: Merve, 30–50.

Spinoza, B., 1963. *Ethics and on the correction of human understanding*. A. Boyle, trans. London: Everyman.

The metaphysics of media: Descartes' sticks, naked communication, and immediacy

Florian Sprenger

ABSTRACT

Continuing longstanding debates in German Media Theory, the article explores the genealogy of the concepts of media and communication and their physico-philosophical background. By referring to Descartes' physics, it shows how concepts of action at a distance were part of the formation of the modern idea of physical mediation, while at the same time leading to phantasms of immediacy, which means the cancellation of mediation. In his Dioptrics, Descartes uses the analogy of a stick to explain how light is transmitted from the sun to the earth. This mediation is described as naked communication because it acts at two places at the same time, thus showing a historical oscillation related to all concepts of mediation.

Introduction

In recent years a growing interest has been expressed in the history of the concept *medium* and that of related terms such as *communication, milieu,* and *environment.* Building upon the now classic works of Spitzer (1948) and Canguilhem (2008), scholars have advanced a number of different perspectives about the importance of these related histories for facing the challenges of our contemporary 'technological condition'.[1] This work has illustrated the ruptures and shifts that these concepts have undergone over time. An approach grounded in the history of concepts and the history of knowledge can analyse these turns and breaks without overlooking the gaps and blanks that necessarily constitute these histories. Such an approach would avoid raising questions about the 'proper' meaning of a concept based on the common error of projecting a contemporary perspective onto the past. As Joseph Vogl writes in a succinct characterization of the circumspection necessary for such an undertaking, one cannot extrapolate 'conceptual continuities' from 'the historical inertia of terms'.[2] This article seeks to find how the tensions between continuities and discontinuities might serve as a symptom offering insight into the promises and plausibilities that adhere to these concepts. Concepts [*Begriffe*] can be understood, following Koselleck (1979), as the smallest unit of an epoch's self-interpretation, and thus can serve as indicators and factors of historical processes. We can find a culture's understanding of itself crystallized in concepts, which also provide an account of how it faces the challenges of its time. Thus, a glimpse at the history of concepts can help in contextualizing these options of self-interpretation. Thus it is not an exaggeration, as I would like to show here, to claim we can learn something about contemporary debates from historical constellations that seem so far away.

1. Mediations of physics

Since Aristotle, the field of physics has been concerned with relations of mediation and communication. Physics asks how forces can be transferred from one body to another, and how something can act, via a medium, somewhere where it is itself not located, as forces of attraction or light do. These problems become especially significant in early modernity. As I will address in what follows, taking Descartes' sticks as an example, media-theoretical issues are not externally imposed onto the field of physics in the seventeenth and eighteenth century. Rather, these issues are central to the physics of these periods.[3] At the very heart of the field, problems of communication and media were disputed; and often even in the same terminology as that used in contemporary media theory. As terms, *medium* and *communication* by no means refer to processes between humans and technological artefacts alone, as is all too frequently suggested today.[4] Furthermore, far too often an artificial division is maintained between debates in philosophy and the natural sciences which, in the case of philosophy, often neglects the epistemology of natural sciences.[5] Historically, this division hardly existed before the twentieth century, and it is precisely in the early modern period that philosophical questions were understood as always also questions of physics, even if physics did begin to distance itself from philosophical postulations at this time. In this convergence between philosophy and the natural sciences lies history's potential for doing theory today.

Since antiquity, thinking about motions and interactions between bodies that come into contact with one another has led to the following problem: how can a moving body and a body that causes motion or a motive force be connected if they are not spatially proximate to one another? This issue is particularly salient for phenomena that became focal interests starting in the early seventeenth century with the development of new instruments like the telescope and microscope and with the emergence of experimental methods – phenomena such as light, gravity, magnetism, and electricity. In this context, 'communication' means a connection between cause and

THINKING MEDIA AND BEYOND

effect, a connection between which a transmission occurs. Every contact between bodies raises the question of whether the separation between both bodies will be maintained or not. This question formed the crux of debates about communication and media at the time. In their historical formations, causality, continuity, and communication were linked in various relationships, and so offer a breeding ground for immediacy, that is, for the cancellation of any separation. A medium, however, cannot be immediate. If it were, it would bring its relational elements – between which the act of communication joining these elements occurs, and between which it mediates in specific ways depending on the case – into an unmediated relation that would eliminate both separation of the elements and the medium's mediation in turn. Media are, of course, the condition for the immediate connection of two elements with each other since immediacy implies a relation between two or more elements.[6] However, in the immediacy of connection, the medial connection of the elements and their presupposed separation are at the same time erased.

The stakes of such immediacies entail historically different prospects of reward: they sublate the uncertainties and contingencies that lie in the separation between elements by promising to substitute multiplicity for unity; they present the prospect of an undivided community; in the form of a metaphysics, they hark back to an originary source [originären Ursprung] from which everything else can be derived; and they strive for an always already-transmitted transmission in which delay or loss play no role. In the context of early modern physics, immediacy meant the continuity of connections of causality, and thereby implied a unity that refers every effect back to its cause, above and beyond separations, delays or differences. This is why early modern physics needed media that presupposed distances – in order to erase them.

In the history of media, one can discern a repeated emphasis on the significance of media that is shot through with the 'reverie' of a media-less immediacy, one that the self-historicization of media studies thus faces the urgent task of clarifying.[7] The paradox of the immediacy of media consists in the negation of its own presuppositions. The 'dangers' of immediacy seem to lie less in its phantasms than in the miraculous way in which its 'reverie' relegates what ought to be explained to a realm of the unexplained, and substitutes uncertainties with too-certain certainties.

It is particularly significant in this regard to consider the entanglement suggested by an immediacy that presupposes, and at the same time erases, media. What should be investigated, accordingly, are the historical technics, discourses and phantasms of this erasure, the conditions of its appearance, and its aporia. They are deeply rooted in the metaphysical household of the Western world. The relation between media and immediacy articulates, to speak with Derrida (1967, p. 280), a 'coherence in contradiction [which] expresses the force of a desire'. The function of this relation can be resolved only historically, and not logically. For this reason, media studies ought to investigate constellations – from Plato's *Phaedrus* and Aristotle's *to metaxy*, to Newtonian physics and the transatlantic cable, to Paul Baran's theory of distributed networks and Marshall McLuhan's media theory – in which media have a constitutive function that is at the same time negated. Such a history would allow us to understand how these phantasms of immediacy live on in the description of our contemporary condition – constituted, as it were, by ubiquitous, omnipresent, and smart media.

2. Chains of continuity

The ambitious project that René Descartes begins to bring to an end in 1644 with his *Principia Philosophia* is a search for inconsistencies in the universe, for places where gaps open up that would point to a *deus malignus*, an evil God who deceives humans and plays tricks on us. As Descartes confesses in the *Meditations* in 1641, his philosophical intervention is driven by a very real fear. In a vivid manner, he depicts how the indistinguishability of waking life from dreams unsettles him to the point at which his methodological skepsis secures a sound foundation in the sentence, 'I think, therefore I am' (Descartes 1999a). Descartes' ultimate cognitive instrument is the evidence that, on the grounds of reflection, leads the *ego cogito* to self-knowledge. On these grounds, Descartes establishes a science whose hidden driving force is a fear of the inconsistent and inexplicable, such as an action at a distance [*Fernwirkung*] or a vacuum.

The vacuum was traditionally understood in antiquity as a horror since a benevolent God could not have created any sort of emptiness. After Aristotle, one of the first rules of physics said that there can be neither vacuum nor void since the world is a continuum.[8] According to a second rule, every movement has a cause in impact or pull. With the mechanistic theories of early modernity, the *causa efficiens* becomes the only valid model of causality in science because it is predictable, can be probed through experiment, and explains movements through cause and effect. It is above all Descartes who equates the *causa efficiens* with the *causa materialis*, and attributes to them a general validity whereby *causa finalis* and *causa formalis* disappear from the table. Following a third rule, these movements must stand in contact with their causes because they occur in a continuum and there exists no external impetus. The insight that no body can have an effect where it is itself not located, unless there is some sort of interceding medium, was formulated in the Aristotelian-influenced late Middle Ages: '*Omnis actio fit per contactum, quo fit ut nihil agat in distans nisi per aliquid medium.* (Every action happens by contact, because nothing can act at a distance if there is no medium.)'[9] For every movement, there must, as a fourth rule, be a prime mover, most often God. Action at a distance, in which cause and effect are spatially separated but occur simultaneously and are communicated without delay, cannot be permitted in this framework of all physical processes, just as a vacuum cannot be. Action at a distance contradicts all foundations because it threatens the nexus of causation and continuity, because conceivably it has no material bearer, and perhaps even implies a vacuum or, in any case, an empty space. Consequently, in order to explain actions at a distance from phenomena such as light, gravity, magnetism, or electricity, a number of media, from ethers to corpuscles to spirits, were invented over the centuries. The task of these media lies in filling such gaps and empty spaces.[10]

In fact, these issues of communication are about more than philosophical-physical niceties – they concern the coherency of the world. The continuity of causality, which ties cause and effect together and was referred to as communication, has to be infinitely divisible, without any empty space, if it is godly and/or rationally ordered. If no gaps can be found, if mechanism and materialism are non-contradictory, and if, therefore, unquestionable foundations exist, then Descartes' universe is in itself consistent, and thus necessarily organized by a benevolent God. God must, as Descartes argues, prove Himself unto rationalism. A science that strives for evidence in this way attempts, one might say, nothing more or less than to prove God's existence and goodness.

With its ungrounded continuity and causality, an immediate action at a distance like that known today from quantum physics would constitute such a feared inconsistency. For this reason, Descartes derives all worldly occurrences from the mechanical interactions of the smallest particles, which do not allow for any in-between space. This approach is closely related to his methodological reduction of composites to their simplest parts. Descartes explains all worldly occurrences from the interacting circular movement or spin of these particles, which are referred to as corpuscles or effluvia, and are not to be confused with atoms. These processes involve bodies that are material, differently sized and shaped, but act beneath the threshold of perception. Their interactions explain the movement of all inanimate matter, as Descartes claims most notably in the *Principia Philosophia*. Through recourse to mechanical explanations of the world via the smallest of particles, explanations that were familiar since pre-Socratic atomism, but revived in early modernity under entirely different auspices, Descartes grapples with the question of whether an action at a distance is possible. This question is addressed time and again in the history of knowledge of physics, but also as this knowledge is implemented in media-technologies. Descartes denies any such action if it cannot be attributed to immediate contact. Only an action in proximity exists, likewise only communication through contact, and only continuous media.

The heteromorphic components of matter are offset from one another through mutual displacement, even if, in contrast to later effluvial theories, they are not active themselves. Movements resulting from pressure and impact are used to explain all phenomena of nature. No force is ever lost in such movements because there are no voids into which an impact might trail off and from which pressure could come. Force in the universe is constant and every effect is equivalent to its cause. For Descartes, there is no demiurgic or thermodynamic intrusion that would rob the universe of force. Yet a vacuum, whose existence was accepted by some and rejected by others during Descartes' time, and actions at a distance, like gravitation (and later electricity), bring gaps into focus: an emptiness that is not supposed to exist and a *causa* without ground. For these problems, which had been addressed since antiquity, Descartes offers attempts at solutions. He conceptualizes the smallest bodies without voids between them. In this, he attempts to introduce a metaphysics different from atomism, which granted reality to being and non-being, atom and void. He carries through a logical exclusion of voids, an exclusion that mutates into fantasy insofar as it meant to fulfil a desire, or rather to sooth a fear:

> For when there is nothing between two bodies they must necessarily touch each other. And it is a manifest contradiction, for them to be apart, or to have a distance between them, when the distance in question is nothing, for every distance is a mode of extension. (Descartes 1999b, p. 231)

3. Communicating sticks

Descartes' world system appears to be closed unto itself due to this desire for contact between bodies and the fear of voids. But the system has one lock keeping it shut – action at a distance. Instantaneity is the key to this lock. Instantaneity implies that something can have an effect at two places at once without any delay in time: immediately, without any medium in between. Using a slender stick as an analogy, one that appears in different variations in his work, Descartes breaks down the universe.

He frequently refers to the blind man's stick and the sense of sight to make his points. On one hand, sight as a primary sense is closely connected to the act of cognition. On the other hand, sight occurs as a transmission across distance without actually transporting anything, and therefore must be immediate. Additionally, and central to the argument of this text, Descartes makes use of the stick to explain action at a distance as well: By substituting light's physical action at a distance with a continuous chain of actions in proximity between corpuscles, actions which necessarily occur at the same time through the entire chain, Descartes introduces the notion of instantaneity. Its mediation ultimately reveals itself as that which is unthought-of in this philosophy. Every symbolic order has its 'disorder' that must be excluded, a disorder that nevertheless renders the system of order effective insofar as the order requires the exclusion to be ordered at all; yet this exclusion continues to haunt the symbolic order.[11] Mediation, communication, and immediacy can be described in this historical formation only in conjunction with one another.

Descartes' order of the universe is pervaded by vortexes, by particle streams, and by different forms of invisible matter. These aspects of the Cartesian system would later be decried by the Newtonians on account of this system's attention to detail and aspiration to explain every event in the universe as 'Philosophical Romances ... contriv'd for the Diversion of the lazy and talkative' (Hales 1727, p. 265). Because Newton assumes other forces than just pressure and impact, the French Cartesians consider him to be anti-mechanistic since the gravitational force Newton argues for is regarded as occult by the Cartesians. Unlike Newton, Descartes seeks to prove without contradiction that the universe consists of interconnected corpuscles, which move in circular motions and can explain all appearances of nature as effects of pressure and impact. Descartes thus takes a different path than that of Newton with the latter's active force of gravitation.

The notion of a gapless plenitude of the universe entails an extremely powerful differentiation that divides *res cogitans*, thinking or mental things, from *res extensa*, extended things, that is, matter entirely describable through analytic geometry. If all matter is extended and anything extended is material, if extension and matter are then identical, there can be no empty space. An empty space would be nothing and nothing cannot exist since only *res cogitans* and *res extensa* exist. The *res extensa* encompass three different types of matter with different degrees of fit and continuities amongst them. The corpuscles of this matter appear in various constellations and forms and explain the complex configurations of physical processes in the world. According to these notions, all space is filled with a *matière subtile*, a concept that harks back to antique notions of the ether. The concept also anticipates the ether theories of nineteenth-century physics, yet with the exception that *matière subtile* not only fills empty space, but also fills spaces already filled with matter of other classes. This concept likewise garners accusations of atheism against Descartes, for it raises the question of where God might be located in a universe that is filled with matter, is mechanical, and is explainable through and through.

Matter transmits actions in proximity through the circular motion of its components. The *matière subtile* is, in a way, a second stratum of the universe. In interaction with other matter it prevents an empty space from occurring when a body moves and leaves behind a void. Since the entire universe is filled with particles, every movement triggers a chain of other movements. If indeed everything is filled with matter and voids are impossible, then every movement in this plenum results in another, and does so instantaneously. This is demonstrated through an analogy in Descartes' *Dioptrique*, a 1637 addendum to his *Discours de la Methode* written as something of a primer for opticians according to the new method. For Descartes, light is:

> a certain movement, or very rapid and lively action, which passes to our eyes through the medium of the air and other transparent bodies, just as the movement or resistance of the bodies encountered by a blind man passes to his hand by the means of his stick. In the first place this will prevent you from finding it strange that this light can extend its ray instantaneously from the sun to us. For you know that the action by which we move one end of a stick must pass instantaneously to the other end, and that the action of light would have to pass from the heavens to the earth in the same way, even though the distance in this case is much greater than that between the ends of a stick. (Descartes 1637/1954, p. 71)

A movement at one end of the stick thus directly, by passing through the stick, generates a movement at the other end of the stick. Cause and effect are necessarily simultaneous. Every movement of particles thrusts the particles that lie in front of the moved particle forward, while those that lie behind it are pulled along. The particle's attribute of being 'viscous' or 'porous' is what enables straight-lined, stick-like movements that do not lose any force. Every contact results in an equally strong reaction.[12] As shown between A and E in the figure below, the stick produces a connection across distances while allowing for impacts as interactions between two ends. The stick itself, however, remains an unalterable transmitter of force. The Cartesian world cannot be squashed (Figure 1).

Descartes' solution to the problem of action at a distance, in this case the communication of light from the sun to the earth, follows the exclusion of immediacy. If everything is filled, there can only be mediating actions in proximity – actions which, as in the case of the stick, are linked with one another.

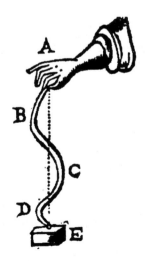

Figure 1. Reproduced by permission of Descartes (1632, p. 220).

This communication nevertheless reintroduces immediacy since the stick, which is supposed to exclude immediate actions at a distance, has an instantaneous effect. In this sense, immediacy builds on a continuity of the medium, on an uninterrupted chain of effluvia, and on a universal matter. Descartes supplements the stick example a few pages later with another analogy between the transmission of light and liquids. In this example, the sides of a container would necessarily collapse and come into immediate contact if something were to be taken out of the container and nothing in turn put in its place (see Descartes 1637/1992, p. 113). Because there is no vacuum and ethereal matter is extended everywhere, there are only actions in proximity, but these actions, because chained together, are necessarily immediate. The transmission of light presupposes a medium, but then in the same move erases the medium.

Even when Descartes accepts a finite velocity of light in other passages in the *Dioptrique* concerning the theory of light refraction, this immediacy does not pose any open contradiction. The stick cannot have velocity since every movement occurs through action in proximity. Following the argument, light does indeed have to pass through media such as glass or water and is diffracted or diverted in the process, but it is instantaneous all the same. The particles of *matière subtile* are constantly exposed to motion and pass on this motion when other particles, triggered from somewhere or other, move. The stick operates by evading any mediating waypoint. Only beginning and end are relevant. The spaces between remain identical with themselves. Because there is no empty space between the particles, the stick is not elastic. It is one piece of matter. If the stick consisted of individual, elastically linked atoms, between which there were a gap, it would be exposed to a transmission of force in which the impacting end of the stick would move earlier than the impacted end since the effect of elasticity would be to transmit the force step-by-step across the individual in-between spaces. The transmission would not be instantaneous. It is precisely this fact that the Jesuit priest and physicist Boscovich (1763/1966, p. 20) brings to our attention a good 100 years later using the same example: 'In nature there are no rods that are rigid, inflexible, totally devoid of weight & inertia & so, neither are there really any laws founded on them.' Descartes' stick, by contrast, has to be constant and inflexible in order for the analogy of its effect to work. Because it is a body, the movement of the stick spreads in the direction of its location and remains constant thereby. The stick can be as long as the universe is: if one end of it is moved, then its other end necessarily moves at the same time since there is no void that has to be filled. No force can be lost. As both medium and its communication, the stick entails an entire worldview.

In order to explain the effects of electricity (hardly researched at the time) and magnetism (more prominent at the time), which appear enigmatically, but also fascinatingly, to act at a distance, Descartes draws not on an electric substance or special effluvia, as many of his contemporaries do. Rather, he integrates these into his general theory of corpuscles. As a mechanical phenomenon, the attraction of a lodestone belongs to the same class of occurrences as that of amber or that of the electrifiable objects hardly known at the time.[13] According to Descartes, both stones consist of a porous material permeated by conduits and channels through which the corkscrew-shaped corpuscles pass. The corpuscles are thrown into streams upon friction. Because these emanating particles belong to the body and remain connected to it, they pull everything along with them when they snap back – like a rubber-band, as it were. Descartes explains this process by bringing analogies with sticks and fluids together:

> Just as we see that a very sticky drop of liquefied fats of this kind, suspended from a rod, can be shaken by slight movement in such a way that one part of the drop still adheres to the rod, while another part descends for some distance and immediately returns of its own accord towards the rest of the drop and also brings with it the tiny straws or other minute bodies which it has encountered. (Descartes 1983, p. 273)

In the process, small circular motions are responsible for the attraction. Magnetic and electric attraction function, too, like sticks (Figure 2).

The difficulties of thinking through such mediations in a vacuum-less universe characterized by plenitude, undermines even the level of representation in the schematic illustrations of invisible processes. Voids appear not only in the world, but also in the representations, which are visible only because of

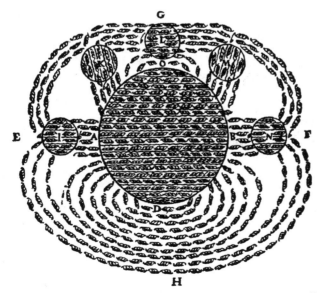

Figure 2. Reproduced by permission of Descartes (1637/1992, Illustrations).

the blank white background. In the illustration, which is meant to serve as an example, a ball magnet can be seen in the form of the earth. Meandering particles move through the channels and pores of this ball parallel to the axis of the earth. Because of their form, the particles are able to pass through the magnet only in a single direction. By continuously spiralling in corkscrew manner, they set a circular motion into effect that carries all other surrounding particles along with it. The balls I, K, L, M, and N are additional small magnets, which are aligned through the movement of the particles relative to the poles of the large (earth) magnet and strengthen the vortex.

The continuity of the filled world cannot be captured in the illustration. Thus, there is a contradiction between text and image, since in the image an empty, white, in-between space is visible, a space that should not exist according to the text. However, the text constantly provides the reader with instructions on how the image is to be read. It states that the reader should imagine the empty space in the image as filled. The image does not display or make anything evident until the text corrects it, because, on its own, the image is wrong. In this way, the discursive nexus of the corpuscularian stick directs its immediacy across the gaps on the paper and through the image description into the image itself. Insofar as the illustrations are meant to show how mechanisms unfold, the theoretical gaps emerge in the mechanism as well.[14]

Descartes uses this and other analogies in order to plausibly transfer certain attributes from one object to another. In many of his works, visual analogies depict the mechanisms he addresses, and thereby elucidate the phenomena. In this sense, the analogy is not meant to be taken literally or as 'true' because it works out some specific attributes of the stick – instant transmission and incompressibility – in order to apply these attributes to the explanation of light. The analogy does not provide any comprehensive explanation, nor is it intended as any sort of ultimate explanation (see Eastwood 1984, p. 487). Because the stick analogy, as Michael Hagner has shown, brings along a number of problems for Descartes' theory of sight that cannot be elaborated upon here, and because the analogy becomes inconsistent, Descartes abandons it in later passages in the text.[15] The analogy is in no way meant to be understood as an explication of his theory of sight. Nevertheless, it does gain a certain effectiveness that renders the analogy plausible even beyond the *Dioptrique*, especially given that the stick example was used as early as antiquity as an explanation for sight and its rays. Already in Simplicius' commentary on Aristotle's *De Anima*, the diaphane as a bearer of light is compared with a stick in order to explain light's instant emanation without referring to atomism.[16]

The mediality of the stick, which transcends all distances, structures a large part of the Cartesian world. The stick requires no time to transcend distance. A body moves only when another body has impacted it. In this way, light reaches instantaneously from the sun to the earth, for the corpuscles fill everything and any distant movement has effects everywhere. At the moment at which light is emitted, it has already arrived, but not because small bodies of light were transported. In this point, Descartes' theory differs from later corpuscle theories, which often assume movements of corpuscles across smaller stretches to explain magnetic or electric attraction for instance. Descartes does not address movement *in* a medium, rather, the movement *of* a medium. There is no bearer of light. Since no two things can be present at two places at the same time, every movement leads to further movements. Movement results in more movement and thereby leads to the circular motions mentioned above. For Descartes, cause and effect are logically and physically connected as a successive reaction. They can be simultaneous. And they can be simultaneously dependent on each other across distances. The transmission of force always occurs mechanically and without loss since there is no theft (of force, for instance) in the universe. The transmission is undisturbed and the issue of whether there could be disturbance at all does not even enter the purview of this discursive formation. The relation between the particles has no intervening medium. The immediacy of instantaneity is logically necessary because there is a frictionless transmission between corpuscles that is continued through a stick at random – for instance from the sun to the earth as an immediate-instantaneous transmission of force.

4. Evidence of instant contact

With the metaphor of the blind man's stick, which Descartes employs in texts besides the *Dioptrique*, the transmitting stick is modified into a medium of distant-action tactility. It immediately links that which touches to that which is touched through the medium: a 'concretization and compression of the *pneuma* into a quasi-tactile prosthetic' (Alloa 2011, p. 147). Following the *Regulae ad directionem ingenii*, the *Rules for the Direction of the Mind*, this touch accounts for the evidence of intuition. According to Descartes, the 'light' of intuitive reason operates immediately in the 'illuminated' evidence of visual cognition. For this reason it does not require any intermediary steps because it apprehends things without any detours. It is linked through the henceforth three-tiered analogy of the blind man's stick to the instant transmission of sunlight, the act of seeing, and the act of touching. The proximity of the sense of touch and the distance of sight, as Serres (1991, p. 169) points out in his reading of Descartes, are coupled in this context. Sight, which presupposes distance and void since one cannot see that which touches the eye, rests on the stick-like communication between corpuscles. As a tactile process communication forms the visual. In the *Regulae*, Descartes expands this to include intuition, which likewise presupposes distance but nevertheless apprehends immediately.

Descartes describes the foundation of perception in one of the rejoinders to the *Meditationes* as 'that through which the bodily organ is immediately affected by external objects' (1642/1972, p. 378). In early modernity, sight is understood, in line with older traditions, as an act that rests on the transmission of corpuscles. The transmission of light, as elucidated by the stick example, underlies this act of sight. Descartes is part of a transition from antique emission theories of sight to an early modern understanding. It involves a change in arguments about media as well. Antiquity assumed that rays of sight emitted from the active eye come into contact with objects and are thus tactile. In contrast, Newtonian optics, especially, posits rays of light that function as a carrier medium and which are later replaced by waves.[17] Though Descartes does not assume the existence of active rays of sight, he does accept corpuscular mediation, albeit a mediation that does not consist of a substance transportable through a medium. Instead, as has been shown, the reciprocal push and pull motion of linked particles accounts for transmission, though nothing is transported in this process. Descartes turns against the scholastic notion that what is transported by light or acoustic impressions must be similar to what is transmitted (Wohlers 2002, p. 72). To be sure, such a notion does not yet explain how an image develops between the eye and the soul. But the comparison between cognition and sight does serve the function of explaining the latter on the grounds of a mechanical transmission of light as tactile, which resembles the stick example. Here too, Descartes describes immediacy as a unity whose division only exists for limited senses, which see a distance and void between the earth and the sun. This void, however, is filled with imperceptible particles and for this reason is indivisibly immediate. Descartes describes this immediate action at a distance very appropriately as 'naked communication'. The skin of the communicating body is exposed and senses what comes into contact with it (1628/1973, p. 60).[18]

In short, sight in Descartes' ninth rule can occur equally physiologically-physically unmediated as it can occur intuitively-immediately as compared to cognition. The stick comes into play with the example of action at a distance:

> For instance, if I move one end of a stick, however long it may be, I can easily conceive that the power which moves that part of the stick necessarily moves every other part of it instantaneously, because it is the bare [*nuda*, naked in Latin; F.S.] power which is transmitted [*quia tunc communicatur nuda*] at that moment [*uno et eodem instanti*], and not the power as it exists in some body, such as a stone which carries it along.[19]

Descartes uses the stick example in this expression to make the point, more on an epistemological level than on a physical level, that, in order to verify the possibility of an *actio in distans*, which occurs 'instantaneously [through the whole medium], [instanti [...] per totum medium], reason ought not resort to complex objects such as magnets or sunlight. Rather reason should refer to the world, perceptible to the senses' (Descartes 1974, p. 34). The knowledge being sought can be ascertained from the world – precisely through the observation of a stick and by working through the analogy which makes clear that there are only effects through contact. For just as intuition, which is the focus of the ninth rule, produces evidence without mediation, so too does the stick transmit something. Just as in intuition we apprehend something without friction, and in sight we perceive the distant object without delay (although in this case a transmission is required between the object and the eye) so does light in this way transmit, since there is a continuous chain of communication. In the words of Serres, 'Touch is that model of sight which is the model of intuition' (1991, p. 167). This interweaving of analogies is held together by the stick, which in turn puts into play the unrest of mediation and immediacy.

This analogy is both physically and epistemologically an analogy of contact or touch. Contact implies here mutual presence. What is on one end of the stick is on the other end as well. The metaphor of the stick brings the presence of touch into relation with the evidence of sight.[20] Accordingly, for a blind man, the stick and the mediating contact with the outer world are – as is made clear when Descartes revisits the analogy at another point – a substitute for eyes:

> For instance, when our blind man touches bodies with his stick, they certainly do not transmit anything to him except in so far as they cause his stick to move in different ways according to the different qualities in them, and thus likewise setting in motion the nerves in his hand, and then the regions of his brain where these nerves originate. This is what occasions his soul to have sensory awareness of just as many different qualities in these bodies as there are differences in the movements caused by them in his brain. (Descartes 1988, p. 66)

The mediation allows the blind man to substitute sight with tactility and to feel out the world. This functions because things come into contact with the retina as they do with a stick. They trigger an impulse that brings forth an image in the soul. As Descartes demonstrates in the *Dioptrique*, in sight the retina is just as tactually stimulated as the skin is in touch. In this manner, blind people see with the stick since sight touches: 'In their lack of the sense of sight, the stick becomes for them a sixth sense' (Descartes 1637/ 1954, p. 60). As Natalie Binczek has shown, sight and touch mutually compensate for one another's deprivation.[21] Sight, touch and intuition, we could say, operate analogous to the communication of sticks, of invisible entities that consist of corpuscles, of material blind man's sticks, and of evident cognition.

In the various stick analogies, the ends of the transmission touch each other in a touchless [*taktlos*] contact that is shared in the epistemological history of both tactility and physics: Both a contact, which presupposes the presence of what is in contact, and a continuity of causality are modified to become an immediacy of light corpuscles between distanced locations whose result is presence. Absence in presence is supplemented. The *relata* – the sun and the earth; two ends of the stick; hand and object; eye and that which is seen – are separated from one another and distanced. But because there is a continuous chain of corpuscles, a stick and instantaneity, the *relata* are present side-by-side without interlude. They can immediately touch one another in spite of their separation. The here of the now and the there of the now can, despite interruption, be immediately linked, just as the blind man experiences with his stick a tactile nearness through which he interacts immediately and intuitively with that which is touched as if he were seeing. Presence is more than a precondition for contact at the same location. It is the result of an action at a distance that links separated locations timelessly. Communication occurs in this way immediately and erases its preconditions. 'Immediacy is derived' (Derrida 1976, p. 157).

As a medium without content, the stick is the communication of communicability: naked communication of force, disguised and revealed by that which is communicated. With the stick analogy, Descartes' sticks can be inserted as nexuses of particles that are dependent on situation and effect. Because this can be done wherever a mediation or effect occurs, all disputes about causality, distance or time may be skirted. The stick analogy leads, in its different variations within Cartesianism, to a stabilization of the oscillation between separation and connection, or presence and absence, an oscillation that results in a balance of causality and a fusion of mediation and immediacy: through 'naked communication'.

5. Media of immediacy

From a media-historical perspective, what I have discussed here with Descartes' sticks concerns an entanglement that one can observe in numerous constellations: media and immediacy are closely linked with one another. While the tension between them has historically been solved in various ways, it often leads to media being erased. What lies between no longer plays a role. This tension becomes problematic whenever media are tied to unity and presence. A media theory of unity prefers, to put it bluntly, identity to difference, and it overlooks the practices of negotiating address and personhood, the delay of transmission, or otherness in today's global networks.

Rather than allowing an absorption by metaphysical unity, it is necessary to consider the differences that exist because there are media. That media operate with delays that they isolate, rather than unify. Wherever they appear, simultaneously or in real time, or in any case where they appear in a *timely* manner, steered by 'cultural technics of synchronization' (Kassung and Macho 2011, Geoghegan 2013), does not enter the picture if media are phantasmatically invested with immediacy. Media are only relationally observable: in other media, in associations and in differences. If media are defined, not as fixed entities, but rather by historical circumstances in which something becomes a medium (Vogl 2009), then such historically grounded particularity allows the multiplicity of the concept of media to gain validity and underscores this concept's transversal moment. Instead of devaluing a metaphoric, and thus secondary, use of the concept of media in sciences such as physics, biology, or information technology, its commonality in difference can be foregrounded in the following way: by being confronted with widely differing constellations of mediation, for example, physics, with action at a distance, biology, with the environment, or information technology, with communication. In this way, the multiplicity of the concept of media can both be historicized and serve as a resource for theory.

In this sense, writing a history of media or of media theory necessarily entails a history of immediacy as well. Even today, this entangled history concerns the modes of operation of media theory – and perhaps all the more so today as the genealogy of the concept of medium threatens to become ever more concealed. When media, and especially transmission media, are meant to serve, to put it abstractly, the overcoming of an abyss, a task whose fulfilment suggests a disappearance, they are always in danger of becoming media of immediacy. If media studies is time and again confronted today with technologies that appear new and always more immediate, in which action at a difference and simultaneity seem to become permanent states, then media studies needs more than new concepts to address objects such as smart phones and implanted RFID chips. It requires knowledge of its history in physics and philosophy. (Translated by Nathan Taylor)

Notes

1. For the English-language context, see Guillory (2010) and Peters (2000); the discussion has been more prevalent and broader in the German-language context. For this see Seitter (2002); Hoffmann (2002); Berz (2010); Hagen (2008) as well as Porath (2008). On the 'technological condition', see the essays in Hörl (2011).
2. Vogl (1997, p. 117). What underlies Vogl's statement is a sense of the German word *Begriff* that is lost in its English rendering as concept, and which makes it difficult to adequately translate the German tradition of *Begriffsgeschichte*, the history of concepts. The approach outlined here demands however a departure from an understanding of the widely prevalent, traditional German-language project of *Begriffsgeschichte*, marked by names like Joachim Ritter, Hans Blumenberg, and Reinhard Koselleck, towards a history of knowledge and historical epistemology.
3. Descartes' sticks have been addressed as objects of several analyses before: Serres (1991, p. 169), Hagner (1990), Bexte (1999), Binczek (2007), Wilke (2010), Eliassen (2010). Such analyses have however not yet been integrated into the

more local context of corpuscle theory and issues of communication and causality.

4. We find such a suggestion in, for instance, the work of John Guillory, who treats media simply as inter-human means of communication. This ultimately results in a narrow concept of media, the historical breadth of which falls from view. The use of this concept for explanations in physics is precisely not derived or metaphoric, as Guillory suggests. See Guillory (2010).

5. This attitude can be seen for instance in the fact that, in the English translation of Descartes' *Principia Philosophia,* the sections on the natural sciences are simply left out, thus instilling an undue and deeply problematic division. In Descartes' case, this is probably exacerbated by the fact that nearly all of his insights have proved to be incorrect. See Descartes (1999b).

6. On this, see Chang (1996).

7. The concept of reverie has been invoked by Gaston Bachelard to describe the relation between the symbolic and the imaginary: Bachelard (1987).

8. For these rules see Hesse (1961, p. 64).

9. Eustachius a Sancto Paulo (1614): Summa Philosophiae, cited in Spitzer (1948, p. 201).

10. An important text in this regard is the exchange between Gottfried Wilhelm Leibniz and Samuel Clarke as representative for Isaac Newton, in which Leibniz offers a brilliant media-theoretical argument: Leibniz and Clarke (1956).

11. Hubert Damisch has described such constellations in regards to central perspective. See Damisch (1974).

12. As Christian Wohlers has emphasized, Descartes does not work out a theory of light, but one of transmission. See Wohlers (2002, p. 72).

13. For a detailed account see Heilbron (1979).

14. As Claus Zittel has shown, Descartes' illustrations are not to be understood as illustrative representations, because, according to Descartes, no image resembles its object. See Zittel (2009).

15. See Hagner (1990). Hagner has demonstrated the extent to which Descartes' theory of sight draws on corpuscularian theory but at the same time assumes a genuine ability of the soul to see. The transmission of light from the seen object to the eye is not based on any process other than the metamorphosis of the impression in the eye into a perception of the soul.

16. See Sambursky (1958). The omnipresence of light is already described by Aristotle and, building on his work, by a long tradition of optics, according to which light is present everywhere, albeit as diaphane, and for this reason is not transmitted or communicated. Communication as dependent on instantaneity is first introduced with Descartes' mechanism. See Aristotle (1986, p. 417b).

17. On theories of sight in early modernity, see Crary (1990).

18. This reference between instantaneity and tactility has itself a historical depth that cannot be traced here, one that reaches to Marshall McLuhan's electric tactility. See Sprenger (2012).

19. Descartes (1999c, p. 34). Unfortunately, the English translation is not a precise rendering of the Latin: 'Verbi Gr., so quantum vis longissimi baculi unam extremitatem moveam, facile concipio potentiam, per quam illa pars baculi movetur, uno & eodem instanti alias etiam omnes ejus partes necessari movere, quia tunc communicator nuda, neque in aliquo corpore existit, ut in lapide a quo deferatur.'

20. Peter Bexte has investigated the significance of the blind man's stick and its iconography (1999). Tobias Wilke concentrates in his interpretation of tactility in

Descartes on the perceptual aspects of light refraction and comes to similar conclusions (Wilke 2010). Knut Ove Eliassen has traced the emergence of concepts of mediation in regards to the philosophical history of the blind man's stick (2010). Philosophy into the twentieth century has also pursued the metaphor of the blind man's stick which one finds in the works of Bateson (1972, p. 318) and Wittgenstein (1990, p. 472).

21. Binczek has meticulously demonstrated the tension and potential of the analogy between sight and the stick, pores and ball, and situated this analogy within a transition of historical orders of knowledge (Binczek 2007).

Disclosure statement

No potential conflict of interest was reported by the author.

Notes on contributor

Florian Sprenger is Professor for Media and Cultural Studies at Goethe University, Germany. He is the author of *Politics of Micro-Decisions: Edward Snowden, Net Neutrality and the Architecture of the Internet* (2015). His research covers topics such as the history of artificial environments and the media of immediacy.

References

Alloa, E., 2011. *Das durchscheinende Bild Konturen einer medialen Phänomenologie.* Berlin: Diaphanes.

Aristotle., 1986. *De anima.* Oxford: Oxford University Press.

Bachelard, G., 1987. *The psychoanalysis of fire.* Boston: Beacon.

Bateson, G., 1972. *Steps to an ecology of mind.* Chicago: University of Chicago Press.

Berz, P., 2010. Die Lebewesen und ihre Medien. *In*: T. Brandstetter and K. Harasser, eds. *Ambiente: Das Leben und seine Räume.* Vienna: Turia + Kant, 23–50.

Bexte, P., 1999. *Blinde Seher: Wahrnehmung von Wahrnehmung in der Kunst des 17. Jahrhunderts.* Dresden: Verlag der Kunst.

Binczek, N., 2007. *Kontakt: Der Tastsinn in Texten der Aufklärung.* Tübingen: Niemeyer.

Boscovich, R., 1763/1966. *A theory of natural philosophy.* Cambridge: MIT Press.

Canguilhem, G., 2008. The living and its Milieu. *In*: G. Canguilhem, ed. *The knowledge of life.* New York: Fordham, 242–279.

Chang, B., 1996. *Deconstructing communication.* Minneapolis: University of Minnesota Press.

Crary, J., 1990. *Techniken des Betrachters: Sehen und Moderne im 19. Jahrhundert.* Dresden: Verlag der Kunst.

Damisch, H., 1974. *Théorie du nuage: Pour une histoire de la peinture.* Paris: Edition du Seuil.

Derrida, J., 1967. Structure, sign, and play in the discourse of the human sciences. *In*: J. Derrida, ed. *Writing and difference.* London: Routledge, 278–294.

Derrida, J., 1976. *Of grammatology.* Boston: John Hopkins University Press.

Descartes, R., 1628/1973. *Regeln zur Ausrichtung der Erkenntniskraft.* Hamburg: Meiner.

Descartes, R., 1632. *Le Monde ou Le Traité de la Lumiere.* Paris: Girard.

THINKING MEDIA AND BEYOND

Descartes, R., 1637/1954. *Dioptrik*. Meisenheim: Hain.

Descartes, R., 1637/1992. *Die Prinzipien der Philosophie*. Hamburg: Meiner.

Descartes, R., 1642/1972. *Meditationen über die Grundlagen der Philosophie*. Hamburg: Meiner.

Descartes, R., 1974. Regulae ad directionem ingenii. *In*: C. Adam and P. Tannary, eds. *Oeuvres*. Vol. 10. Paris: Vrin, 359–469.

Descartes, R., 1983. *Principles of philosophy*. Boston: Kluwer.

Descartes, R., 1988. *Selected philosophical writings. Volume 1*. Cambridge: Cambridge University Press.

Descartes, R., 1999a. Meditations on first philosophy. *In*: J. Cottingham, R. Stoothof, and D. Murdoch, eds. *The philosophical writings*. Cambridge: Cambridge University Press, 1–62.

Descartes, R., 1999b. Principles of philosophy. *In*: J. Cottingham, R. Stoothof, and D. Murdoch, eds. *The philosophical writings*. Cambridge: Cambridge University Press, 177–294.

Descartes, R., 1999c. Rules for the direction of the mind. *In*: J. Cottingham, R. Stoothof, and D. Murdoch, eds. *The philosophical writings*. Cambridge: Cambridge University Press, 7–78.

Eastwood, B.S., 1984. Descartes on refraction: scientific versus rhetorical method. *Isis*, 75 (3), 481–502.

Eliassen, K.O., 2010. Remarks on the historicity of the media concept. *In*: V. Nünning, A. Nünning, and B. Neumann, eds. *Cultural ways of worldmaking: media and narratives*. New York: De Gruyter, 119–136.

Geoghegan, B., 2013. After Kittler: on the cultural techniques of recent German media theory. *Theory culture society*, 30 (6), 66–82.

Guillory, J., 2010. Genesis of the media concept. *Critical inquiry*, 36, 321–362.

Hagen, W., 2008. Metaxy: Eine historiosemantische Fußnote zum Medienbegriff. *In*: S. Münker and A. Roesler, eds. *Was ist ein Medium?* Frankfurt/Main: Suhrkamp, 13–29.

Hagner, M., 1990. Die Entfaltung der cartesischen "Mechanik des Sehens" und ihre Grenzen. *Sudhoffs Archiv*, 74 (2), 148–171.

Hales, S., 1727. An account of a book entitul'd vegetable staticks. *Philosophical transactions of the royal society of London*, 34 (34), 264–291.

Heilbron, J.L., 1979. *Electricity in the 17th and 18th centuries: a study in early modern physics*. Berkeley: University of California Press.

Hesse, M.B., 1961. *Forces and fields: the concept of action at a distance in the history of physics*. London: Nelson.

Hoffmann, S., 2002. *Geschichte des Medienbegriffs*. Hamburg: Meiner.

Hörl, E., ed., 2011. *Die technologische Bedingung: Beiträge zur Beschreibung der technischen Welt*. Frankfurt/Main: Suhrkamp.

Kassung, C. and Macho, T., 2011. *Kulturtechniken der Synchronisation*. Munich: Fink.

Koselleck, R., 1979. Begriffsgeschichte und Sozialgeschichte. *In*: R. Suhrkamp, ed. *Vergangene Zukunft: Zur Semantik geschichtlicher Zeiten*. 1st ed. Frankfurt/Main: Kosselleck, 107–129.

Leibniz, G.W. and Clarke, S., 1956. *The Leibniz-Clarke correspondence*. Manchester, NY: Manchester University Press.

Peters, J.D., 2000. *Speaking into the air: a history of the idea of communication*. Chicago: University of Chicago Press.

Porath, E., 2008. Begriffsgeschichte des Mediums oder Mediengeschichte von Begriffen? Methodologische Überlegungen. *In*: E. Müller, ed. *Begriffsgeschichte der*

Naturwissenschaften: Zur historischen und kulturellen Dimension naturwissenschaftlicher. Berlin: De Gruyter, 253–274.

Sambursky, S., 1958. Philoponus' interpretation of Aristotle's theory of light. *Osiris*, 13 (13), 114–126.

Seitter, W., 2002. Vom Licht zum Äther: Der Einfluss der Medienphysik auf die Elementenlehre. *In*: L. Engell, B. Siegert, and J. Vogl, eds. *Licht und Leitung*. Weimar: Universitätsverlag, 47–60.

Serres, M., 1991. *Hermes I: Kommunikation*. Berlin: Merve.

Spitzer, L., 1948. Milieu and ambiance. *In*: L. Spitzer, ed. *Essays in historical semantics*. New York: Vanni, 179–316.

Sprenger, F., 2012. *Medien des Immediaten: Elektrizität, Telegraphie, McLuhan*. Berlin: Kadmos.

Vogl, J., 1997. Für eine Poetologie des Wissens. *In*: K. Richter, ed. *Die Literatur und die Wissenschaften 1770–1930*. Stuttgart: Metzler, 107–127.

Vogl, J., 2009. Becoming media: Galileo's telescope. *Grey Room*, 27, 14–25.

Wilke, T., 2010. *Medien der Unmittelbarkeit, Dingkonzepte und Wahrnehmungstechniken 1918 – 1939*. Fink: Munich.

Wittgenstein, L., 1990. *Philosophische Untersuchungen*. Frankfurt/Main: Suhrkamp.

Wohlers, C., 2002. *Wie unnütz ist Descartes?: Zur Frage metaphysischer Wurzeln der Physik*. Würzburg: Königshausen & Neumann.

Zittel, C., 2009. *Theatrum philosophicum: Descartes und die Rolle ästhetischer Formen in der Wissenschaft*. Berlin: Akademie.

Meta/dia two different approaches to the medial

Dieter Mersch

ABSTRACT

In media philosophy since Benjamin, the concept of 'medium' is conceived in terms of translation or transport. In a similar vein, Christoph Tholen has brought the literal sense of metaphor as metapherein into focus. In this paper, I argue that Tholen's approach misses the 'meta' ('middle' or 'beyond') of metaphor, corresponding to the Latin *trans*. This is contrasted with the Greek *dia* that allows the development of a performative notion of medium, which orients itself at material practices of transition.

Introduction: locating 'medium' in the cultural discourse

In his rare remarks on the question of the 'medium', Gadamer (1989, p. 715) assesses above all that it is – as he somewhat complacently put it – an 'interesting' concept (Begriff). The philosophical interest in it is derived from its proximity to expressions such as 'mediation' or *Vermitteltheit* ('mediatedness'), which also play a prominent role in Hegelian dialectics and can be read as the basic function of the 'medial'. All terms – the 'medium' as well as 'mediation' and the 'medial' – belong together and turn out to be fundamental for the entire tradition of Western thought; however, it remains unclear if there is a specific structure – either to the 'medial' or to its 'mediality' – that conveys any process of mediation (or 'mediatedness'). I therefore begin my discussion of the full circle of notions by reconstructing their interconnections with other fundamental concepts of cultural philosophy, such as the symbolic and the performative, in order to reveal its peculiarity.

In the most general sense of a 'mediator', the 'medium' remains literally 'in the middle', that is, between two entities or processes and objects, and creates transitions between them. Culture seems impossible without this transitiveness. The concept of 'medium' thus has the potential to become a universal category or interface. It creates connections as well as differences and divisions just as much as it functions as a 'condition of the possible' for each and every cultural practice. Concepts of medium therefore prove to be indispensable where we deal with signs, representations and translations, as well as with processes of understanding, communication and memory. Since men can actually do nothing but mediate, that is to say, interpose 'concepts' (Hegel) or 'distances' (Cassirer) in order to posit a kind of spacing so as to displace their displacements, and in this way approach that which is new. Mediations and relationships belong together; referentiality requires mediality. The ability to differentiate, to cut in, to break or to rupture is then an essential part of the *conditio humana*, for any determination, meaning or cultural order requires differences, just as the form of the *Unter-Schiede* (dif-ferences)[1] can be said to originate in its historicity and constitute it (see Tholen 2002). However, there is still the question of whether or not the concept of media is adequately modelled by these approaches; or put differently, if we are seeking it in a place where it does not even belong.

From the perspective taken thus far, we would be confronted with the medial, the 'middle' or with differentiality as the most fundamental guarantee of culturality, just as, inversely, mediation amalgamated with the symbolic and the performative cannot be separated from them. The context has origins in the philosophy of language and art. It is thus not surprising that in particular Georg Wilhelm Friedrich Hegel and Ernst Cassirer, or also Martin Heidegger and the French structuralists and post-structuralists, are among the foremost contributors to a general media philosophy. Walter Benjamin and Theodor W. Adorno, whose considerations might be suitable for those models, which are concerned with the intimate interconnection between art and language, should also be included here. Both art and language obey an *ursprüngliche* (primordial) differentiality which, as Heidegger and Jacques Derrida equally emphasized, does not refer to *anything* primordial, but rather to an *Ur-Sprung* (a primordial leap),[2] a movement generating a continual differentiation, which time and time again is 'over-written' and 'shifted' by new differences. Every *Über-Tragung* (trans-mission; literally: over-carrying) and every *Über-setzung* (trans-lation; literally: over-setting)[3] already imply a differentiation, as they modify both the transmitted or transferred as well as the process of transmission, thus initiating a process that continues infinitely without finding a 'reference point', a point of arrival or an *adequation* (see esp. Derrida 1984). In one of his first essays, *On language as such and the languages of man* (1916), Benjamin developed this notion in connection with that in Jewish theology regarding the opposition between the 'pure' languages of the divine and the languages of man (Benjamin 1977a, see also Mennighaus 1995). Underlying it is a direct naming of the name, which reveals, so to speak, the singularity of the 'being' at every moment, and which would only be suitable to a divine nature. In relation to the language of man, this requires an incessant translation (latin: *transferre*), which at the same time suffers from an ongoing breach such as that specified in the preface to *Origin of the*

German tragedy (Benjamin 1977b, p. 214). Consequently, every expression, like every cognition, proves to be expelled from the paradise of immediacy and dependent on mediation, just as every mediation in turn is rooted in the process of a transmission which refuses its fulfilment and, as Benjamin adds, determines the basis 'of all sadness and (seen from the perspective of things) all silence of nature'.[4] Then, as Benjamin (2008, p. 35) writes in the essay *The task of the translator* published five years later, the specific feat of the medial also exists in testifying to the difference between the languages, as well as their 'supra-historical relatedness'. However, this refers to a vague longing ultimately attached to the idea of a divine criterion lost forever to mankind, and which can at best be touched through art that stems from 'certain types of thing-languages' in order to save the 'connection with languages of nature' from new ones.[5]

It is illuminating that Adorno pursues this idea meticulously in his writings on aesthetics, intensified by a dialectic that puts art – and in particular music – at the mercy of the same adjustment or shift. A key passage in *Music and language: a fragment* (2002) states, 'intentional language wants to mediate the absolute, and the absolute escapes language for every specific intention, leaves one behind because each is limited. Music finds the absolute immediately, but at the moment of discovery it becomes obscured [...]'. Music thus reveals its similarity to language in:

> that, as a medium facing shipwreck, it is sent like intentional language on an odyssey of unending mediation in order to bring the impossible back home. But its form of mediation and the mediation of intentional language unfold according to different laws [...]. (Adorno 2002, pp. 4–5)

Once again we are confronted with the opposition between the naming of the divine name as the only suitable word for evoking the 'non-identical', and the concept always estranged from the divine name as a universal inherent to the irrevocable sign (*signum*) of an 'idealistic pre-decision', as Adorno (2007, pp. 6–11, 2004) writes in his *Negative dialectics*. There is no conceivable place where justice can be done to the materiality of things themselves: 'What the philosophical concept will not abandon is the yearning that animates the nonconceptual side of art [...]' (Adorno 2007, p. 15) – an art that to the same degree exposes its own supposed immediacy as appearance. The true, like the symbolic, owes much to an inescapable mediation, and like the medial, it will always contain the trace of an irreparable fissure, yet at the same time continue to refer to an interminability that seals the fate of humankind and its cultural practices.

One can reject this type of inherent theologism, its latent messianism, as well as its hidden reference to an absolute – or the difference between a medial and an immediacy that resonates within it, and upon which the former measures itself. It is not the questionable difference that is of importance in developing a philosophy of the medial, but rather the interwoven figure of mediation as an original alienation, because mediation seeks to fulfil not only the notion of a *necessary mediatedness* of all human relations – the inner correlation between culturality and mediality – but also the chronic *non-fulfilment* of human relations. Benjamin, like Adorno, has tried to derive these particulars from an irreconcilable break in the ontological, from a disparity between the sphere of the divine and the domain of men, in order to finally transform the tasks of mediation into political practice. Nonetheless, the actual volatility exists in that a radical concept of media is thus formulated for the first time – one that defines the medial as an indispensable condition or a priori. Moreover, it is done in a way such that the medium always already impacts the mediatized, transforms it and forges it. It is this 'art of forging', a literal 'forgery',[6] first systematically developed by Marshall McLuhan, that is a guide for all further media theory, and at the same time poses a challenge for it – whether it be to decipher an inadequacy or a lack in the medial, to account for its permanent transitoriness, or, as McLuhan ironically expresses it, to posit a 'massage' in mediation which works over all social and cultural domains (2003, p. 26). Media philosophy involves the systematic spelling-out and reflection on this 'working over'. The relevance of media philosophy is primarily measured by the clarification of its transcendental indispensability, as argued by McLuhan in *Understanding media*, where media are said to have the power to modify perception, thought, knowledge or action. The remarks made here are meant as a contribution to this work of clarification.

Locality of the medial

I would now like to consider the systematic difficulty caused by a concept of media, whereby mediation is granted a type of universal status, and where every possibility of differentiating between the medial and non-medial withers, such that mediation itself disappears. It should be added here that the terms 'medium' and 'mediation', as well as 'the medial' and 'mediality', form a circle that allows them to be separated from one another just as little as it allows them to replace one another. All of them occupy an interim space, a 'milieu', as McLuhan said, referring to Spitzer (1968, pp. 179–316), within which we move. This milieu also shapes us, which is precisely why it seems difficult to fully fathom its concept because, as *tertium* (or as a third), it can only be localized by virtue of a differentiation. Neither internal nor external, the medial is like a phantom that refuses to materialize precisely at the moment when we try to get hold of it. However, unlike the symbolic, the medial does not describe a relation that would be decipherable; nonetheless, the concept of relation presupposes both the familiarity of the *relata* as well as its structure and rules for connections – the common mathematical formalization 'aRb' characterizes exactly that. The same does not apply to

THINKING MEDIA AND BEYOND

the notion of media, because it basically sets *three* unknowns in relation to one another, whose places, moreover, are first constituted through the mediation. Formally it should concern the sequence (a)–(M)–(b), whose places all have to remain in parentheses, insofar as both 'a' and 'b' are literally *be-dingt*, that is, conditioned by, M;[7] their undecidable centre, just as, inversely, the structure of 'M' can only be determined by 'a' and 'b', which already bear the medial as an index. In other words, all of the places remain unknown because that which is mediatized cannot be represented without the medium, just as, inversely, the medium can only be represented by reverting to the mediatized. Obviously, we are moving in a circle created by a series of negations, which identifies the concept of mediation itself as well as its various facets as a 'negative'.[8]

Consequently, neither the medium nor the medial can be allocated a precise locality – a problem which has been seen as a characteristic 'uncertainty' or 'indeterminability theorem' of 'media theory' from the beginning: This is reminiscent of McLuhan's notion of media's constitutional blindness, since the effect is always a hidden ground and never part of a figure. McLuhan points out that, although what one sees is the figure, it is the ground that creates the impact. Ultimately this is the meaning behind 'The medium is the message': The medium is hidden, the content obvious (McLuhan 2001). No place is in the real that can be identified *as such*. The real can only be spoken of *indirectly* or through a persistent negativity by the mediation around it. And this mediality, moreover, is one that always withdraws from what it is able to accomplish in terms of its positive determination. For example, what would be the mediality of language? Would it be its propositional structure, as some philosophers allege, the figural power of rhetoric, its communicative function, the 'illocutionary force' of the speech act, the entire scene of communication, the infinite creativity of syntactic and semantic concatenation, the voice that lends its presence, the writing, or the order of signifiers, which ensures the duration and historicity 'beyond … (the author's) life itself', as Derrida (1982, p. 313) formulated? Granted, all of these qualifications deliver 'contributions' to what can be identified as the mediality of language; however, any determination or viewpoint already means the exclusion or subsumption of the others, and with that comes a kind of reductionism – just as, on the other hand, the recognition of all the aspects together would constitute a tautology: the mediality of language is language itself. Is this not also the reason why Heidegger reverted to the level of this tautological equation, to resist any attempt at a universal comment 'about' the linguisticality of language? 'We encounter language everywhere'; 'language itself is – language'; 'language speaks', as Heidegger (2001, p. 187) says in *Poetry, language, thought*. There is no exhaustive media philosophy of language that does not fundamentally narrow it or truncate its own possibilities. For the same reason, Ludwig Wittgenstein recommended in his *Philosophical investigations* that the practice of speaking shall be understood as based on 'language-games', instead of drawing on language itself. Consequently, Wittgenstein (2001, p. IX) ask us to 'travel over a wide field of thought criss-cross in every direction' and to consider a 'number of sketches of landscapes which were made in the course of these long and involved journeyings'. One therefore could say that Wittgenstein's *Philosophical investigations* demonstrate the mediality of language in an exemplary manner; language, in its mediality, reveals itself only by virtue of a plurality of uses, which can only be analysed performatively. The medial then *appears through its use*, without being manifested *as* such: 'I am only *describing* language, not *explaining* anything'[9] (Wittgenstein 1974, p. 66).

McLuhan attempted to solve this problem by anchoring all of the ontological qualifications of the medial in relation to anthropological features of man, declaring mediality a basic condition of human culture in general. Consequently, McLuhan does not provide any general definition of media based on general properties; rather, all such properties are extensions of the senses or the human body – whether clothing, instruments, glasses, books or artificial light sources (McLuhan 2001, p. 8, McLuhan 2003, p. 26). With that he returns to the early philosophy of technology of the Hegelian Ernst Kapp, who already interpreted weapons and tools as projections of human organs in conjunction with an older anthropological concept of humans as being inherently deficient and in need of enhancement – as developed particularly by Johann Gottfried Herder. Herder's influence can be traced from Friedrich Nietzsche to Arnold Gehlen, and especially in the understanding of technology in the 1950s, according to which men – the 'wild beast' (Nietzsche) – produced art and technology as compensatory qualities in order to overcome their inadequacy, and to be able to survive. Furthermore, Freud (2002, p. 29) interpreted the prothetic nature of technology in *Civilization and its discontents* as an expression of the wretchedness of mankind, insofar as mankind set itself up as a 'god with artificial limbs' who is 'quite impressive when he dons all his ancillary organs', but is nevertheless pitiful because these organs have 'not become a part of him'. McLuhan too noted the ambivalence of the prosthetic, in the sense that it enables as much as it restricts: 'Any invention of technology is an extension or self-amputation of our physical bodies [...]' (McLuhan 2001, p. 48). The intervention is characteristic of the dialectical thinking of McLuhan, which remains frequently unrecognized. The moment we supplement our body through technology, we expose it to anaesthesia or desensitization. The gain suddenly changes into a loss; medial technologies do not submit to any clear position because they are paradoxically constituted.

Nevertheless, there is something not quite right with the image of the prosthesis. The medial principle runs counter to it because every prosthesis also functions as a source of vexation. Technology-based organ extensions supplement the human, just as, inversely, technology is extended into humans. The tool that extends the hand is reflected in the hand that extends the tool.[10] The medial then functions as a hybrid that does not take the interface into consideration, a hinge so to speak, or a 'change of aspect' (Wittgenstein) from apparatus and body. In particular, a fissure or a difference arises in the seam that joins the two, which as it were would be the place of reflection relevant from a media philosophical perspective, but which is again systematically faded out due to the subject of the extension. One might say: At the transition, there, where the machine projects into the flesh and the flesh into the machine, a monstrosity arises, a wound that gapes between men and medial technology. This wound emerges exemplarily based on the artificial hand that emulates the movement of the natural, though the whirr of the motor or the characteristic rigidity and coldness inherent in the prosthesis makes it shocking in many respects. Where the metaphor of 'extension' strives to adapt the medial to the human and to reconcile itself with it, its necessary obverse side would be its irreconcilability. This chasm admittedly say less about the medial itself than about the inadequacy of the prosthetic, that fixes its position precisely at the point where – literally – the gap remains open. McLuhan's theory leaves more questions unanswered than it can answer.

Nietzsche's typewriter again

In order to approach this difficulty of appropriately localizing the medial, we will first make a small detour that discusses the 'solution' to this paradox as exemplified in the positions of two of the most prominent media theorists in German-speaking countries. We will discuss Friedrich Kittler's media materialism and Georg Christoph Tholen's 'metaphorology of the medial' followed by positing a third approach opposite to both. Both theorists take as their point of departure Nietzsche's frequently cited (in German at least) dictum: 'our writing tools are also working on our thoughts'.[11] From this Kittler (1999, p. 109) derives no less than an emphasis on a mediatic a priori, that is, the assertion that technical means do not just extend the possibility of our thoughts, but rather directly intervene in them. The context of the passage to which Kittler alludes seems clear: 'You are right', notes Nietzsche in his reply to a letter from Heinrich Köselitz: 'Our writing tools collaborate on our thoughts. When will I manage to convey a longer sentence with my fingers […].'[12] A few days before, Köselitz had written to Nietzsche:

> I would like to see how manipulation occurs with and through the writing tool. […] Perhaps you will find you express yourself differently with the instrument […] I do not deny that my 'thoughts' in music and language are often dependent on the quality of the feather and paper.[13]

THINKING MEDIA AND BEYOND

Hence, the original idea stems from Köselitz, who suggested that 'writing tools' intervene not only in our thoughts, but also in our creative processes. It is not philological correctness that is important so much as the problem of constitution, which arose from it. It is vested above all in the prefix *mit*. What does the *mit* in *Mitarbeit* (collaboration) mean, and what is its specific epistemic surplus? Often overlooked, it refers to the practice of the medial in the sense of its impact, its influence on thought. *That* mediality and thinking are entangled in one another seems to be trivial; nonetheless, it is critical to understand *what type* of entanglement this is, that is, its particular modality.

Kittler does not hesitate to infer from *Mitarbeit* that all thought is a function of technology and thus 'always already' mediatized, that is, that subsequent to the *mit* ('with/co-') a transcendental sense is added. However, is it obvious what 'always already' means in this context, and what status the 'aprioritic perfect' has in the medial? The prepositional *mit* (with/co-) connotes here, not a cooperation, but an instrumentality in which both sides of the process, the thinking as well as the tool, participate. Kittler infers from it what he calls the 'exorcism of the spirit' due to the triumph of the machine.[14] Here, he asserts a dependency, a one-sided determination, so that the specific modality of the *mit* (with/co-) leads to a technical 'condition of the possible' in a Kantian sense, a *conditio sine qua non* which we cannot do without – a historical 'a priori'. Or is this just a discursive postulate, a claim that we have to fulfil when we want to speak of mediation as a basal structure of cultural practice? Even though Strawson (1972) discussed the transcendental conditions from the perspective of *conditiones sine quibus non* in his analysis of *individuals*, this still needs to be differentiated from the Kantian (Kant 1998) 'conditions of the possible' as formulated in his *Critique* because the title 'transcendental' is consistently only used in consideration of a subject and its capacity for reflexivity. Transcendental arguments would then be reflexive arguments. It remains questionable though what their equivalent in relation to media and their technical determinants would be. In particular, what can be referred to as 'conditions of the possible', requires a reconstructive gesture that reflects on its own inherent necessary presuppositions. A medial transcendental, however, especially in its technical guise, points to real conditions or 'material' requirements, which, in the form of apparatuses or technical arrangements, enter into the symbolic and its production. Nevertheless, once again the questions arise: from which location we can gain access to the transcendental and the media-apriori, which discursive formation is responsible for it, and who or what vouches for its validity.[15]

Consequently, we are either confronted with a theoretical gap, which we are still unsure how to close, or we need to be more precise about what *Bedingungen* (conditions; literally, 'be-thinging') means in the context of media theory. Does the *mit* (with/co-) used by Nietzsche and Köselitz only mean an influence, a coincidence, or a 'contemporariness', or does it mean a

THINKING MEDIA AND BEYOND

conditioning in the strict sense, a 'condition of the possible'? Interactions are indisputably present; nevertheless, their presence, and their 'present' or contribution, prove to be as mysterious as the other formulations, especially where these only call on an existence – a 'that' that veils the 'how' relevant in this context. Influences, interactions or coincidences have to be separated from *conditiones sine quibus non* (indispensible conditions), just as these, in the strict sense, need to be separated from generativity and transcendentality. On one hand, a claim that thought, perception, space and time, and the symbolic cannot manage without media would only imply an arrival at a negative conclusion, one that refuses to provide an answer to the question regarding *in what sense* mediation is necessary. On the other hand, to speak of the media as generating meaning leads to numerous antinomies and inconsistencies – insofar as each construction of meaning needs an analysis that sees through it – and moreover to a phantasm of sovereignty that, because media and technology triumph over knowledge itself, credits mediation with 'too much' power. A strict constructivism refuses its own premises, which can only function as axioms, unless we are dealing with a mathematics, which nonetheless does not speak *about something*, but rather analyses only the consequences of its self-generated structures.

Thus, the *mit* (with/co-), in the sense of inscribing the technical in our thinking, raises more questions than it answers. Evidently, most literature in the field of media theory converges, at least with regard to the thesis of constitution, in the assumption of a genuine productivity of the medial, as indicated in both Benjamin's and Adorno's philosophy of language and art, there, however, with respect to the dialectic between creating and limiting or enabling and refusing, just as they are felt, and in the same sense with reference to art, in Heidegger's (2008a) 'struggle' between 'earth' and 'world' (see also my interpretation Mersch, 2010a, pp. 109–112). If we are dealing with a primordial chiasm, the significance of the productivity, its specific modality – not unlike the *Mitarbeit* (collaboration) of Nietzsche's writing tools – remains undefined. Moreover, it also remains undefined how the productivity of production or the generativity of generation can be reconstructed without falling back on the generativity of reconstruction itself, and without taking into account their own mediality. Transcendental theories of experience or cognition always include both, because the ability of perception or knowledge coincides with their reflection, just as Michel Foucault's archives and their 'historical a priori' operate within the register of discursive formations. Transcendentality addresses the conditions found in reality, which in turn have to be differentiated from the way they are addressed. Language speaks 'of' or 'about' language in the medium of language. Comparatively, uncovering the constituitivity of media requires a theory of media that actualizes the insight in the discursive, that is, in another medium. Hence, the exemplary position of language in philosophical discourse, which forms a challenge for

110

THINKING MEDIA AND BEYOND

every strict media theory, just as it acts as a model for it, because, as Heidegger (2008b, p. 398) expressed it in his later philosophy, we are always already reflecting 'within language and with language.' All speaking of language remains subject to the systematic limitation of trying to speak about language with language, and by doing so entering into a circle. This proves that, right from the start, even before language becomes a topic, we are already moving on its terrain. Obviously, this circle resists being easily transferred to a general concept of media; at the same time it raises doubts regarding the durability of the generativity thesis and its postulation about constitution. A philosophy of language is unable to grasp language – just as a philosophy of media cannot seize the mediality of the medium – but rather only the 'ways' in which speaking marks 'furrows' or intervenes into language (p. 408), and how it is necessary to continually put these into motion again in order to coax other surprising or still unexpected ways from them. Moreover, a philosophy of media grasps how important it is to observe the medium as it 'works', that is, through the practices that it performs. There is, however, nothing obvious about what the term 'generation' should mean with regard to language or mediality. This is true not only because it is not clear which place the medial occupies in language, but also because 'speech acts', 'conversation', 'understanding' and the structure or repetition (de Saussure, Derrida) in language are able to keep awake, but not constitute, such *Be-Wegungen* (movements),[16] let alone thoughts, the communicativity of communication or the social and so on.

Between information theory and structuralism

In order to do justice to Kittler, I add here that this way of understanding mediality captures the concept of technology in the original sense of *techné* to a very large extent, and at the same time refers to Heidegger, especially to his essay *The question concerning technology*. The expression *techné* invokes the entire circle of 'art', 'craftmanship', right up to 'knowledge' and 'science', as well as *techniké*, technology in the actual sense, *tektonia*, *architektonia* and *teknosis*, the basis of architecture and likewise procreation. Aristotle refers to it as the virtue of *poiesis*, the true creation to which the created work, or *ergon*, also belongs (see Aristotles 2011, p. 1140a). This is why Heidegger generally understood technology as a thought, while at the same time making clear that technological culture had launched the nineteenth century into a 'frenzy' that radically changed the 'sense of being' and its obscurity. What Nietzsche diagnosed as the 'devaluation of what is most valuable' whose 'malaise' spread in the form of European nihilism (Nietzsche 2005, pp. 165, 119; see also Heidegger 1982) turns into its actual recognizability for Heidegger through the reign of technology, and plunges mankind into the 'homelessness' of the abandonment of being (Heidegger 2008c).

Kittler removed the critique of technology and moved the technological itself into a truth-occurrence which, in the meaning of the Heideggerian *Aletheia*, shows the 'unconcealment' of the world, and thereby superimposes the technological. It is based on operations rooted in formal algorithms, which in turn take on the positions of language, thought and the symbolic (esp. Kittler 1993, pp. 58–80). From there Kittler is able to delve into the entire history of Western culture, once more based on mathematics as well as the cultural and media technology derived from it: Neither content nor symbolic orders play a role, rather, according to the provocative response in *Grammophone, Film, Typewriter*, nothing but letters, signals and data processing. *(N) ichts ist, was nicht schaltbar ist*,[17] as Kittler writes in his essay *Vom Take Off der Operatoren* in *Draculas Vermächtnis* : The sceptical attack is aimed at traditional metaphysics, so that Kittler finally formulates a media technological critique of rationality, on whose back an 'informationstheoretischer Materialismus'[18] can be erected. This dissolves the traditional *Geschichte der Seelen und ihrer Nosologien* in the arsenal of news technologies, which *das Innere nach außen gekehrt oder eben implementiert hat*.[19] Therefore, not only do perceptions, thoughts or memories prove to be mediations in the most general sense, but also even their theoretizations form the effects of technologies, which are thus at the start of it all and dictate their conditions, instead of pursuing human directives: *Was Mensch heißt, bestimmen keine Attribute* [...], *sondern technische Standards*.[20]

The radicalism of the tone feeds on the conviction of belonging to an 'axial age' and being at the threshold of a new age, one in which all of the former medial formats begin to amalgamate into a single universal medial machinery. Kittler now holds the abbreviation UDM, the 'Universal Discrete Machine', ready for them: *Mit der Universalen Diskreten Maschine ist das Mediensystem geschlossen. Speicher- und Übertragungsmedien gehen beide in einer Prinzipienschaltung auf* [...]. *Eine menschenleere Bürokratie übernimmt alle Funktionen, die zur formalen Definition von Intelligenz hinreichend und notwendig sind*.[21] This polemic finding is nevertheless due to a hypothesis whose supposed plausibility stems from the reductive conclusion that information theory, like structuralism and post-structuralism, further the same developments. This assessment was particularly virulent in the 1960s and early 1970s, because both blocks of theory seem to refrain from meanings and interpretations on their surface, in order to instead pay attention to the 'how' of the processes or structures. Already on the first page of his essay *A mathemtical theory of communication*, Shannon writes the highly consequential statement that 'these semantic aspects of communication are irrelevant to the engineering problem' (1948, p. 379). They are irrelevant, not because of engineering per se, but rather to the task in question. Correspondingly, the link to structuralism was forged by Benoit Mandelbrot (with Apostel *et al.* 1957) and Moles (1973, p. 12) as well as Bense (1998, p. 404) in Germany, and earlier Helmut Heißenbüttel in his analysis of Marshall McLuhan's media theory. The latter stated in his essay *Das Medium ist die Botschaft. Anmerkungen zu Marshall McLuhan* (1969), that *Understanding media* replaces, on the basis of the Shannon-Weaver-model (which McLuhan in fact refused), the 'traditional difference between content and form [...] in favour of an absolute and permanent in itself declining formalization' in order to pass on a general structuralism, 'for which every single meaning and content can dissolve in a function of the structure'.[22] The initial reception thus created a series of misunderstandings intensified by both an insufficient image of the mathematical and the mistaken hope of a global understanding, similar to the one that seemed to be promised by the digital media technology revolution.[23]

In various respects Jacques Lacan also succumbed to the same fascination, when, in his seminar *Psychoanalysis and cybernetics*, he sets the logic of binary numbers in relation to the fundamental oppositions of the symbolic register. In doing he allocates cybernetics to that 'indefinite' area which includes heterogeneous theories such as probability theory, game theory, combinatorics and information theory, as well as, in the actual sense of Norbert Wiener's control theory (Lacan 1990, p. 295), an operation, which, since the collaboration between Claude Lévi-Strauss and Henry Weil regarding a mathematical theory of the 'elementary structures of kinship', seemed to speak for itself. Lacan, however, used it on one hand to refer to difference, and on the other to lower the conceptual foundation of psychoanalysis, especially the standing of the concept of unconscious as an 'order of signs'. This is why he prefers to speak of a correlation between 'chance' and 'determinism', between conjecture and combinatorics, and their relation to the 'real', and the 'correlation of absence and presence' in the 'world of the symbol', and their related 'erection' through binary structures. All the same, the 'convergence', as he at the same time perceptively admits, finds its limits when confronted with 'sense', the 'imaginary' and in particular 'the extreme difficulty [...] in translating cybernetically the functions of *Gestalt* [...]'. For Lacan, these point to the 'image', the 'body' and 'desire' as primary psychological functions (Lacan 1990, p. 302 and esp. p. 306). Kittler (1993, p. 59) willingly takes up the convergence notion in particular, in order to align the 'world of the symbolic' with the 'world of the machine' and to foist onto Lacan a media – 'materialism', whose essential point is the homology between digital units and the structures of nothing but signifiers – the circuit pattern 0/1 or on/off is nothing more than the hinge between 'absence' and 'presence', allowing Lacan's psychoanalytical structuralism to be reduced 'to information technology': *Das Symbolische [...] ist einfach eine Verzifferung des Reellen in Kardinalzahlen. Es ist, expressis verbis, die Welt der Informationsmaschinen.*[24]

This is why media technology *constitutes* language, thought, perception, as well as the experience of the real, and why, inversely, the illusion of sense and

THINKING MEDIA AND BEYOND

the 'so-called' human as *zoon logikon* or *animal symbolicum* can be reduced to technologies and a piece of information theory (Kittler 1993, p. 232). The fallacy here follows the outer appearance of an analogy that mistakes structural linkage with the syntax of digital codes, and mistakes the fundamental difference between absence and presence with the digital 0–1 sequence.[25] Even at the level of information theory, a transmission would have to differentiate between 'news' as a coded message and 'information' as a statistical measure. This differentiation is true all the more between the structuralist idea of 'structure' and the order matrix of a Turing machine. Although they both seem to be algebraic in nature, the former only lives off of the metaphor of algebra, whereas the latter stems from algebraic models. There is of course proximity, in the case of structuralism, between the mathematics of Nicolas Bourbaki and the linguistics of Émile Benveniste, or between Bourbaki and the structural anthropologist Lévi-Strauss, to give another comparative example between the symbolic language of Georges-Théodule Guilbaud and Lacan.[26] Nevertheless, there are more differences between them than similarities. Every random series of numbers or functions can be traced back to a digital schema. The difference between absence and presence, however, leads to questions about the threshold and transition, that is, the 'not unambiguous', to which nothing corresponds in the digital: Lacan complied with this in his reflections on the door schema, the 'symbol par excellence' as far as the door simultaneously includes and excludes. But he does so particularly in the final passage of his remarks about *Psychoanalysis and cybernetics*, where he establishes that 'the fundamental relation of man to this symbolic order' consists in the 'relation of non-being to being'. Thus, in the end he gives absolute priority to nothingness, the 'non-being', that is, the occurrence (*Ereignis*) as opposed to the pure formal game of cybernetics (Lacan 1990, pp. 302, 308).

Without différance

At this point one can go a step further since mathematics and mathematic codes, or symbolic languages such as 'semi-Thue systems' based only on alphabetic and production rules, exclusively generate that which Wiener (1990, esp. p. 43, p. 61, p. 73) referred to as *flache Formalismen* (flat formalisms). They follow the principles of logic, first and foremost the 'law of identity', whose absoluteness is in turn necessary for the validity of the *principium contradictionis*, the avoidance of contradiction. Hence, the role that negation takes as formal operator: it obeys the equations non (non) 1 = 1 as well as non 1 = 0 and non 0 = 1, in order to cancel out all intermediate shades, especially the inclusion of a non-identical or *tertium*. Iteration means *identical* repetition; every repetition in information theory produces the same and is a matter of redundancy, whereas in the symbolic, repetition means difference, and according to Derrida (1982, p. 313) always includes an alteration. Signs in their chronological sequence refer to other signs and thus include the actualization of a memory, which, despite their iterability, makes something else out of it. Each repetition is – and here Derrida's Grammatology joins up with psychoanalysis – a *Wieder-Holung* (re-petition), a *Zurückholung* (retrieval) or a shift to another register, which marks the primacy of the difference in it, since, according to Derrida in *Writing and difference* (1967, p. 246), a sign is 'divided by repetition' from its first use and bears the mark of a primordial division: A sign is not one, but rather one that already contains a folded two. It is, as Derrida puts it, '*two* with no *one*. Always one extra or one too few' (1981, p. 274). Hence: 'Three is the first figure of repetition' (Derrida 1967, p. 299). There is no equivalent for the priority of the third in the mechanical, just as there is no *différance* principle in information theory that covers such processing, because there can be no 'between' in the digital. Instead, every informational transmission and every algorithm has already excluded the productive differentiation. In comparison, the symbolic unfolds by virtue of a continuous figuration that is always shifting from metaphor to metonymy, and from metonymy to metaphor, without ever being able to return to its initial state or to find closure. With that the motion of the differentiality of the symbolic – the *différance* as generativity – is neither present nor absent: 'The hyphen of the symbolic comes, so to speak, in-between', as Tholen (2002, p. 188) puts it. Between symbolic language and Turing machine on one hand and the structural linguistic or post-structuralist theory of difference on the other lies an unbridgeable gap, because neither the iteration of the sign nor the process of figuration follows rules in a strict mathematical sense. Instead of 'iterability' it would thus be better to speak of 'recursivity' in mathematics, which not only presupposes identity, but also the strict application of rules. Such rules Wittgenstein (2001, p. 195) links in the same way to commands as to machines, and their fulfilment presupposes a specific type of 'training'. This is why Tholen resolutely put language *before* the machine: '(T)he structure of exchangeability and replaceability which is *inherent* to language, is the non-technical, unassailable requirement of technological media itself.'[27] This is not just a claim; it can be derived from the perspective of basic mathematical research, insofar as symbolic language, Turing machines, and recursive functions can all be mutually converted into one another. The 'grammatical' basis of symbolic language as well as the language of types referred to as 'Chomsky's grammars' forms a set of transformation rules, which in turn correspond to the instruction sets of the Turing machines. In the end, it is not digitalization that forms its core – this applies only to the notations of its elements –rather, the algorithm of its syntactic linkages. In the repertoire of language it is provided by a figurality that is not totally absorbed in functions and their predictability. The mistake in comparing information theory and structuralism lies primarily in focusing on the similarity between bits and signifiers, rather than on the difference between rules and figures. In other words: The paradigm of the analogy is based on the consideration of the units – on the 'ontology' of the systems, just as if languages were based on configurations of their pieces or rules – and not on the *practitioners and their performances*.

Here, Tholen's 'metaphorology of the medial' comes into effect because it is linguistic right from the start. In particular, it tries to link three different operations with one another: first, the historically received metaphors of the 'medium' and of the 'in-between', which stretch through the history of philosophy since Aristotle and are continually 'recast' (Blumenberg) or dislocated; second, the deconstruction of the key metaphysical difference between 'notion' and 'metaphor', 'proper' and 'improper' speech, as can be found in Heidegger and Derrida and third, the 'metaphorization' of the medial itself with recourse to the literal meaning *metapherein*, the 'carrying over' or 'transferring' from one domain to another. With that Tholen spells out the metaphorics of 'transmission', of transgression, transport, or of transfer, just as they had become key for Innis (2008, p. 62), McLuhan, and more recently again for Krämer (2008, p. 9). The focus remains on language, whose own 'metaphor' offers the concept of mediation, but also the method for analysing it, just as it simultaneously works on its own 'transfer'. Namely, the translation and mediation processes between languages and the digital transmission process of technological media. The *transfer–transmission–transformation relationship* itself then changes into a universal media model that – beyond all intentionality and technological teleology – provides nothing but transitions, in the sense of an equally placeless and continuous movement of the *metapherein*. In this way, Tholen tries to establish a non-technological and non-metaphysical concept of media, which attaches the problem of constitution to a space of a permanent transitionality, whose basic principle is mobility or continuous processuality itself. At the same time, he radicalizes what Benjamin and Adorno already suggested: the consolidation of the medial in the *Über-Tragung* (trans-mission) or *Über-Setzung* (trans-lation) which lives less from concrete or technological transmission and transference processes, than it emphasizes the *Hinüber-Tragen* (carrying over) and *Hinüber-Setzen* (transferring over) as an equally differential and mediating practice.

Nevertheless, the 'meta' of *metapherein* remains unaddressed in this conception – and consequently so does the meaning of the 'over' in its actual sense. If the core structure of mediation is decisively due to a series of prepositions or prefixes, which always come into effect where a relation is to be identified, whose *relata* implies a change of level – *meta* in Greek, *trans* in Latin, also *trans* or *over* in English and *über* in German – their own structure would still need to be investigated. Prepositions refer to relationships; they posit the nouns in play in a topological relation to one another. In this sense, a theory of prepositions can be understood as a general topology of relations: 'after', 'over', 'under', 'through' and so on designating specific spatial or temporal orders. If one questions the nature of these orders, one ends up with relational modalities, which can be linked to a general theory of media (see esp. Hubig 2006). The medial, as discussed above, cannot be allocated a precise position – according to Weber (1999), it appears to be nothing but virtual; there is thus nothing real about it, but rather only a scattering of possibilities. However, they 'un-fold' in the form of relational *modi* in order to literally generate 'folds' between the *relata*. In turn, it cannot be said of these modalities that they already constitute thoughts or experiences. In the same way, the expression 'ex-perience' corresponds (as does the related term 'experiment') to the Latin terms *experiens*, *experientia* or *experior* that all convey the same connotation: Suddenly the eyes are opened up, new relationships are visible or conceivable, not unlike the performative, which is much less about the generation of meaning in a speech act than it is about the generation of variations of its practical modi. The performative then does not form 'conditions of the possible' nor a transcendental, but rather forms a co-determination or *Mitarbeit* (collaboration) just as Nietzsche's writing tools and their collaboration in thinking can be understood as a modelling of a practice, whose differences are each delivered differently in the symbolic. However, with that, we have already anticipated too much.

'Dia' versus 'meta'

If we now turn to the meaning of 'meta' in a narrower sense, its various adverbial and prepositional applications have to be differentiated. Depending on how the expression is used, it connotes 'after', 'over (there)', 'from … up', 'in the middle', 'below' and so on; however, it always implies that a boundary has to be crossed. In particular the prefix – like the *metapherein* itself – implies a transition, thus bridging the disparate, as it were, such that the medial serves as a leap, a displacement of its non-causal mediation. This applies to the metaphor of the actual 'transfer' to another place, which in turn contains the image of the ferryman, who carries passengers over to the Isle of the Dead. Something similar can be said about expressions such as *metaballon*, meaning displacement, permutation or inversion, *metamelos*, a change of heart or a transition between notes, or *metastasis*, a rapid transition to proliferation or migration to a foreign place. There is always the difficulty that the succeeding metaphor has to re-connect the separated without it being clear what the re-connection actually accomplishes. The concept of media seems to step in precisely at this point. If, according to Tholen and following McLuhan, mediation is determined from the process of *metapherein*, then it itself takes on the act of a leap, and with that the 'unmediated middle'. At the same time, we are left in the dark as to where the leap or the mediation occurs, because the leap of mediation cannot itself be mediated: 'to leap', as Heidegger (2002, p. 32) accurately states in *Identity and difference*, means to let oneself go 'into an abyss'. It is thus striking that we are once again dealing with a metaphorization, which itself has already 'leapt over' the possibility of the leap. As a result the medial as 'meta' is due to a difference, whose difference itself remains open. It performs, so to speak, a *metabasis eis allo genos* (a shift or leap to a foreign domain or type), whose transition closes off all further analysis. Tholen, like McLuhan, seems to want to assign this difference to the *conditio humana*: we cannot perceive, experience or identify without difference, without differences that 'make the difference'. It is thinking itself that is the productive constitutive difference, because thinking already means making distinctions, so that a difference is already given, even before thinking, understanding or identifying comes to be. In other words: Difference is – and here Tholen follows Derrida – the first script before the script; it is so to say the *prescript* or 'primordial' script of the medial, which already precedes every single medium and already divides the space of the symbolic in order to continually further divide itself.

Nonetheless, the way of 'leaping over', the unrepresentability of the break, which literally 'happened' is not yet the answer, but rather the question. This is especially clear with the Latin translation of 'meta' into 'trans' since every *Über-Setzung* (*transferre*) – the embodiment of the medial as translation since Benjamin – performs a leap between the translated languages which impacts the two, both the one transferred to and the one transferred from. 'Meta' thus literally implies a risk because there is no criterion, no *tertium comparationis* (common point for comparison) that can guarantee its success. In the same sense, every *trans*mission *trans*ports not only something from one place to another, but also 'displaces' and converts the 'mission', inscribes into it an alteration – similar to the way that a *trans*formation does not just mean reshaping the form, but also the creation of something completely new in the sense of a *meta-morphosis*. This may explain the many analogue expressions available to invoke the central function of the medial in addition to *transmissio* and *transferre*, *transgression* or *transposition*, as well as *transsubstantiation* (as Hörisch 1991, 2004 suggested in view of the Catholic ritual of converting bread and wine). *Meta* or *trans*, depending on the language, then expresses more a *transcendence* than a 'transcendentality' in a philosophical sense, which at the same time inherently contains the seductive idea that 'meta' or 'trans' concerns a site of a 'prim-ordial' transformation, be it from matter into an immaterial form, from things into symbols, or from markings on vinyl into sounds (see Kittler 1999, p. 27). One could say that there is a theological moment in the theory of the medial, which, in the middle of the figure of the leap and the *meta*, touches upon an enigma in order to defer the mediality of the medium to an unknown, almost 'uncanny' place. In this sense

THINKING MEDIA AND BEYOND

the concept of media – the way media are constituted – carries the entire burden of all the unsolved riddles of metaphysics, of the chasm between nature and culture, between body and soul, up to the difference between matter and form, meaning and structure, or the line that separates signified and signifier. With one stroke these seem to disappear, as soon as these are related to a 'third' – an 'in-between'– which provides mediation in order to simultaneously fail to do so. Thus the differentiality of the medial seems to conjure away the mystery of the difference, just as at other moments differences return like the undead, because the medium itself, like a black box, is taking on the aura of spectrality.

The problem of the medium's constitution cannot be solved in this way. Rather it seems to be necessary to replace the problematic prefix with another preposition, whose direction proceeds less vertically and is less *sprunghaft*, that is, is less prone to 'leaping', and thus flatter and more decisive. This leads to a consideration of the materiality of transitions as well as methods of transforming *one thing into another 'through' (or by means of) something else*. With 'through' (or 'by means of') here, I am referring to that which corresponds to the Latin *per*, indicated in related expressions like cost per person, miles per hour – *per* also in the sense of *performare* or 'per-locutionary' – the latter referring to the speech act's impact on language. The Greek expression 'dia' would be allocated to it, which also means 'through' or 'by means of' and which differs only at times from 'meta' in nuance – for example *diapraxis* for mediation itself (in addition to *hermeneuein*) or *diallattein* for the equalization, the reconciliation of two persons. Moreover *dihairesis* for separating or differing, *diáthesis* for arranging and classifying, or splitting and removing, *diabasis* for a bridge's passageway, and also *dioryx* for the canal, the literal process of burrowing. All of these examples are related to the *Be-Dingungen* (conditions), as they are literally conditioned by some-*thing* real, which actualizes them, thus making possible an inner connection, a space.[28]

The prefixes and prepositions that I have listed here take on a far greater role as it initially appears when applied to the medial: *per*-sona thus refers to the mediality of the mask, by which the voice articulates itself, 'through' (or by means of) (*per*) sounds (*sono*). Similarly, the *per*-spective means 'to see through' (Dürer)[29] by means of a mathematical structure, rather than a transparency. The same holds true for the Platonian *dialogoi*, the 'speaking through' (*dialogizomai*), which actualizes a discussion by means of *logos*, in order to see a way through the divided truth of a thought or conviction. *Dialegerein* also means interpreting a text or remark 'through' its being read in a specific way. One can say the same for thinking, *dianoia*, in the sense of an understanding by virtue of the *nous* and its analytical abilities, as well as for *diáphora*, the dispersion or spreading that is reminiscent of the seed and semen, that is, the primal scene of dissemination.[30] A difference or a separation thus underlies all of these forms; however, in such a way that this difference is never elided, but rather is worked 'through' by means of a *poiesis* and its material conditions.[31]

Performativity of the medial

In playing two Greek prefixes – *meta* und *dia* – off of one another, the purpose is not to value one more than the other, but rather to ground the transcendence of the 'leap' methodologically in practices as well as in materiality. On another level, this play of prefixes returns us to the notion of poeisis and its connections to 'dia' and 'per.' As already mentioned, Aristotle considers *techné* to be the virtue or highest fulfilment of *poiesis*. Nevertheless, it is not so much its instrumental character, as much as its creative or artistic side that is emphasized – just as art and aesthetics in general are fundamental to the concept of media presented here. Whereas *meta, trans* or *über* (over) refer to a transfer or transmission whose basis remains questionable, various ways or modalities of ensuring transition are indicated by *dia* or *per*. All of them are rooted in the real. Situated in the world, they continuously provide new and different linkages, passages and detours. Connected to a network of things and actions, the medial is consequently based on *performative practices* rather than in the occurrence of *différance*. Therefore the emphasis here is on practices in the arts: instead of a *metabasis*, the transition from one to another order undertakes a *diabasis*. *Diabasis* also names a transition, but one that *is to be actualized in the material*, to the extent that it requires a passage based on concrete 'architectures'.[32] The material is then allowed into the medial, so to speak, just as inversely the medial is allowed into the material. We are thus dealing with a mutual *osmosis*. The same applies to the difference between *transformare* and *performare*: the first completely transforms its objects, so that we are dealing with entirely new forms, whereas the latter strives to perform or embody something by using services of the material world. This results, not in transformation, but in representation, which includes presence as well as the work of presentation, the exposition of a presence. The 'transfer' or the *metapherein* is therefore no longer paradigmatic for the process of mediation; rather, those forms of *experiens* or experimentation, *through* which something appears, are 'posed' or 'exposed' in order to manifest *themselves* in reality just as much as to 'transpose' it.[33]

These can be explained further based on two other compounds formed with the prefixes 'dia' and 'per': Aristotle's *diaphane* and the concept of the performative as introduced to philosophy by John Austin and John Searle. Instead of drawing on Plato's critique of writing and the ambiguous notion of *chora* in the *Timaeus,* as well as the subsequent question of the *pharmakon*, to return finally to the 'meta' in the name of a media theory of difference,[34] we turn to Aristotle's teachings on *aesthesis*, from whose Latin translation the term media is historically derived.[35] These teachings, moreover, are related to theories of performativity, which are capable of integrating the dimension of the practical with the medial. In Aristotle, the *diaphane* initially functions as a guiding thread for another understanding of media, which downplays the idea of their constitution without completely abandoning it. In particular, Aristotle's treatment of perception and seeing, on the central position of his argumentation, inserts the notion of *metaxu*, a 'laying between' that maintains the 'contact' between the eye and thing, in order, almost without warning, to proceed to the concept derived from older theories of perception: *diaphane*, the 'shining through' (*diaphaino*), is almost analogous to the 'seeing through' of *per-spectiva*. If the hypothetically introduced concept of *metaxu*, which again emphasizes the 'meta' and marks 'betweeness', follows the idea that the perceived has to communicate with the perceiver in order to be perceived, then the *metapherein* is less able to represent it than the process of a 'thoroughfare' or passage *through* a space, in whose empty place the *diaphane* steps. Once again we are confronted with the contrast between 'meta' and 'dia', whereby the *diaphane* names *that which causes appearance in the first place* – *diaphaino* names the 'appearance' (*phaino*) *through* something. Aristotle does not leave any doubt regarding the materiality of this *diaphane*, and it is no coincidence that the idea of 'ether' subsequently developed from it. In other words, something, a materiality, enables an appearance, just as inversely appearance is only possible by virtue of a foil that makes it possible in the first place. Once again an ambiguity between a foil as an obstruction and as facilitation of appearance results – however, the notion of a 'material shining through' may ultimately lead us astray. Appearance itself instead proves to be transparent or 'see-through', provided that something is indeed *made* visible *through* it. 'Appearance' and 'shining through' thus mean the same thing: unlike the superficial Latin translation of *diaphane* as 'transparency', suggesting that something opaque reveals itself through a veil or screen, *diaphane* refers to the place of visualization itself. It is not something 'not-visible' that makes itself visible through something else, but rather the visualization itself remains invisible, which is why Aristotle connects the *diaphane* with the dialectic: something is both revealed and veiled in it. As he says in *De Anima* 'that which, though visible, is not properly speaking visible but by reason of extrinsic colour' (Aristotle 1991, p. 418b).

In this way, the analysis of the *diaphane* can be seen as a touchstone for the further explanation of the notion of media. In continually referring to a materiality and the practices of visualization, *diaphane* first and foremost clarifies the 'modal' aspect of 'dia'. This emerges also through the 'per' of Austin's performative linguistics, particularly in view of the aspect of perlocution that has been ignored after Searle. As we know, based on performative actions, Austin

(1975, p. 99) differentiates between illocutionary and perlocutionary statements: the first do something 'in saying something' (e.g. assert, direct, express), the latter do something '*by* saying' – *through* something being said (e.g. the effect of impressing, following, persuading). Accordingly, illocutions inaugurate speech acts, which themselves have consequences for social relationships, whereas perlocutions cause effects that are not actually in the acts themselves – the two move in opposite directions. The first therefore contains a figure of identity, the latter a process of difference;[36] in both cases though, the 'per' in performativity changes the modus of either statement as well as the act itself.[37] It is obvious that perlocution is of greater interest than illocution for the concept of media being discussed here. Accordingly, the mediality of speech acts would have to be connected to the structure of performative modalities. In other words, the medial practice of speech fails to fulfil itself both in its production of sense as well as the order of signification or the occurrence of figurality, as far as these are both constitutively attached to difference. This means, furthermore, the *Unter-Schied* (difference)[38] *between* signified and signifier, its unfathomable 'in-between' signalled by the hyphen, which – literally – 'comes between' to identify the actual position of the medial and thus, sign and medium are ultimately confused with one another. Instead, mediality *appears* with the aid of different performative practices and the modi induced by them, which *qua* practice so to speak, include a difference. What we have here first concerns a vertical difference, which corresponds to the 'meta' and which directs a figurative plumb line between language and world, or medium and reality. Second, there is an uninterrupted chain of horizontal shifts that should be assumed, which does not take on any constitutive function, but rather whose constitutive effect needs to be verified in every single case. Correspondingly, rules and conventions which locate the verbal in the real are less interesting than the effects that these have 'on the communicative scene' and, in fact, what the *expressis verbis* want to say is not *directly* available. Neither the question of the symbolic nor of the semiotic is therefore particularly relevant to the medial; instead, what is important are the practices that are tied to actors and contexts, just as to discourses, materialities and 'dispositifs' (Foucault). Ultimately it is the question of *scene* or milieu that unveils the ways of mediation, rather than the 'auctorial' practices of the speaker. Moreover, it is not the media that constitute situations, but rather a mediality that appears as a result of the totality of conditions that enable it, while at the same time constraining it. An example would be the 'example' itself, which, depending on the context, reveals some facets while foreclosing others. It is neither the act nor an *apparatus* that mediatizes in order to 'leap over' the site of differences, but rather their *Ver-Wendung* (use), in which they 'change' (*wenden*), contort (*ver-wenden*), and turn into something completely different.[39]

Nietzsche's typewriter – *once again*

The step from 'meta' to 'dia' thus leads to a *performative understanding of the medial* – though in itself the medial remains chronically opaque. This step implies a 'crossing-over' from the transcendental and the problem of constitution to the question of production as a poetic practice and its occurrence. These are now to be understood as separate from teleology as well as from intentionality. If we are then talking about 'occurrences', we need to do this in order to resist the seduction of the subject and its intentionality as well as its technological means-ends reductions. For example, a person can hurt someone else by offering help because the offer itself is already an act of superiority. In that case, the assistance *mediatizes* superiority through the – perhaps habitualized – resort to innocent politeness. The 'medium of the mediatization' here is not to be found; rather it proves to be inherently entangled in the scene and only to be found in the way it is set within the entire field of practicalities. This includes the complete 'arrangement', the order of things as well as the 'opportunities' the field of practicalities presents, the occasionality of structures and conditions and the accompanying discourses and the orders of power, as they have deposited themselves in the social. It is not the offer of support itself, but rather *how* it transforms into disdain *through* its *Ver-Wendung* and becomes degradation. Turns (*Wendungen*) such as this 'happen' so to speak *as* 'perlocutionary' shifts, whose *mediality* constitutes the intended courtesy as a gesture of violence. However, their mediality does not already mean that the act is constituted *as* act or that its symbolic dimension is constituted *through* its mediation, as that would imply a symbolization beyond the aforementioned *scene* and to already sanction it as such without drawing upon its situatedness.

The medial is thus not fulfilled in the extension of our body or our perceptions, as McLuhan suggests. It is also not fulfilled in technological apparatuses, and in the materiality of their *hard-ware* and the software it would support, as Kittler formulates. Instead, mediation occurs ultimately in ineluctable practice, its endless possibility, in which the 'means' or instruments are as intertwined just as much as they can be changed into continually new and different *Ver-Wendungen* along each of the performative modi. In leading to this conclusion, my reading does not negate the possibility of the constitution of the medial per se. However, it seems to run contrary to the connection of the medial with 'apriority' – the view that there is only perception or significance because there is media and that, for example, Nietzsche's typewriter thinks itself, or the technological-medial complex of a transmission determines the possibility of communication. *Instead, the question of constitution transforms itself into a procedural issue*: methods produce effects, which allow something to appear *as* something, and in which the question has less to do with the 'appearing' of the appearance, as it does with the *occurrence of the 'as'*, which, depending on the *scene of the performative*, first transcribes itself into a *medial 'as'*. The medial therefore does not function as a prime-ordinal hypothesis, but rather always only as a function of those methods and materialities whose *Ver-Wendung* of the medial invariably applies it in new ways, that is, 'changes' (*wendet*) it into something new. At the same time the orthographic chasm that divides the *Ver-Wendung* points to the withdrawal of control – the withdrawal of sovereignty. We cannot say *what* the medial *is* – there is no ontology of mediation, other than to say it persistently refuses its determination.[40] However, it is possible to partially reconstruct the 'movements' of the medial since they reveal themselves *through* its changes (*Wendungen*). The medial then proves to be a function, so to speak, of a scattering or distribution of folds, within which these, literally, 'un-fold'. They tolerate a synopsis just as little as they do a universal theory; instead, they produce at best 'regional' studies from case to case similar to Wittgenstein's investigations of language-games. Media situate themselves, beyond preset operative structures, in an indeterminate field of potentialities, which is why Samuel Weber looks to them to emphasize the perspective of virtuality and delocalization: they *are* not in the sense of a *being – rather they are a becoming*.

At the same time, this measures the 'extent' of their reflexivity. Unlike the discursive notion of reflection and its anchoring in transcendental arguments, we must deal with a performative concept of reflection. This has the advantage that we avoid falling into a fundamental separation between medial processes and their reflection in other media – the apparently enlightening dictum of systems theory that media can only be thematized in other media or can only be analysed in predetermined discourses. Instead, performative reflexivities refer to disruptions or subversions, to the notion of counter-programmes and contrary *Ver-Wendungen* that exploit contradictions and paradoxes, in order to continually reveal new and surprising elements.[41] The 'negativity of the medial' means nothing more than this. It reveals itself alone on the basis of interventions going against the grain, which intervene in medial practices, 'breaking them down', perforating them and thus making identifiable that which obstructs conventional detection. Heidegger forged the apt expression *Aufriss* (a breaching incision) – instead of its totalization through a kind of 'blueprint', offering a structural synopsis, and without exposing its 'realness', its continual *Ver-Wendungen* leads to nothing but disparate views which reveal a series of recorded moments, just as their 'sights' are 'cut' *through* by their different uses.[42] The paradox of reflection – in the sense of a simple 'birds eye view' – would not be solved, but rather at best be by-passed and 'annulled' through various facets and fragments. Its focal point is art. Accordingly, the forms of medial reflexivity as well as the possibilities of their *Ver-Wendung* prove to be as unpredictable as artistic practice. The reflexive discovery of the medial finds its model in its incompleteness and its experimental character.

THINKING MEDIA AND BEYOND

What then does Nietzsche's and von Köselitz's insight, that writing tools or the quality of the feather and paper collaborate (*mitarbeitet*) in our thoughts, mean? It is not the discrete tableau of the typewriter, the keys as a mechanical alphabet, which already anticipate digitalization, that changes our thoughts, but rather the different modalities of the typewriter's use and counter-use which the technological invites, just as the 'notion' of a non-technological creativity also belongs to it. Both technological use and non-technological creativity – on the basis of performative practices – go hand in hand. The 'pressing' of the typewriter keys *be-dingt* (is conditional on) the effort of the unpractised, not only for the aggregation and concentration of thinking, as an idea that is reminiscent of the early Pre-Socratics, but it also releases a completely new potential for our dexterity, for example, in the generation of endless textual interlinkages, their ironic misappropriation (*Ent-Wendung*) through random processes, and their becoming images as with earlier image transmissions, for example, via telex machines and so on.[43]

In summary, the collaboration of writing tools in thinking has less to do with the apriority of the medial, than with the inexhaustible potential of their *Ver-Wendung* which at the same time collaborates in the unveiling and veiling of the medium itself. However, what does this ultimately mean for the *mit* (with/co-) of the *Mitarbeit* (collaboration)? It does not signify any kind of 'between', or 'meta', just as it does not refer to a transcendence or transcendental, but rather, it designates a way of practice that is integrated into our processes of perception and recognition. We are not thinking in the loneliness of our soul, just as inversely we are not 'thought' 'through' the medial. Rather we experience the world by means of those practices with which we process it, and whose alienness and materiality strikes back at us in reverse, thus registering an equally uncontrollable and obdurate element in it (translated by Clemens Ackermann).

Notes

1. [Translators note: Originated by Heidegger the term '*Unter-Schiede*' emphasizes the division, the separation as it were (symbolized by the hyphen) that occurs in differing one object from another.]
2. [Translators note: The German *Ur-Sprung* (origin) allows for a primordial leap or act and allows for an opening up, as well as a singular appearance.]
3. [Translators note: *Über-Tragung* and *Über-Setzung* both carry with them the sense of transferring something (in the sense of the Latin *trans-ferre*), for example, from one thing to another, from one point to another, or from one language to another.]
4. '*aller Traurigkeit und (vom Ding aus betrachtet) allen Verstummens*' (Benjamin 1977a, p. 155). [Translators note: All English translations found in the footnotes are my own.]
5. '*gewissen Art von Dingsprachen* [...] *Zusammenhang mit Natursprachen*' (Benjamin 1977a, p. 156).

125

THINKING MEDIA AND BEYOND

6. The Cynic, Diogenes, was accused of this (see Laertius 1967, p. 304).
7. [Translator's note: Whereas *be-dingt* can be translated as 'conditioned by' it also inherently contains a reference to *Dinge* or things.]
8. This insight at the same time forms the insertion point of a 'negative' media theory, which attempts to systematically develop these; see for now my own attempts in Mersch (2004, 2005, 2008).
9. See also Wittgenstein (1999, p. 84) and Wittgenstein (2001, p. 66): 'And we may not advance any kind of theory. [...] We must do away with all *explanation*, and description alone must take its place.'
10. See also Mitchell: 'If there is to be mediation, the tool itself can no longer function as intermediary but must itself be transformed' (2010, p. 77).
11. Cited here according to Kittler (1999, p. 200). Nietzsche wrote this in a letter to Peter Gast (a pseudonym used by Heinrich Köselitz) in February 1882.
12. 'Sie haben recht, unser Schreibzeug arbeitet mit an unseren Gedanken. Wann werde ich es über meine Finger bringen, einen langen Satz zu drücken [...] Können Sie das auch lesen!' (Nietzsche 2002, p. 172) [Translators note: Whereas the Winthrop-Young translated Kittlerian quotation states that (RSol: verify edit) the tools 'work on' our thoughts, I prefer to use 'collaborate' here in order to emphasize the *mit* (with) aspect of Nietzsche's *mitarbeiten*].
13. 'Nun ich möchte gerne sehen wie mit dem Schreibapparat manipuliert wird. [...] Vielleicht gewöhnen Sie sich mit dem Instrument eine neue Ausdrucksweise an [...], ich leugne nicht, dass meine "Gedanken" in der Musik und Sprache oft von der Qualität der Feder und des Papiers abhängen [...]' (Nietzsche 2002, p. 229).
14. '[...] the exorcism of the spirit' (Kittler 1992).
15. This does not mean that we would debate the possibility of medial selfreflexivity – art does nothing but that. What is meant, however, is that in the medial, the discursive reflections on its conditions are not the subject of the mediation. Consequently, discursivity and mediality need to be differentiated.
16. [Translator's note: *Be-Wegungen* also carries with it a sense of creating paths].
17. '[...] there is nothing that is not switchable' (Kittler 1993, p. 152).
18. '[...] information theoretical materialism [...]' (Kittler 1993, p. 182).
19. '[...] history of souls and their nosologies [...] turned or just implemented the inner outside' (Kittler 1995, p. 10).
20. 'What it means to be human is not defined by attributes [...] but rather by technical standards' (Kittler 1993, p. 61).
21.

> With the Universal Discrete Machine the media system is closed. Storage and transmitting media are absorbed in a circuit of principles [...]. A bureaucracy devoid of humans takes over all the functions sufficient and necessary for the formal definition of intelligence. (Kittler 1989, p. 196)

The same findings are found in Coy: The computer as a programmable machine becomes the 'integrator of all previous media' (1989, p. 30), as well as Tholen, insofar that cultural scientists and media theorists unanimously found that in 'the age of electronic media and computers [...] their binary principle circuits' could be emulated 'according to all previous machines and media' (2002, p. 191).

THINKING MEDIA AND BEYOND

22. Heißenbüttel (1969, pp. 294 and 302). See also Hörl (2005), although with Hörl it is more in reference to the contemporaries of structural anthropology, linguistics, information theory and cybernetics.

23. Hans Magnus Enzensbergers *Baukasten zu einer Theorie der Medien* in the end follows the same assessment: The text triggered a debate that is reprinted in Engell et al. (2002, pp. 264–299). Art projects such as Nam June Paiks *Global groove* point in the same direction. In fact, the history of this reception and its fallacies is not yet written.

24. 'The symbolic […] is simply a digitization of the real into cardinal numbers. It is *expressis verbis*, the world of information machines' (Kittler 1993, pp. 69, 73).

25. For his part Tholen had pointed out a related problem, even when he tends towards the same mistake. Thus he writes: '(F)ür die Bestimmung der Medialität der Medien ist die Nähe von Signifikant und Information keine nur vordergründige: Die "kleinste" Einheit – ein Bit – ist nach Gregory Bateson der Unterschied, der einen Unterschied macht' [In determining the mediality of the media, the proximity of signifiers and information are not just superficial: According to Gregory Bateson, the 'smallest' unit – a bit – *is* the difference that makes a difference'] (Tholen 2002, p 187). In the same sense he maintains there is a correlation between digitalness and arbitrariness in structural linguistics – nevertheless he grants language the unlimited priority.

26. With regards to the relation between mathematics and structuralism, see Dosse (1996, p. 132); as well as Aczel (2006).

27. '(D)ie Struktur der Austauschbarkeit und Ersetzbarkeit, die der Sprache zukommt, ist die nicht-technische, uneinholbare Voraussetzung der technischen Medien selbst' (Tholen 2002, p. 187).

28. [See translator's note – note 18].

29. See Panofsky (1998, p. 99). Belting (2008, p. 23) seems similar. Whereas, the word 'perspectiva' is already attested to by Boethius, it first finds its dominant interpretation in view of the mediality of figurativeness as *Durchsicht* (looking through) a transparent world in Dürer. In turn Alberti associated it with the metaphor of a window: A window, its frame, releases a view, makes us through that sighted, opens up for us our own image space. To this extend, one can say: the 'perspectives" form performative *picture acts*; the space that they erect is not created by any arrangement of places and signs, but rather something that can be scanned, controlled and captured through the movement of the eye.

30. See Derrida (1981). In particular, Derrida refers to Plato's motif of the sower, as well as to the older myth of Demeter and the figure of Triptolemos as the cultivators proper. Durham Peters in turn recognizes the actual productivity of the medial in the dissemination (see 2000).

31. For initial considerations about these differences see my essay in Mersch (2010a).

32. The reader is reminded here that *architektonia* literally means the 'basic' technique or art.

33. With regards to the concept of positing in relation to the performative, see my comments in Mersch (2002). In particular, the occurrence of a *Setzung* (positing) is understood to be from the threefold moment of *Einsetzung* (instantiation), *Aussetzung* (exposition) and *Entsetzung* (transposition).

34. The return to Plato forms the background for a media theory following Derrida (1981) as well as Derrida (2005), whereby, both the *pharmakon* as well as the

Chora call forth figures of the ambivalent, which ultimately try to legitimate the 'leap' of the 'meta'.

35. See Hagen (2008), as well as my remarks in Mersch (2006, p. 18).
36. See esp. my examination of Austin and Searle in Mersch (2010b, pp. 220–245, esp. p. 240).
37. Regarding modal interpretations of the performative, see Davidson (2001, p. 109).
38. [See translator's note – note 2].
39. [Translator's note: While *Ver-Wendung* can be translated here as 'use', in German it also carries the sense of a change or a turn (*Wendung*) which through the prefix '*ver*' takes on the sense of a contortion].
40. Regarding the withdrawal of the medial, see my comments in (2010b, p. 148–169).
41. In his essay on *Bilderstatus*, Flusser argues quite similarly: This requires the 'list' of counter-changes, to outwit the apparatus and by means of 'agility' of art or *Ars* to bring the status of images in the old and new media to light. '*Ars* is usually translated as "art" but one should not forget the importance of the "manoeuvrability"' (Flusser 1997, p. 77).
42. Heidegger (2008b, p. 408) and elsewhere. See also my considerations Mersch (2010b, p. 164).
43. Ihde also points this out: 'Technologies, by providing a framework for action, do form intentionalities and inclinations within which use-patterns take dominant shape' (1990, p. 141). The writing process did indeed become faster first with the typewriter, but then all the more so with the computer, so that one's writing style also changed and became more like spoken language. In the end with the computer – even when we use it as a writing tool – the forming of thoughts and writing go hand in hand, just as at the same time the text becomes something that is permanently re-worked, rewritten and corrected, so that it retains, so to speak, the status of a provisional nature or crudity.

Disclosure statement

No potential conflict of interest was reported by the author.

Notes on contributor

Dieter Mersch is director of the Institute for Theory at the Zurich University of Arts, Switzerland. His writings cover philosophy of media, philosophy of language, aesthetics, semiotics, hermeneutics, structuralism and media theory.

References

Aczel, A.D., 2006. *The artist and the mathematician*. New York: Basic.
Adorno, T.W., 2002. Music and language: a fragment. *In*: T.W. Adorno, ed. *Quasi una Fantasia*. R. Livingstone, trans. London: Verso, 1–6.
Adorno, T.W., 2004. *Aesthetic theory*. R. Hullot-Kentor, trans. London: Continuum.
Adorno, T.W., 2007. *Negative dialectics*. E. B. Ashton, trans. London: Continuum.

THINKING MEDIA AND BEYOND

Apostel, L., Mandelbrot, B., and Morf, A., 1957. *Logique, language et Théorie de L'information*. Paris: Presses Universitaires de France.

Aristotle 1991. *De anima*. R.D. Hicks, trans. New York: Prometheus Books.

Aristotle 2011. *Nicomachean ethics*. R.C. Bartlett and S.D. Collins, trans. Chicago, IL: University of Chicago Press.

Austin, J.L., 1975. *How to do things with words*. Cambridge, MA: Harvard University Press.

Belting, H., 2008. *Florenz und Bagdad. Eine westöstliche Geschichte des Blicks*. Munich: Fink.

Benjamin, W., 1977a. *Über Sprache überhaupt und über die Sprache des Menschen. In*: W. Benjamin, ed. *Gesammelte Schriften*. Frankfurt/Main: Suhrkamp, vol. II.1., 140–157.

Benjamin, W., 1977b. *Ursprung des deutschen Trauerspiels. In*: W. Benjamin, ed. *Gesammelte Schriften*. Frankfurt/Main: Suhrkamp, vol. I.1, 202–430.

Benjamin, W., 2008. The task of the translator. *In*: W. Benjamin, ed. *One-way street and other writings*. J.A. Underwood, trans. London: Penguin, 29–45.

Bense, M., 1998. *Einführung in die informationstheoretische Ästhetik. In*: M. Bense, ed. *Ausgewählte Schriften*, Stuttgart: Metzler, vol. 3, 251–417.

Coy, W., 1989. Aus der Vorgeschichte des mediums computer. *In*: F. Kittler and G.C. Tholen, eds. *Arsenale der Seele*. Munich: Fink, 19–38.

Davidson, D., 2001. *Inquiries into truth and interpretation*. Oxford: Clarendon Press.

Derrida, J., 1967. *Writing and difference*. London: Routledge.

Derrida, J., 1981. *Dissemination*. B. Johnson, trans. Chicago, IL: University of Chicago Press.

Derrida, J., 1982. Signature event context. *In*: J. Derrida, ed. *Margins of philosophy*. A. Bass, trans. Chicago, IL: University of Chicago Press, 307–330.

Derrida, J., 1984. Différance. *In*: J. Derrida, ed. *Margins of philosophy*. A. Bass, trans, Chicago, IL: University of Chicago Press, 1–27.

Derrida, J., 2005. *Chora*. Vienna: Passagen.

Dosse, F., 1996. *Geschichte des Strukturalismus*. vol. 1. Hamburg: Junius.

Durham Peters, John, 2000. *Speaking into the air: a history of the idea of communication*. Chicago, IL: University of Chicago Press.

Engell, L., *et al.*, eds., 2002. *Kursbuch Medienkultur*. 4th ed. Stuttgart: DVA, 264–299.

Flusser, V., 1997. *Medienkultur*. Frankfurt/Main: Fischer.

Freud, S., 2002. *Civilization and its discontents*. D. McLintock, trans. London: Penguin Books.

Gadamer, H.G., 1989. Kultur und Medien. *In*: A. Honneth et al., ed. *Zwischenbetrachtungen. Im Prozeß der Aufklärung. Jürgen Habermas zum 60. Geburtstag*. Frankfurt/Main: Suhrkamp, 715–732.

Hagen, W., 2008. *Metaxy. Eine historiosemantische Fußnote zu einem Medienbegriff. In*: S. Münker and A. Roesler, eds. *Was ist ein Medium?* Frankfurt/Main: Suhrkamp, 13–29.

Heißenbüttel, H., 1969. Das Medium ist die Botschaft, Anmerkungen zu Marshall McLuhan. *In*: G.E. Düsseldorf, ed. *MERKUR vol. XII, No. 11 1968, reprinted in and cited here according to McLuhan. Für und Wider (1969)*. Vienna: Stern, 293–314.

Heidegger, M., 1982. The word of Nietzsche: 'god is dead'. *In*: M. Heidegger, ed. *The question concerning technology, and other essays*. W. Lovitt, trans. New York: Harper Perennial, 53–112.

Heidegger, M., 2001. *Poetry, language, thought*. A. Hofstadter, trans. New York: Perennial Classics.

Heidegger, M., 2002. *Identity and difference*. J. Stambaugh, trans. Chicago, IL: University of Chicago Press.

THINKING MEDIA AND BEYOND

Heidegger, M., 2008a. The origin of the work of art. *In*: M. Heidegger, ed. *Basic writings*. New York: Harper Perennial, 139–212.

Heidegger, M., 2008b. The way to language. *In*: M. Heidegger, ed. *Basic writings*. New York: Harper Perennial, 397–426.

Heidegger, M., 2008c. Letter on humanism. *In*: M. Heidegger, ed. *Basic writings*. New York: Harper Perennial, 241–243.

Hörisch, J., 1991. *Brot und Wein. Die Poesie des Abendmahls*. Frankfurt/Main: Suhrkamp.

Hörisch, J., 2004. *Gott, Geld und Medien*. Frankfurt/Main: Suhrkamp.

Hörl, E., 2005. *Die heiligen Kanäle*. Berlin: Diaphanes.

Hubig, C., 2006. *Die Kunst des Möglichen I. Technikphilosophie als Reflexion der Medialität*. Bielefeld: Transcript.

Ihde, D., 1990. *Technology in the lifeworld. From garden to earth*. Bloomington: Indiana University Press.

Innis, H., 2008. *The bias of communication*. Toronto: University of Toronto Press.

Kant, I., 1998. *Critique of pure reason*. P. Guyer and A.W. Wood, trans. Cambridge: Cambridge University Press.

Kittler, F., 1989. *Die künstliche Intelligenz des Weltkrieges: Alan Turing*. *In*: F. Kittler and G. C. Tholen, eds. *Arsenale der Seele*. Munich: Fink, 187–202.

Kittler, F., 1992. *Austreibung des Geistes aus den Geisteswissenschaften*. Stuttgart: Schöningh.

Kittler, F., 1993. *Draculas Vermächtnis. Technische Schriften*. Leipzig: Reclam.

Kittler, F., 1995. *Aufschreibesysteme*. 3rd ed. Munich: Fink.

Kittler, F., 1999. *Gramophone, film, typewriter*. G. Winthrop-Young and M. Wutz, trans. Stanford, CA: Stanford University Press.

Krämer, S., 2008. *Medium, Bote, Übertragung. Kleine Metaphysik der Medialität*. Frankfurt/ Main: Suhrkamp.

Lacan, J., 1990. Psychoanalysis and cybernetics, or on the nature of language. *In*: J. Lacan, ed. S. Tomaselli, trans. *The seminar of Jacques Lacan, book II, XXIII*. New York: Norton, 294–308.

Laertius, D., 1967. *Leben und Meinungen berühmter Philosophen*. Hamburg: Meiner.

McLuhan, M., 2001. *Understanding media*. London: Routledge.

McLuhan, M. and Fiore, Q., 2003. *The medium is the massage. Pinguin design series*. Corte Madera, CA: Gingko Press.

Mennighaus, W., 1995. *Walter Benjamins Theorie der Sprachmagie*. Frankfurt/Main: Suhrkamp.

Mersch, D., 2002. *Das Ereignis der Setzung*. *In*: E. Fischer-Lichte, C. Horn, and M. Warstat, eds. *Performativität und Ereignis*. Tübingen Basel: Francke, 41–56.

Mersch, D., 2004. Medialität und Undarstellbarkeit. Einleitung in eine 'negative' Medientheorie. *In*: S. Krämer, ed. *Performativität und Medialität*. Munich: Fink, 75–96.

Mersch, D., 2005. Negative Medialität. Derridas Différance und Heideggers Weg zur Sprache. *Journal Phänomenologie. Jacques Derrida*, 23, 14–22.

Mersch, D., 2006. *Medientheorien zur Einführung*. Hamburg: Junius.

Mersch, D., 2008. *Tertium datur. Einleitung in eine negative Medientheorie*. *In*: S. Münker and A. Roesler, eds. *Was ist ein Medium*. Frankfurt/Main: Suhrkamp, 304–321.

Mersch, D., 2010a. *Posthermeneutik*. Berlin: Akademie.

Mersch, D., 2010b. *Irrfahrten. Labyrinthe, Netze und die Unentscheidbarkeit der Welt*. *In*: G. Mein and S. Börnchen, eds. *Weltliche Wallfahrten*. Munich: Fink, 41–56.

Mitchell, A.J., 2010. *Heidegger among the sculptors*. Stanford, CA: Stanford University Press.

Moles, A., 1973. *Kunst und computer*. Cologne: DuMont.

Nietzsche, F., 2002. *Kritische Gesamtausgabe. Band III.1*. Berlin: De Gruyter.

Nietzsche, F., 2005. *The gay science*. J. Nauckhoff, trans. Cambridge: Cambridge University Press.

Panofsky, E., 1998. Die Perspektive als 'symbolische form'. *In*: E. Panofsky ed. *Aufsätze zu Grundfragen der Kunstwissenschaft*. Berlin: Spiess, 99–167.

Shannon, C., 1948. A mathematical theory of communication. *The bell system technical journal*, 27, 379–423, 623–656.

Spitzer, L., 1968. *Milieu and ambiance*. *In*: L. Spitzer, ed. *Essays in historical semantics*. New York: Vanni, 179–225.

Strawson, P., 1972. *Einzelding und logisches Subjekt. Ein Beitrag zur deskriptiven Metaphysik*. Stuttgart: Reclam.

Tholen, G.C., 2002. *Die Zäsur der Medien*. Suhrkamp: Frankfurt/Main.

Weber, S., 1999. *Virtualität der Medien*. *In*: S. Schade and G.C. Tholen, eds. *Konfigurationen. Zwischen Kunst und Medien*. Munich: Fink, 35–49.

Wiener, O., 1990. *Probleme der künstlichen Intelligenz*. Berlin: Merve.

Wittgenstein, L., 1974. *Philosophical grammar*. A. Kenny, trans. Berkeley: University of California Press.

Wittgenstein, L., 1999. *Denkbewegungen, Tagebücher*. Frankfurt/Main: Fischer.

Wittgenstein, L., 2001. *Philosophical investigations*. G.E.M. Anscombe, trans. London: Blackwell.

Historical, technological and medial a priori: on the belatedness of media

Anna Tuschling

ABSTRACT

This essay addresses German-language media theory through the lens of its central concept, the technological a priori. The technological a priori is a concept developed most prominently in the work of Friedrich Kittler out of the historical a priori of Michel Foucault's discourse analysis. The focus of the technological a priori is historically significant materialities, that is, media technologies. This essay argues that the technological a priori precisely cannot be reduced to analysing specific materialities, such as individual media technologies, the computer, gramophone, telephone, etc. in terms of their fundamental significance for sense-making and history. The technological a priori entails not only a concept of materiality but also a concept of time. The media studies to come should expand the technological a priori towards a more general media a priori by incorporating more complex theories of time such as those offered by various approaches to belatedness. This task would prove especially compelling for the history of media and the disciplinary history of media studies.

Synopsis

The epistemological potential of media studies tends to come from how the field treats media as a precondition for informational knowledge subsequent to these media. The defining force of all media is expressed in the priority of their capacity for mediation, a priority that also entails a specific temporal advantage. One finds a particular sensorium for this, in connection with Foucault's historical a priori, in the form of a technological a priori. Several critiques target a purported anti-humanism at stake in assuming a preconditionality for media technology and in disregarding theories of language and signification in favour of a pure 'thinking of hardware'. Modern enlightenment concepts of the human, however, do not harbour a programme for the future of media studies. Nor is an exclusive focus on linguistic concepts of signification sufficient. Rather, the following essay will offer a critical inquiry into the implicit temporal concept of a technological a priori; through theories of belatedness, this inquiry aims to make the concept available in the context of media a priori. Such an approach seems promising not only for foundational theories, but also for the temporal schema of historiographies of media and the disciplines in particular. Because the discipline of media studies is poised to record its beginnings, and in doing so necessarily rewrites history, it faces the task of reflecting on ideas of origin, as it outlines belatedness from trauma research, cryptonomy, grammatology and game theory in ever different ways. It is worthwhile to consider relinquishing altogether talk of the a priori – whether formal, historical, technological or medial – in favour of a systematization of belatedness. Connected to this is the hope that such a systematization might prove to be influential for the theoretical foundations of media studies.

Media studies' intervention

The emancipation of media research

As the idiosyncrasies of media come more clearly into focus in the course of the twentieth century, media studies all the more emphatically lays claim to a place amongst the disciplines. Media studies is the name for the institutional response to real and imaginary effects, particularly those of informational–technological upheavals. The discipline gains an increasingly sharp profile; however, the more it emancipates itself from the expectations of the public, that is, by not catering to a wide-spread fear of technologies with studies on the negative influence of digital media. It is only through a transformative appropriation of social responsibility, so it seems that the young discipline can secure its own instruments and theoretical spaces. Media studies begins at the point at which it comments on more than just the technologically self-evident manipulability of digital and analogue footage, or the ostensible amplification of violence through computer games. It must also devote itself to erratic mediality in all of its forms and historical figurations, for it is precisely the unusual and occasionally alarming singularity of medial functions that the most important philosophies and historiographies of media target. It is only when media no longer vanish together with, or exhaust themselves through, the transmission, storage or processing of their content that their achievements become visible ones that elevate media as the legitimate object of an autonomous discipline with a recognizable purpose within the academic division of labour.

Media as objects of knowledge in media studies

As evident as the idiosyncrasy of media might be within the field of media studies, the idea that media in a certain sense precede every form of perception and signification is not self-evident. This is the point at which the inner and the outer of media studies part ways. While fields such as jurisprudence, sociology and psychology establish new areas of research in media rights, media sociology or media psychology, respectively, they do not actually engage in media studies. It would be astoundingly misguided if the individual disciplines wanted to resist, for instance, the encroachment of computers in their areas of knowledge. Internet transactions raise legal questions, just as they enable modes of consultation that can be approached and studied as either forms of new psychological services, or as the upheaval of such services, depending on one's perspective. The immeasurable methodological scope of information technologies in the natural and life sciences is simply worth mentioning here. The computer as 'all-pulverizer' ['*Alleszermalmer*'] rearranged the world anew and redefined precisely the spaces of knowledge production as well.[1] Yet, the established disciplines turn their attention to the Internet and (the now not-so) New Media mostly with the intention of utilizing these fields of research in the service of their already well-tried methods and bodies of knowledge. Media studies proceeds in a very different way. Its point of departure lies for the most part in opposing a narrow conception of media and mediality, one that tends to reduce media and mediality to individual technologies and arrangements, such as the PC, computer networks or mobile telephones. Nevertheless, the PC, Internet and mobile media serve as important objects of study for media studies. Yet media, as the epistemological object of media studies, are in no way concretely defined products of what is regarded as the age of computers. Media theory explicitly emerged as a critique of the redundant talk of New Media and rescued the question of medial functions from an exclusive consideration of the present as well as from a strict definition of media concepts in terms of information technologies of the twentieth and twenty-first century.

The computer: a trickster

Just as work in media studies need not remain limited to the study of digital media, it is likewise unnecessary for them to have a singular focus on modernity, pre-modernity or antiquity. Nevertheless, it is hard to resist having the impression that the computer, with the implementation of a discipline wholly devoted to it, somehow appears on the scene as a troublemaker and a trickster. Just as the computer undoubtedly served alongside radio, telephone, film and television as one of the most important reasons for the formation of the field, it certainly also operated subversively in the production of media theory from the beginning. The Universal machine embodies one of the most peculiar 'architectonic ensamples' with which the mind imitates the 'system of the universe' (Leibniz 1979, p. 33), or with which the mind transposes the operations and workings of the universe that it captures onto everything programmable in the digital age. This signals a decisive turning point in comparison to earlier technologies of 'prosthetic gods' (Freud 1999, p. 451). Experiments [*Versuche*] – which were condensed to the singular and given the title computer – unfurl their own efforts at imitation. Indeed, they become totalizing imitations of all analogue or technological media. Digital media usurp any individual medium; they are veritable 'generica' (Schanze 2004, p. 72). The reason why the discourse analysis of technological media could, with Kittler (1999), be declared finished at its own beginning is that precisely this total amalgamation of digital media is in a position to 'swallow up [kassieren]' the concept of medium. However, one chooses to go about this, programmes of media studies cannot help but subsume themselves critically to such an influential enterprise of media theory, which in the course of writing its history has, as it were, consumed itself. It is not easy for a discipline to appeal to systems of thought that deny their very continuation in such a pointed way. Media theory after Kittler, through the discovery in cultural studies of general programmability, dismantles any sort of programme of knowledge from the start, insofar as media, and thus their concept, are meant to end with the computer. Nevertheless, media theory provides a precise instrument that, while preserving productive differences, reveals a common thread amongst the many experiments in media studies. It does this insofar as it uses the concept of the technological a priori to formulate what is likely the strongest and still most provocative case for the priority of media. The temporal–theoretical inquiry into the technological a priori[2] or the 'technological-media a priori' (Spreen 1998; Winthrop-Young 2005, p. 76; Horn 2007, p. 7) which is undertaken in what follows surprisingly does not bring to light a simple positing of materiality, but rather a highly contradictory treatment of time.

Media theory as an implicit theory of time

Every concept of media implicates a specific notion of time, even, and especially, when it aims to analyse the measurement of time in a media-technological manner. Innis (1951) already insisted on a media-historical investigation of time and asserted that all historians are compelled to accept a 'time factor', which would reflect their attitudes towards the time of the epoch in which they write. His plea applies not only to historical research and media history but to nearly any area of studies. Yet the most important theories of media already present implicit theories of time precisely because they grasp media as literally *imperfect*[3] preconditions of knowledge, and thus grasp media according to their own understanding as a priori. However, many approaches fail to reflect on their own temporality, with the result that their concepts of time remain unacknowledged and often underdeveloped.

Media-technological analysis and media archaeologies in and after Kittler adapt French discourse analysis. Foucault's (1989, p. 172; 1972, p. 141) historical a priori, which for its part can be understood only through its difference from a formal a priori, is correctly considered a key concept of early German-language media historiography in particular. The conditions of possibility for thought, perception and signification cannot, according to Foucault, be extracted from time nor placed prior to any experience. They are, rather, embedded in the concrete history and historical knowledge of their time. The separation of a formal from a historical a priori in Foucault, and later in Kittler, leads, however, to the very loss of any understanding of temporality, which to this day has shaped and defined conceptions of time in media theory and media philosophy.

The term 'a priori' itself entertains a contradictory relationship to time. And according to several readings, including those of Foucault, as a 'formal' a priori the term negates its own temporal ties, since a priori categories logically precede the empirical time of historical events and, as is frequently suggested, are independent of such events. As a word, a priori means nothing other than 'from what comes earlier' (Ritter and Gründer 1971, p. 462). Both Foucault's historical a priori and Kittler's technological a priori play with the philosophical undertones of the term, while simultaneously rejecting its idealist systematic.[4] Thus far, media theories have uncritically adopted the verdicts and convictions of postmodernism, particularly with regard to the philosophy of Kant and Hegel. If, in the future, one desires to engage in a provocative reading of a priori categories commencing with Kant, as for instance Foucault does in his archeology, then one would have to, perhaps to his or her own surprise, engage in a discussion of a priori structures in media and cultural studies under new auspices at the very least and, in part, with new adversaries, an endeavor that can unfortunately only be hinted at here without further elaboration (Bürger 2008).

Transition from historical to technological a priori

The temporal ties of any archaeology

With recourse to his other studies in histories of knowledge, Foucault emphasizes in *The Archaeology of Knowledge* the positivity of a discourse's statements as a historical a priori, which represents a 'purely empirical figure' (1972, p. 144). Adaptations of Foucault's discourse analysis for media studies have been defined by this 'happy positivism', which rings of Nietzsche, and have been defined by an effort to assert preconditioning structures, that is, a-priori patterns. Such patterns, however, are not *timeless*, but themselves subsumed to historical change (Foucault 1972, p. 141). Since the middle of the 1980s at the latest, media materialities that embody technological media, and programmable hardware still more, have functioned as a-priori structures in this sense. For all the emphasis on the specificity of material, Foucault desired to generate with the historical a priori a concept for what different discourses and the statements that support them have in common, that is, for a discourse's 'unity throughout time', beyond the individual works of any disciplinary field (1972, p. 142). What connects a discourse, its preconditionality or its 'condition of reality [*"Realitätsbedingung"*]' in other words is determined as much by a non-concordance of suppositions and assertions within a field as it is by the transformability of a field at historic junctures (Foucault 1972, p. 143). As carefully as this method devotes itself to addressing the description, comparison and contrast of statements and their 'dispersion', archaeology can little afford to forgo the two conditions it sets for itself: non-concordance of statements within a given field and the transformability of this field (Foucault 1989, p. 172). In other words, there must after all exist contrasts to investigate, both between different stages in time and within the investigated time frame. Foucault's comments allow only the following conclusion: according to discourse-analytic conceptions, under appropriately impartial consideration, distinct states effectively emerge out of the material in question or even the time period itself. In this process, the conditions of differentiation that media studies seeks to investigate remain once again undisclosed and as a methodological problem underestimated. This results in a loss of reflection on the specific temporality of those differentiations that reside in historiography as concealed presuppositions. As the contradictions at stake in its name suggest, the formulation of the historical a priori entails something that precedes history anew: inclusion in or exclusion from the archive, or perhaps a portal with opening and closing mechanisms. Both in Nietzsche and Foucault something is assumed that switches [*schaltet*] – regardless of whether certain histories, or perhaps even certain a priori, are switched on or off, as Ebeling (2009, p. 318) suggests. Notable in this regard is that Foucault constructs his archaeological method above all *ex negativo*. Greater emphasis seems to lie on what his method cannot be than on actually describing its approach. One of the few positive aspects of his method, by contrast, is how archaeology grasps 'discourse as praxis' with rules that encompass the regularities and patterns of inclusions and exclusions in the respective enunciative fields (Bürger 2008, p. 127). The rules of discourse imply neither a spatial nor temporal 'deep stratum', which is why the language of the positivity of the analyzed discourses in terms of 'pure surfaces' is so fitting (Bürger 2008). Foucault's archaeology proceeds from nothing less than the historicization of meaning-carrying differences themselves. With Foucault, historicity is even more determined by preceding history and the selection mechanisms of the archive already mentioned. In order to designate the precondition of the historical a priori itself, one thus requires in a double sense historicity as such, which for Foucault (1972, p. 143), however, ought always to remain 'a specific history'. On one hand, media-theoretical endeavours follow this strict historicization. On the other hand, they shift the emphasis from the statements of a discourse and its rules to media technologies. As a precondition of a precondition that goes by the name of history, Kittler (2005) in turn introduces 'Discourse Networks' [*Aufschreibesysteme*]. The shift from the historical to the technological a priori implies the shift from the ability to make a statement [*Aussagbarkeit*] to the ability to notate [*Aufschreibbarkeit*], or to programmability (Foucault 1972).[5] No longer does the historicization of difference alone stand in the foreground, one could say, but rather the 'reification of difference', which is always understood, however, as the material precipitate of history. An understanding of what Kittler considers the most exemplary hardware, namely, the inverter, complicates this sort of object-oriented historiography, a historiography that is programmatically oriented towards materialities of communication; the issue of the 'door'[6] is directly related to this. Already in Lacan, the door embodies the symbolic since it serves not only as a factual, but also always simultaneously immaterial, condition of possibility for any ability to distinguish or posit difference.

The Foucauldian endeavor thus does not escape the antinomies of the a priori in the way that its use of historicization and inner-discursivity would lead one to hope. But this essay is not meant as a critique of Foucault. Neither is its focus the foreseeable objections from the field of history, which suggest that Foucault positions the shifts he works out in a historically incorrect manner or that he outlines these shifts at the cost of historical accuracy. Rather, this essay is concerned with the methodological consequences for media studies that result, not only from the specificities of discourse-analytical and archaeological approaches, but likewise through the shift from a historical to a technological a priori.

Near or far

History in and after Foucault no longer desires to recognize any outside or any overarching structures in the sense of a formal a priori. The historical a priori is thus concerned with the rules of discourse that are implicated in what connects them (Foucault 1972, p. 144). This strict inner-discursivity, which is already central in Foucault, is elaborated in 'media a priorism', according to which there is no outside of media (Krämer 2008, p. 66–67). It remains necessary for discourse analysis and media theory, according to their own claims, to reflect on their own historical and medial preconditions. For this reason, the historical a priori connects 'the priority of the a priori with the belatedness of the historical' – though this connection implies a weak notion of belatedness as simply that which is subsequent (Ebeling 2009, p. 312). Even Foucault (1972, p. 147) is aware that one's own archive forms the blind spot of any analysis, and for this reason he regards historical, and therefore temporal, distance as the condition of possibility for all archaeology. The archive of a society or culture cannot be grasped in its totality. Nor can an archive be described that serves as the precondition of its own analysis, and which thus grounds the existence of the analysis (Foucault 1972).

Therefore, neither the current moment nor antique eras are suitable for archaeology. In this way, Foucault calls that which encompasses the analysis of the archive neither exclusively current nor entirely distant. And not incidentally, this characterizes the threshold of time to which Foucault primarily dedicates his work: from early modernity to the end of the monopoly of writing around 1850. Kittler's continuation of the discourse analysis of technological media begins at the historical moment with which Foucault ends (Krämer 2006, p. 97). Against the purported atemporality, immobility and thus immutability of a formal a priori, discourse analysis sets the historical embeddedness of its own concepts. As the differential and volatile movement of an unforeseeable historical sequence, time serves as the basis for the later concept of the archive, which discourse analysis of technological media inverts into the dependency of the contemporary on presupposed material matrixes or media technologies. Whereas the historical a priori is constituted solely retroactively, the technological a priori, as conscious mimicry of media technology, increasingly determines its contemporary and future observation from its respective moment. If the historical a priori was understood as the 'agent of the elimination of all a prioris', at least with regard to its own objectives, then one can conclude that media are now again elevated to 'transcendentals' (Ebeling 2006, pp. 313, 317). The inversion, or at least complication, of perspectives is by itself not crucial to the analysis here. In studying the shift from the historical to the technological a priori, there needs to be a more serious assessment of the fact that, in stark contrast to Foucault, one no longer vaunts the ironic positivism of one's own archaeology. Rather, negligent of the foundational theories that subtend one's position, one must consider a view that gives room to the dictum of the observable, and thereby gives into an emphatic positivism. In this sense, Ebeling sees the positivization of philosophy as a merit of projects in media studies and the history of knowledge.

Today we can see what sort of knowledge was able to be developed with these philosophical–historical ingredients: it is a historicized, positivized and often spatialized knowledge – a positivization of philosophy. The negativity of philosophical concepts has for instance been positivized through the gesture of historicization. The beyond of the a priori has been transformed into the here of historical and discursive, medial and technological processes. (Ebeling 2006, p. 319)

In contrast to the self-evidence of these historiographies, the epistemological struggle for absolute historicization has a number of predecessors. By way of these predecessors, one would essentially be aware of what German-language media studies and cultural studies seem to hint at: that the complete historicization of knowledge, by making knowledge empirical, threatens to turn into positivism. Not without reason, Foucault flirts with, though never ever affirms, a self-designation as positivist, all the while keeping in mind the undisguised positivistic belief in the observable and measurable that, for instance, characterizes many works of historical materialism. Pairing materialism and positivism has a long tradition.[7] At the moment, the risk of a surreptitious paradigm shift seems to be forming in the overall field of media and cultural studies through the increased emergence of positivisms and the more amiable treatment of positivistic sciences. A reading of Kittler's media-technological analysis that conflates his analysis with positivistic materialism fosters this tendency, whether willingly or not.

The other legacy of economic critique

History of knowledge and discourse analysis pick up where classical historical materialism makes a decisive exception: with the historicity of intellectual labour, the sciences and in particular the natural sciences and their laws, which themselves were necessary for the creation of technological and digital media. Sohn-Rethel (1978, p. 2), for instance, critiques the fact that in Marx's work, even as late as in *Capital*, the natural sciences were 'not given a place' such that Marx takes their 'intrinsic methodological possibilities ... for granted'. On the one hand, Marxian analysis is characterized by how it understands 'all phenomena contained in the world of consciousness, whether past, present or future ... historically' and thus as 'time-bound' (Sohn-Rethel 1978). On the other hand, for Marxism, 'questions of logic, mathematics and science are seen as ruled by timeless standards' (Sohn-Rethel 1978., see also Schmidt 1993). In this way, a Marxist historiography approaches natural laws and natural sciences with precisely the timelessness that Foucault ascribes to the formal a priori, and which Foucault seeks to avoid with the historical a priori. Like Foucault, Sohn-Rethel sees it as absolutely necessary to reflect on the temporal ties of his own thought. It is precisely with this point that Sohn-Rethel draws a line between materialism and idealism.

Is a Marxist thus a materialist as far as historical truth is concerned but an idealist when confronted by the truth of nature! Is his thought split between two concepts of truth: the one dialectical and time-bound, the other undialectical, consigning any awareness of historical time to oblivion! (Sohn-Rethel 1972, p. 2–3)

Related projects of discourse analysis, science studies, gender studies and media studies each address in their own ways what becomes noticeable here as a blind spot of Marxism. Marx refrains from historically situating natural laws. Moreover, Marx imagines he can block out the unforeseen and contingent with his thesis of systemic contradiction, which takes the form of an antagonism between personified classes. However, recent Marxian analysis wrongly remains reduced to this axiom of class contradiction, as has been evident in recent years with the so-called new Marx readers and, among others, Badiou. In this way, the temporal determinism with regard to the probability of revolutionary change comprises, together with the thesis of alienation, the problematic legacy of Marxian work. The critique of political economy offers an excellent example of how self-reflexive thought threatens to go awry whenever it attempts to outpace time in the sense of deterministic development. In terms of perspective, media-theoretical and philosophical approaches must also start treating an awareness of their origins in economic critiques as interesting, if not extremely important, origins that often receive little acknowledgement. At the same time, one cannot yet again overlook the fact that even absolute historicization still faces the dilemma of not being able to get a whole picture of its own pre-conditions. In addition, critical theory offers a reminder that tracing elements of knowledge back to particular historical formations is not an end in itself. Historicization works determinedly against the ossification of epistemic and social relations as natural, immutable and predetermined; for a circumstance and a power relation prove to be changeable only to the degree that they can be thought of as emerging historically. Two sex theory, above all, is worth mentioning in this regard. Nevertheless, debates in media studies demonstrate that an exclusive historicization runs up against its limits as soon as it lapses into what are themselves unquestioned, pure descriptions of seemingly factual media technologies. Furthermore, the genesis of these technologies can no longer be understood if these 'thing-a prioris' are essentially posited at specific points in time. Concepts of belatedness that call to mind the contribution of basic research in media studies demand a skewed position towards the Scylla of ahistoric structures and the Charybdis of historicism insofar as they do not attempt to grasp the coming into being of their own structures solely in terms of positivizable statements. In this way, belatedness faces the dilemma of all efforts to historicize, namely, the need to translate the genesis and coming into being of the investigated formations into empirical, that is sequential, temporal concepts.

The technological a priori or the price of programmability

Time is hardware

Discourse analysis continues to represent one of the most important tools of contemporary media theory. The formation of German-language analyses of media technologies occurred under the aegis of a reinterpretation of a historical inquiry into a technological a priori. What appears to be a careful reconstruction of previous historical constellations in Foucault takes on the shrewd form of a 'timer', or even a time manipulation, in Kittler that emerges under the name of media technology. While Kittler primarily takes the media of the nineteenth century into account, the media-technological a priori is exhibited paradigmatically in the form of the computer or in universally programmable machines, for which Kittler demonstrates an 'indispensability and, consequently, the priority of hardware in general' (Kittler 1997b, p. 152). The development of the technological a priori occurs in various stages as a disentanglement, not only from discourse-analytic historiography, but also from structural psychoanalysis. In his reading of Freud's interpretation of E.T.A. Hoffman's 'Sandmann', Kittler insists on the literalness of psychoanalytic concepts and offers a symbolic a priori as the precondition of subsequent signification. Language is not exhausted 'in the informational-exchange double' (Kittler 1997b, p. 155). Later, Kittler demands a media-technological, non-metaphoric reading of Daniel Paul Schreber, from whose writings Kittler adopts the expression 'Aufschreibesystem [Discourse Networks]'.

The paradox of programmable hardware

Kittler pointedly and relentlessly insists on the priority of the technological, and thus on a certain notion of time, albeit one that remains implicit. To the same degree, his temporal–theoretical analysis of hardware is concise and nuanced in its details. Thus the concern that an 'information-technological materialism' reduces the concept of materialism to a simple notion of fixed *physis*, or matter, is out of the question, even though Kittler (1993, p. 182) seems himself to stray in this direction at times. Indeed, upon closer consideration, programmable hardware not only appears to be a paradox, but also to be an issue of time, as will be demonstrated in what follows (Kittler 1998, p. 119).

Kittler was decisive in promoting the study of a media-theoretical helix comprised of the intertwining functions of storage, transmission and the consolidation of the two in processing. Yet Kittler (1998, p. 123) nevertheless consistently stressed that 'the computer-technologically indispensible function of storage is unrealizable as mere software'. The priority of hardware is thus derived from the indispensability of the storage function. And the indispensability of materially realized switches, however miniature these might be, is the defining feature of a strong technological a priori. Because of their factual ineluctability, the material attributes of hardware embody the insurmountable framework of the will to store, to transmit and to process. However, as a technological a priori, hardware is not simply given. Programmability first makes hardware into what it is and forces it to turn into its opposite and to become replaceable: 'For structurally programmable machines, certain physical parameters are apparently as necessary as they are replaceable' (p. 123). While the aspects of material resistance and dependence on hardware as a 'structure in its own right' still garner much attention in all areas of media studies research, the paradox of programmability is far too often ignored in media studies (p. 127). In no way can hardware be separated from its replaceability; and in fact programmability necessarily implies the universal replaceability of what is programmable in hardware: 'As irreplaceable as hardware remains in general, for computational purposes and storage capacity, any individual hardware has become just as replaceable' (p. 123). We might ask whether this '[has] become' does not entirely shift the meaning of the statement in a way that deserves to be revoked. Then we might find that hardware's irreplaceability is per se coupled with replaceability. In any case, no single actor appears to be responsible for hardware's decline – this is the case in contrast to Kittler's (1994, pp. 209–220) treatment of Protected Mode. The 'price of programmability' that hardware must pay for those attributes that characterize it as a technological a priori is the following: it is condemned to be an 'unknown being' (Kittler 1997b, p. 153; 1997a, p. 92; 1998, p. 142). Thus its own programmability precludes structurally programmable hardware from analysis and renders it a great unknown before which 'whole towers of software hierarchies' collect since its invention (Kittler 1994, p. 124). 'What programs the computer cannot be a computer'; nor can that which makes a computer programmable in the first place be a computer (Hagen 1994, p. 148). This precludes the computer's simple givenness *qua* matter and in no way coincides with the dichotomy of hardware and software.

Discreteness of time

Upon first glance the heart of all programming consists in nothing other than time itself; indeed the implementation of the switch leads, as the 'cornerstone of all executable digital computers', to 'measured time' (Kittler 1998, p. 127). In the light of the project of investigating the technological a priori with regard to issues of time, we can come to the following intermediary conclusion: hardware appears to be inextricably linked to the problem of time since the programmability of hardware and hence even the hardware itself represents a particular form of temporality. Switching (regardless of how this is realized technologically) is a crucial activity of all computers and presumes the measurability of time, that is, a clock, as well as the recurring syntagmatization of time, namely through timing [*Taktung*] or, more precisely, the discretization of time.[8]

We might say that the clock enables us to introduce a discreteness into time, so that time for some purposes can be regarded as a succession of instants instead of a continuous flow. A digital machine must essentially deal with discrete objects, and in the case of the ACE [Automatic Computing Engine] this is made possible by the use of the clock (Turing 1986; 1987, p. 192).

This last sentence reminds us that digital machines do not necessarily operate electronically, just as, conversely, not every computer functions digitally. What has become especially powerful in the form of a digital computer is based on the electronic realization of switchability and thus on precisely the discretization of time that Turing mentions. Turing pits two forms of time against one another as epitomes of the digital/analogue dichotomy: the continuous flow of analogue time versus a series of discrete instances as properties of digital processing par excellence.

Not only does the digital stand in need of clarification, the analogue, as its opposite, is just as puzzling. Even for the participants of the Macy conference, defining what distinguishes analogue from digital presented unexpected difficulties (Pflüger 2005). Going forward, one could relate the diagnosed 'ambiguity of analogue' to its delayed consideration, and perhaps account for this ambiguity with the fact that the analogue can only ever be formulated belatedly (Pflüger 2005, p. 28). Kittler resorts to the dichotomy of time-flow and time-series when he calls the combinatorics of instances time axis manipulation, which has validity for digital media, technological media and alphabetical writing (including, though not explicitly, language in itself). Both Turing and Kittler falsely presume a seamlessness of analogue time, even when this remains hypothetical, as in Kittler. Noteworthy here is the fact that Turing declares a special handling [*Handhabung*] of time to be the defining characteristic of the Universal machine: the treatment of time 'als diskret' (Kittler 1998, p. 128).[9] Treating time as discrete means nothing other than switching.

Leaps and clicks

In his discussion of the machine's ability to think, Turing (1950) establishes the universality of digital computers through their capacity for discretization and ultimately through their switchability. Digital computers do not move continuously from one state to the next; Rather, they operate in sudden 'jumps' or 'clicks' (Turing 1950, p. 439). Strictly speaking, there are no discrete machines because in an analogue period of time everything moves continuously. We could, however, think of many kinds of machines *as* discrete state machines even if there is always an 'intermediate position' between two states of switching (p. 439). Turing's description of discreteness in terms of 'as' or 'as if' recalls, if distantly, what will later be described in cultural studies through the metaphorics of digital media (Tholen 2002). 'Only that which is switchable is at all' subsequently becomes Kittler's maxim – a logical one for a Lacanian. However, this maxim now appears to leave Turing's prudence behind by easily assuming discrete states and with them, switchability (Kittler 1993, p. 182). Kittler ties the capacity for discretization strictly to the inherent logic of the utilized matter, or, more precisely, to the matter's inherent movements, as for instance becomes clear with Kittler's (1998, p. 127) paradigmatic inverter switch, in which input and output signals can never be aligned: because 'there is, since Einstein, absolute velocity, input and output are never completely synchronized'. The 'minute delay' that enables this type of switch comes close to a media-technologically inflected concept of *belatedness* insofar as it threatens to short-circuit the concept by conflating it literally with absolute speed (Kittler 1993, p. 193). As much as the factual autonomy of matter is necessary for certain technologically realized switches, such autonomy does not go far enough to be called hardware or a computer. Indeed, only through the incommensurability between input and output does this autonomy become what, according to Kittler's account, defines all running computers hitherto, namely, clocked time [*getakte Zeit*], that is, discretized time. Therefore, an 'immateriality' comes to occupy the place of the 'most material', not simply in a historically or computer-politically determined way, but in an always already and necessary manner (Kittler 1998, p. 124). Furthermore, matter in itself does not constitute the necessary condition or hardware that enables it to become a carrier of universal difference; rather its unavailability as an internal dynamic does. Even the expression 'time' proves to be inadequate and misleading considering the fact that the switch is what provides a difference-giving absolute difference – the quintessence of the medial – a real home, which is what then leads to a treatment of time as discrete. Even in the case of electric switches, the price of programmability remains such that the materiality of what is called hardware can only be defined negatively through the limits that it mutely represents. This makes it necessary to consider again Derrida's insistence on the silent difference of sound, which opens up phonemes to perception and which characterizes *différance* no longer only as difference but rather in Derrida's (1997, p. 84) own words as 'medial form'.[10] The 'electricity fairy' does not fulfill all tasks but is central to the emergence of a new science of control [*Steuerung*], which Lacan (1988, p. 302) takes as an occasion to analyze doors. The ability to operate with discrete objects remains decisive for Turing's definition of Universal machines, that is, to operate as a 'door' in Lacan's sense, whether electronically realized or not.

The door is a real symbol, the symbol *par excellence*, that symbol in which man's passing, through the cross is sketches, intersecting access and closure, can always be recognized.

Once it has become possible to fold the two characteristics together, to construct an enclosure, that is to say a circuit, so that something passes when it is closed, and does not when it is open, that is when the science of the conjecture passes into the realm of realization of cybernetics (Lacan 1988).

The computer stands both for a general precondition of the processing of chains of signs and for the incredibly improved reversibility, or moreover, the free assemblage of serial orders. Even technological media can intervene in the series with respect to the temporal order of the stored and transmitted contents, for which Kittler coins the term 'time axis manipulation'. No discussion or critical appraisal of the technological a priori as a form of time would be complete without including Kittler's (1993) reflections on the opposition between hypothetical 'real time analysis' and 'time axis manipulation'. On the one hand, Kittler's time axis manipulation entails a strong division of time and space. On the other hand, it juxtaposes its concept of time with a concept of seriality; not without reason, Kittler (1993, p. 183) largely speaks of 'temporally serial'. Not only does 'Real Time Analysis' not exist (p. 200); strictly speaking, neither does real time since the manipulable time axis, with its chain of what are only purportedly continuous moments, is itself the product of a particular time axis manipulation, that is the product of the belated workings of signs (Porge 1989, p. 77; Tholen and Scholl 1990).

Upon closer consideration, the historical and especially the technological a priori prove to be far more complex and time-reflexive insofar as they are more contradictory than is generally suggested. For this reason, it will become important in the future to more strongly reflect on the issue of belatedness and to open the way for a medial a priori. Mediality cannot be equated with material conditions of possibility alone but, as Tholen (1999, p. 15) suggests, outlines the 'axiomatic possibility' of precisely these conditions. Foucault takes up the difference-generating precondition of knowledge as time in the sense of empirical history; Kittler equates it with technologically realized discreteness, time-coding or switching. Both accounts, however, still do not go far enough to approach the conditions of possibility for medial functions.

Passageways to a medial a priori

One can study only what one has first dreamed about. (Bachelard 1964, p. 22)

A wealth of foundational studies demonstrates the instructive force and benefit of both the historical and the technological a priori for media studies. The project of expanding the historical and technological a priori to a medial a priori is justified when it takes on the task of addressing the central issue of the priority and preconditionality of media in a nuanced manner, and when it responds to this issue in the most rigorous way possible. It can do this only if it brings the accentuated perspectives of the historical and technological a priori into confrontation with one another, retroactively on one hand and preemptively on the other. Notions of belatedness borrowed from structural–analytical research on trauma (Laplanche and Pontalis 1992; Bronfen et al. 1999), cryptonomy (Abraham and Torok 1979), grammatology and game theory lend themselves to this task. Trauma theory vividly describes the disintegration of time in two scenes, one of which is presupposed while the other belatedly enacts the 'coming into effect' of the primary scene. What goes here by the name of belatedness both shapes and carries not only memory, writing and signification but all media insofar as we have knowledge of them. For this reason, a strong concept of belatedness resides at the heart of all media studies. Because a clinical concept of belatedness mediates between the 'too soon' of traumatic encounters and the always 'delayed' of traumatic apprehension, belatedness as a concept might generally attempt to tie a priori formations to their a posteriori effects. The aim of the previous sections of this essay was to demonstrate the limits of a media-technological sense of belatedness. Media-technological analysis reformulates belatedness as a physical condition of possibility for certain switches and thus subsumes them to its own paradigm, which valorizes the factual device as the premise of subsequent social and epistemological constellations. In the media studies to come, one would have to more strongly elaborate this through further theories of belatedness. The first reflections on belatedness emerged almost simultaneously in early trauma research and in theories of memory at the end of the nineteenth century. The focus of these medical and theoretical–foundational models was the puzzling question of why certain experiences appear inconsequential at the moment they come into being, but as memories lead to traumatic effects. These psychic long-term effects demand sophisticated models of cause and effect, such as those offered for instance by concepts of belatedness. Yet even Freud's work tends to generalize concepts of trauma, and as a consequence tends to single out belatedness as a specifically psychic mode of time. The metapsychological generalization of belatedness-thought is first carried out in the twentieth century by French research that emphasizes, in addition to belatedness, the future *antérieur*, *après-coup* and later, the '*tertium datur*' in Weber's (1980) sense. In the English-language context, by contrast, the term is not taken up, and there thus occurs no nuancing of the classic concept of belatedness. But even the translation of the term belatedness causes many difficulties. The editors of the Standard Edition of Freud's works render belatedness from German to English in a makeshift way as 'deferred action' or 'action at a distance' (Benjamin 1997, p. 231). Strong readings of belatedness, such as those that inform Derrida's concept of *différance* and Lacan's concept of desire, differentiate themselves on a number of fronts: a strong concept of belatedness does not assume a temporally progressing sequence of stages in which an earlier occurrence determines a later fate after a period of latency; nor is belated deferral a matter of simple retrograde 'fantasizing-back', as Jung suggested.

In the simplest readings, belatedness designates the psychic echo of critical experience. Adequate understanding of the context of the origin of psychic suffering requires complex accounts of time and models of effect, because the symptom often arises at a specific point in time without any recognizable external cause. A cause for the suffering, which often lies far in the past, can only be adduced through the reconstruction of a very mediated chain of effect. Concepts of belatedness inquire into this constellation, and into the precise connection between earlier, though only mediated, causes, and a subsequent effect. Between the past primary experience and the triggered psychic reaction lies for the most part a considerable latency. Trauma is generally considered paradigmatic for the staggered, or even belated influence of an experienced situation, one that leads to a traumatic reaction only in combination with a subsequent experience. Trauma cannot be exclusively traced to the primary situation as its determinant; nor can it be understood as the sum of both experiences. Instead, trauma is realized precisely in the specific dual-temporality of different states.

From trauma to a strong concept of belatedness

If trauma likely offers the first chance to introduce complex accounts of time into discourses on the psyche, its *conception* already entails a belatedness that is no longer bound to the field of pathology: in particular the belated process of the wish as that which gives the psyche its pulse. Belatedness becomes a designation for the 'matrix for the historicity of the subject' (Weber 1978, p. 10) and thus for the 'temporal form of the psychic' itself (Görling 2001, p. 567). In no way does this mean that the unconscious consists of ahistoric structures, and that the unconscious could as such be understood as set apart from time, as is accused of the formal a priori. The timelessness of the unconscious can only be determined in opposition to a 'common concept of time', 'the time of mechanics or the time of consciousness' Derrida (1976, p. 215) suggests, for the unconscious is ultimately only timeless 'from the standpoint of a certain vulgar conception of time'. '*Nachträglichkeit* [belatedness]' and '*Verspätung* [delaying]' are for Derrida nothing less than the conceptual bearers of the Freudian project; he designates them as 'concepts which govern the whole of Freud's thought', capable of defining all other concepts of the psychoanalytic canon (p. 203). Deferral, as the most important articulation of belatedness, underlies Derrida's concept of *différance* as a temporal factor. Conditionally, deferral constitutes the 'essence of life', to the extent that one can speak of essence here at all (Derrida 1976). In an aside, Derrida subsequently defines deferral, or delay, as 'a present which does not constitute but is originally reconstituted from "signs" of memory' (p. 206). Just as the 'sup-plemental' ['*nach-tragende*'] unconscious, figured here as a medial a priori of consciousness, cannot be removed from society and culture, and in this sense cannot be considered timeless, likewise it cannot manage to symbolize the origin of the psychic. If the modus operandi of the psyche consists solely in perpetual deferral as a 'temporal moment of the secondary processes', as the early Freud and Derrida suggest, then it erases any origin at all (Tholen 1992, p. 42): 'It is a non-origin which is originary' (Derrida 1976, p. 203). Precisely this 'irreducibility of the "effect of deferral"' is the discovery of Freud that has validity not only for individual psychology, but also for the entirety of cultural history (p. 203). However, the present essay is not solely concerned with emphasizing the critique of origins. Derrida's remarks additionally present a possible response to the dispute about a-priori constellations. Whether general, historically specific, or technological, any originary precondition, and with it, any condition of possibility – such as those that dominate inquiries into the medial – are consequently transformed through accounts of belatedness, especially those of Derrida, into a gesture of preconditioning. The 'postscript' of the 'supplementary delay [nach-träglichen (bzw. –tragenden) Verspätung' does not reveal a past presence or furnish a past presence with some sort of accessory; rather this 'postscript' produces past presence (Derrida 1976, p. 214). In spite of its literal meaning and proximity to the after-effect, belatedness attempts to mediate between presupposed assumptions and subsequent events. It is clear that the discussion of trauma and belatedness now connects to foundational disputes in media studies in a number of ways. Most notably, the concept of belatedness involves an unusual theory of temporality that offers its own response to philosophical and discourse-analytical disputes about the genesis of a-priori structures. It is in no way an obstacle for the general media-theoretical use of these concepts that they were first developed in the context of psychologies and anthropologies. In its (belated) functioning, writing shows the way here: it is for this reason that invoking Derrida's frequently addressed text is justified, though his grammatology and concept of writing are precisely not exhausted in an external history of writing as the horizon of possibility for Western thought.

The belatedness of media studies

Expanding the programme

The programme that this essay foresees cannot be conceptualized *ex nihilo*. It represents first of all the demand not to hastily overlook certain bodies of knowledge in the large canon of media theory. However, we might proceed from a research desideratum within the scope of belatedness, particularly because the cautious description of its micro-architecture is still outstanding; a thorough dissemination of concepts of belatedness in media theory is also missing – even in Derrida this is only partially visible. The next step would be to programmatically reconstruct the abundant thought on belatedness, and in doing so to underline a stronger concept of belatedness. Such a concept would lend itself equally to any contemplation of mediality and to the self-reflection on one's own understanding of history and the history of the discipline. It would seem valuable to further probe the special coexistence of psychoanalysis and mathematics in discussions of logical temporality, including Lacan's (1994) prisoner's dilemma. Concepts of belatedness offer hope for a complex connection between various fields, including the further confrontation of second-order cybernetics and psychoanalysis. Worthy of investigation are not only the similarities, but also the incompatibilities between belatedness, on one hand, and the recursive systems of cybernetics on the other, the recursive systems of temporalized 'central paradoxes' (Baecker 1996, p. 20; Pias 2008). Görling (2001, p. 565) draws attention to the implicit connection between mathematics, chaos theory and belatedness-approaches in particular. Emergence as a phenomenon and problem in theories of complex systems most easily lends itself to being thought in terms of belatedness. If one wanted to translate this mode of time back into models of emergence, it could be understood as a 'relation of recursion and bifurcation' (Görling 2001, p. 566). We are still awaiting a discussion of whether belatedness is really congruent with the concepts mentioned here. It certainly presents a common point of departure, a point of fundamental unobservability.

To give oneself over to history

Along with the attempts mentioned here to revise research on belatedness through other approaches, such as that of chaos theory and advanced cybernetics, other endeavours might be fruitful that reconsider historical research through the lens of theories of belatedness. Kettner's (1998) work, for instance, outlines the possibility of understanding history or historiography as fundamentally belated. This should be taken into account in the field of media studies and expanded for research on media. Media analysis in the German-language world initially entailed a fundamental rereading of various theories, as well as the transformation of numerous bodies of knowledge into a history of media, most often into a prehistory of the computer (to steal and extend the title of an early essay (Coy 1994)). That is, it consisted of an interdisciplinary transcoding of not only historical, but also social and human-scientific thought. Simultaneously, it was a matter of precisely advancing and rededicating that which immediately preceded media theory, namely, structural psychoanalysis, the so-called postmodernism and deconstruction; additionally, it focused on ideology critique, the novel and actual manic systems. In particular, works that continue to consider their objects of knowledge as dependent on their conditions of possibility, or that inquire into the preconditions of their own cognitive formation, lend

THINKING MEDIA AND BEYOND

themselves to being read as media theory *avant la lettre*.[11] This includes a number of other projects as well: for instance, Benjamin's aesthetic theory, which explicitly designates technology as its condition of possibility; or Marx's theory of value, according to which society is formed as a precondition for equivalence through the act of exchange; or semiotics and philosophies of language that investigate the autonomy of signification and the materiality of the signifier as conditions of possibility for any formation of meaning; or, finally, structural psychoanalysis and its understanding of the unconscious as *sine qua non* of consciousness and memory.

The disciplinary history of media studies can be grasped as part of a 'distorting action' [*entstellende Aktion*]' through which the discipline gives itself history belatedly. Media studies would certainly benefit from confronting the hurried development of computer technology according to Moore's law, and the impressions of general haste and acceleration that result from it, if not with reservation than certainly at its own pace and tempo. In the fields of disciplinary history and media historiography, a strong notion of belatedness promises to accomplish at least two things: (1) rereadings of older bodies of knowledge as media theories *avant la lettre* could be defined as the rewriting and movement of belated apprehension; (2) media history demands a conception of time that would be able to carefully incorporate previously blocked out histories of failure and dead-ends as arsenals of the future and inventions twice over (Butis 2009).

Above all, media studies must clarify how one can write the history of the digital without falling into a historical automatism. For example, how can we adequately understand the fact that discrete units (of sound) already operate with the spoken word, an operation which once electronically implemented under the name digital computer rewrites history? On the one hand, the digital is always already housed in any so-called natural language, and therefore in the human who uses language. On the other hand, it seems that this can only be retroactively deduced, or in this simple sense, belatedly deduced, from the perspective of the computerized age. All the same, it remains necessary to hold open as thinkable alternative histories and alternative developments in the world and to not exclude contingency from these (translated by Nathan Taylor).

Notes

1. 'All-pulverizer' is what Moses Mendelssohn calls Immanuel Kant, who, in Mendelssohn's eyes, revolutionizes the world of the mind in an overwhelming and thus oppressive/distressing way (see Mendelssohn 1785).
2. Hardly any introduction to media theory and media history fails to refer to the technological a priori, which again may demonstrate the persistent virulence of the issue for the development of the discipline. For a selection of more specific accounts in recent years, see Stiegler (2005, p. 82), Ebeling (2006) and

Bergermann (2009, p. 307). For an earlier critique, see Sebastian and Geerke (1990); Hickethier's modest critique (2003). For important further developments, see Engell and Vogl (2001) and Vogl (2007).

3. The use of 'imperfect' here plays, both in English and German, with the multiple meanings of the word, both with its colloquial sense of not perfect, and with its status as a grammatical tense.

4. In his later lectures, Foucault firmly positions himself in the philosophical tradition of the Enlightenment and subsequent critical projects in Hegel, the Frankfurt School, Nietzsche and Max Weber. See for instance Foucault (2008, p. 22).

5. For a discussion of Benjamin as the first thinker of these abilities, see Weber (2008). The shift from a formal to a historical a priori can unfortunately be only suggested here, as mentioned. Examining this shift comprehensively would seem worthwhile and is undertaken to some extent in Bürger's work. Bürger demonstrates how French philosophy of the twentieth century struggles against restricted readings of Hegel and even of Kant, a struggle that is due to the reception history of these thinkers harking back to Kojève. For Bürger, French postmodernity presupposes a caricature of Hegel in particular as its own counterpart in order then to be able to set itself apart from this counterpart.

6. On the door as a basic cultural technique, see Siegert (2010).

7. It seems to have been forgotten that materialism has many variations. In many cases materialism does not assume a fixed physical form or material as the reduction of materialism to materiality in media studies would seem to suggest.

8. Without mentioning this technological implementation of a universal discreteness of time, an entire tradition of philosophical critiques of time developed simultaneously, which defended themselves against the objectification of time represented through the discretization of time; in particular these critiques are offered by Bergson and Heidegger (see Langlitz 2005, p. 57). Even Lacan divided the analytical movement through his reluctance to accept the clock as the quintessence of time's objectification and as an external instrument of analytical speech, as Langlitz suggests. On the cultural and media history of timekeeping, see the works of Innis, Koyré, Peters, Macho, Mumford and Thomson.

9. To ask generally 'what is discrete?' is neither banal nor is it a settled matter. In fact, it presents a number of diverse tasks. The question itself contains precisely a problem of time. Furthermore, discreteness demands modularization and standardization, something that has been addressed in several media-historical and media-theoretical works.

10. For a technological–philosophical reading of Derrida, see Stiegler (2009).

11. For an example in the case of psychoanalysis, see Tuschling (2007).

Disclosure statement

No potential conflict of interest was reported by the authors.

Notes on contributor

Anna Tuschling is a Professor in the Media Studies Department at Ruhr-University Bochum, Germany.

THINKING MEDIA AND BEYOND

References

Abraham, N. and Torok, M., 1979. *Kryptonymie. Das Verbarium des Wolfsmanns. Mit einem Beitrag von Jacques Derrida*. Frankfurt/Main: Engler.

Bachelard, G., 1964. *Psychoanalysis of fire*. Trans. A.C.M. Ross. London: Routledge.

Baecker, D., 1996. Kybernetik zweiter Ordnung. *In*: S.J. Schmidt, ed. *Heinz von Foerster: Wissen und Gewissen*. 3rd ed. Frankfurt/Main: Suhrkamp, 17–23.

Benjamin, A., 1997. Ursprünge übersetzen: Psychoanalyse und Philosophie. *In*: A. Hirsch, ed. *Übersetzung und Dekonstruktion*. Frankfurt/Main: Suhrkamp, 231–262.

Bergermann, U., 2009. Konrad Zuses Computerdraht und Programmierschleifen in der Medienwissenschaft. *In*: H. von Butis Butis, ed. *Goofy History. Fehler machen Geschichte*. Cologne-Weimar-Vienna: Böhlau, 298–313.

Bronfen, E., Erdle, B.R., and Weigel, S., ed., 1999. *Trauma. Zwischen Psychoanalyse und kulturellem Deutungsmuster*. Cologne: Böhlau.

Bürger, P., 2008. *Ursprung des postmodernen Denkens*. Weilerswist: Velbrück.

Butis, H. von B., ed., 2009. *Goofy History: Fehler machen Geschichte*. 1, Cologne-Weimar-Vienna: Böhlau.

Coy, W., 1994. Aus der Vorgeschichte des Mediums Computer. *In*: N. Bolz, F. Kittler and G.C. Tholen, eds. *Computer als Medium*. Munich: Fink, 19–37.

Derrida, J., 1976. Freud and the scene of writing. *In*: J. Derrida, ed. *Writing and difference*. London: Routledge, 196–231.

Derrida, J., 1997. Die difference. In: P. Engelmann, ed. *Postmoderne und Dekonstruktion. Texte französischer Philosophen der Gegenwart*. Leipzig: P. Reclam, 76–113.

Ebeling, K., 2006. Das technische Apriori: Kulturgeschichte als Mediengeschichte (oder vice versa?). *Archiv für Mediengeschichte*, 6, 11–22.

Ebeling, K., 2009. Der Thron des Transzendentalen oder Das historische Apriori. *In*: C. Pornschlegel and M. Stingelin, eds. *Nietzsche und Frankreich*. Berlin: De Gruyter, 305–322.

Engell, L. and Vogl, J., 2001. Editorial: mediale historiographien. *Archiv für Mediengeschichte*, 1, 5–8.

Foucault, M., 1972. *The archaeology of knowledge*. Trans. A.M. Sheridan Smith. London: Routledge.

Foucault, M., 1989. *The order of things: an archaeology of the human sciences*. London: Routledge.

Foucault, M., 2008. *Le Gouvernement de Soi et des Autres*. Seuil: Cours au Collège de France 1982–1983.

Freud, S., 1999. *Das Unbehagen in der Kultur, Gesammelte Werke XIV*. Frankfurt: Fischer.

Görling, R., 2001. Eine Maschine, die nächstens von selber geht: Über Nachträglichkeit und Emergenz. *Psyche*, 55/6, 560–576.

Hagen, W., 1994. Computerpolitik. *In*: N. Bolz, F. Kittler and G.C. Tolen, eds. *Computer als Medium Fink*. Munich: Wilhelm Fink, 139–160.

Hickethier, K., 2003. Gibt es ein medientechnisches Apriori? Technikdeterminismus und Medienkonfiguration in historischen Prozessen. *In*: M. Behmer, et al., eds. *Medienentwicklung und gesellschaftlicher Wandel. Beiträge zu einer theoretischen und empirischen Herausforderung*. Wiesbaden: VS, 39–52.

Horn, E., 2007. Editor's introduction: "there are no media". *Grey room*, 29, 6–13.

Innis, H.A., 1951. A plea for time. *In: The bias of communication.* Toronto: University of Toronto Press, 61–91.

Kettner, M., 1998. Nachträglichkeit. Freuds brisante Erinnerungstheorie. *In:* J. Rüsen and J. Straub, eds. *Die dunkle Spur der Vergangenheit. Psychoanalytische Zugänge zum Geschichtsbewusstsein.* Frankfurt/Main: Suhrkamp, 12–32.

Kittler, F., 1993. Real time analysis, time axis manipulation. *In: Draculas Vermächtnis. Technische Schriften.* Leipzig: Reclamm, 182–207.

Kittler, F., 1994. Protected mode. *In:* N. Bolz, F. Kittler and G.C. Tolen, eds. *Computer als Medium Fink.* Munich: Wilhelm Fink, 209–220.

Kittler, F., 1997a. Farben und /oder Maschinen denken. *In:* M. Warnke, W. Coy and C.G. Tholen, eds. *HyperKult: Geschichte, Theorie und Kontext digitaler Medien.* Basel: Stroemfeld, 83–97.

Kittler, F., 1997b. There is no software. *In:* J. Johnston, ed. *Literature, Media, Information Systems.* London: Routledge, 147–155.

Kittler, F., 1998. Hardware, das unbekannte Wesen. *In:* S. Krämer, ed. *Medien, Computer, Realität: Wirklichkeitsvorstellungen und Neue Medien.* Frankfurt/Main: Suhrkamp, 119–132.

Kittler, F., 1999. *Gramophone, typewriter, film.* Stanford: Stanford University Press.

Kittler, F., 2005. *Discourse networks 1800/1900.* Stanford: Stanford University Press.

Krämer, S., 2006. The cultural techniques of time axis manipulation. On Friedrich Kittler's conception of media. *Theory, Culture & Society,* 23 (7–8), 93–109 Verlag, Ort.

Krämer, S., 2008. Medien, Boten, Spuren. Wenig mehr als ein Literaturbericht. *In:* S. Münker and A. Roesler, eds. *Was ist ein Medium?* Frankfurt/Main: Suhrkamp, 65–90.

Lacan, J., 1988. Psychoanalysis and cybernetics, or on the nature of language. *In:* J.-A. Miller, ed. Trans. S. Tomaselli. *The seminar of Jacques Lacan: Book II: The ego in Freud's theory and in the technique of psychoanalysis, 1954–1955.* Cambridge: Norton, 294–308.

Lacan, J., 1994. Die logische Zeit und die Assertion der antizipierten Gewissheit. Ein neues Sophisma. *In: Schriften III.* Weinheim/Berlin: Quadriga, 101–121.

Langlitz, N., 2005. *Die Zeit der Psychoanalyse.* Frankfurt/Main: Suhrkamp.

Laplanche, J. and Pontalis, J.-B., 1992. *Urphantasie. Phantasien über den Ursprung, Ursprünge der Phantasie.* Frankfurt/Main: Fischer.

Leibniz, G.W., 1979. *Monadologie.* Trans. H. Glockner. Stuttgart: Reclam.

Mendelssohn, M., 1785. *Morgenstunden.* Berlin: Voß.

Pflüger, J., 2005. Wo die Quantität in Qualität umschlägt: Notizen zum Verhältnis von Analogem und Digitalem. *In:* M. Warnke, W. Coy and G.C. Tholen, eds. *Hyperkult II: Zur Ortsbestimmung analoger und digitaler Medien.* Bielefeld: Transcript, 27–94.

Pias, C., 2008. Die Welt des Schmoo. Computer als Medium - nach, mit und neben McLuhan. *In:* D. de Kerckhove, M. Leeker and K. Schmidt, eds. *McLuhan neu lesen, 1st edition.* Bielefeld: Transcript, 140–157.

Porge, E., 1989. *Se compter trois: Le temps logique de Lacan.* Toulouse: Eres.

Ritter, J. and Gründer, K., ed., 1971. *Historisches Wörterbuch der Philosophie, vol. 1.* Basel: Schwabe.

Schanze, H., 2004. Gibt es ein digitales Apriori? *In:* J. Schröter and A. Bielefeld, eds. *Analog/Digital - Opposition oder Kontinuum? Zur Theorie und Geschichte einer Unterscheidung.* Bielefeld: Transcript, 67–79.

Schmidt, A., 1993. *Der Begriff der Natur in der Lehre von Marx.* 4th ed. Hamburg: Europäische Verlagsanstalt.

Sebastian, T. and Geerke, J., 1990. Technology romanticized: Friedrich Kittler's discourse networks 1800/1900. *MLN,* 105 (3), 583–595.

THINKING MEDIA AND BEYOND

Siegert, B., 2010. Türen. Zur Materialität des Symbolischen. *Zeitschrift für Medien-und Kulturforschung*, 1, 151–170.

Sohn-Rethel, A., 1972. *Geistige und körperliche Arbeit*. Frankfurt/Main: Suhrkamp.

Sohn-Rethel, A., 1978. *Intellectual and manual labor: a critique of epistemology*. London: Macmillan/Atlantic Highlands, NJ: Humanities Press.

Spreen, D., 1998. *Tausch, Technik, Krieg. Die Geburt der Gesellschaft in Technisch-medialen Apriori*. Hamburg: Argument.

Stiegler, B., 2005. Hardware/software. *In*: A. Roesler and B. Stiegler, eds. *Grundbegriffe der Medientheorie*. Munich: Fink, 82–85.

Stiegler, B., 2009. *Technik und Zeit: Der Fehler des Epimetheus*. Berlin: Diaphanes.

Tholen, G.C., 1992. Traumverloren und lückenhaft - zur Atopik des Unbewussten, Traum und Trauma. *Fragmente. Schriftenreihe zur Psychoanalyse*, 38, 41–57.

Tholen, G.C., 1999. Überschneidungen. Konturen einer Theorie der Medialität. *In*: S. Schade and C.G. Tholen, eds. *Konfigurationen. Zwischen Kunst und Medien*. Munich: Fink, 15–34.

Tholen, G.C., 2002. *Die Zäsur der Medien: Kulturphilosophische Konturen*. Frankfurt/Main: Suhrkamp.

Tholen, G.C. and Scholl, M.O., eds., 1990. *Zeit-Zeichen. Aufschübe und Interferenzen zwischen Endzeit und Echtzeit*. Acta Weinheim: Humaniora.

Turing, A.M., 1950. Computing machinery and intelligence. *Mind: A Quarterly Review of Psychology and Philosophy*, LIX (236), 433–460.

Turing, A.M., 1986. Lecture to the London mathematical society on 20 February 1947. *In*: B.E. Carpenter and B.W. Doran, eds. *A. M. Turing's ACE Report of 1946 and Other Papers*. Cambridge: MIT Press.

Turing, A.M., 1987. The state of the art: Vortrag vor der London Mathematical Society am 20. Februar 1947. *In*: B. Dotzler and F. Kittler, eds. *Intelligence Service. Schriften/ Alan M. Turing*. Berlin: Brinkmann und Bose, 183–207.

Tuschling, A., 2007. Psychoanalyse als Medientheorie avant la lettre. *Psychoanalyse*, 2 (21), 198–222.

Vogl, J., 2007. Becoming-media: Galileo's Telescope. *Grey room*, 29, 14–25.

Weber, S., 1978. *Rückkehr zu Freud. Jacques Lacans Ent-stellung der Psychoanalyse*. Vienna: Passagen.

Weber, S., 1980. Tertium datur'. *In*: F. Kittler, ed. *Austreibung des Geistes aus den Geisteswissenschaften*. Munich: Fink, 204–221.

Weber, S., 2008. *Benjamin's – abilities*. Harvard: Harvard University Press.

Winthrop-Young, G., 2005. *Friedrich Kittler zur Einführung*. Hamburg: Junius.

Synthesis as mediation: inner touch and eccentric sensation

Karin Harrasser [iD]

ABSTRACT
The article inquires into how the tactile sense became a promising area of investigation in media theory, particularly to counteract notions of linear, mechanical culture. I take two starting points: (1) Modern psychology and the arts, unlike Post-Kantian philosophy, are interested in the structure and efficiency of synthetic processes as an effect of a certain medial constitution of sensual perception. (2) Since antiquity, the sense of touch is hardly ever connected with immediacy. On the contrary, since Aristotle it possesses a deeply mediating and reflexive character. Aristotle grasps the sense of touch in two ways: as *koine aisthesis*, common sense – which will later also be known as the sensus communis – and as 'inner touch', which synthesizes the individual sense perceptions. This notion of the sense of touch still resonates in Marshall McLuhan's interest in the haptic sense: 'Tactile' is the word he uses to refer to those percepts that require a strong inner involvement of the perceiving subject. Drawing on Gestalt theory (modern psychology) and avant-garde art, McLuhan unites the two strands of discourse. The article therefore traces a number of versions of the conception of tactility since antiquity and focuses on two distinct fields: physiology and psychology of prosthetics and the classical avant-gardes of the early twentieth century, particularly Raoul Hausmann's thought experiments with Ernst Marcus' concept of 'eccentric sensation'. It argues that with media theory in a strong sense the antique tradition that considered skin and flesh as medium is connected with Avant-garde sensibilities and helps to develop a diagnostic perspective on the effects of media technologies on human agency.

Introduction

Unlike in post-Kantian philosophy, questions about the structure and efficiency of synthetic processes are often approached in psychology and in the arts with an eye towards a certain medial constitution of sensual perception. Central to the discourses addressed here has, since antiquity, been the sense of touch. In the system of sensory qualities that Aristotle lays out in *De Anima* , the sense of touch is hardly connected with immediacy. On the contrary, it possesses a deeply mediating character. Aristotle grasps the sense of touch in two ways: as *koine aisthesis*, common sense – which will later also be known as the sensus communis – and as 'inner touch', which synthesizes the individual sense perceptions. This notion of the sense of touch still resonates in Marshall McLuhan's vote for the haptic sense: 'Tactile' is the word he uses to refer to those percepts that require a strong inner involvement of the perceiving subject. Drawing on Gestalt theory, McLuhan speculates about the ability to complete figures and 'gestalts' mentally. In his framework, 'cool' media demand participation, whereas 'hot' media inundate and paralyse sense perception. In what follows, I will trace various versions of this conception of tactility in two areas: in physiology and psychology of prosthetics and in the classical avant-gardes of the early twentieth century, particularly in Raoul Haussman's thought experiments with Ernst Marcus' concept of 'eccentric sensation'.

Skin and flesh as medium

To approach the theme of tactility through the lens of prosthetics is on one hand a rather obvious approach. On the other, however, such an approach is not as obvious as it might seem, for, if we trace the technological and cultural history of the prosthesis, we find that the very lack of tactility is one of the greatest problems in constructing artificial limbs. This becomes clear in artistic and cultural treatments of prostheses, in which the prosthesis comes to represent the insensibility, monomania, emotional defects, socially marginal position, or radically misanthropic obstinacy of its users, from Götz von Berlichingen's 'iron hand' to Captain Ahab's whalebone prosthesis to the prostheses of various James Bond villains.

The lack of tactile sensation of prostheses has always posed a veritable problem for their development and use. And this is the case, not because the engineers of prostheses are concerned with the balancing of the sensory economy of their patients, but because it is difficult to manage the control and operation of artificial extremities after the loss of the sense of touch and, with this, proprioceptive perception. The technical problem of response arises in prosthetics not only when the prosthesis is no longer thought of in cosmetic terms, that is, with an attention to aesthetic-social concerns, but also and especially when the prosthesis is meant to aid in everyday life, for example, in working or in sports. Tactility is a central mode of self-reference, even more so when the body is in motion and meant to act purposefully. In prosthetics, this became very apparent. The medicinal and psychological literature of the 1920s takes note of the problem that many disabled war soldiers displayed a lacking impetus to use their prosthesis because they perceived it as an impractical 'foreign body' in the most literal sense. For this reason, there was a call as early as the 1920s for 'sensitive prostheses' for the soldiers.

Many of these problems that were so central in the twentieth century for the theorization of the body and its medial character (and also central to the construction of prostheses) were already dealt with in Aristotle's *De anima* (1986). Aristotle faced the difficulty of bringing the sense of touch into accord with his system of sensory qualities and perceptions. The sense of touch is more complex than the other senses, and for this reason is characterized in *De anima* as the sense that makes the 'perceiving that one is perceiving' possible. In the process of sensual perception, *aisthesis* is thus already reflexive (and not so only through secondary cognitive processes). The sense of touch first produces a fundamental and fragile 'self-reference' or self-awareness; second, it inaugurates the body as 'medium'; and third, due to its protean nature, it enables the 'differentiation' of various sensory qualities. Because the sense of touch perceives sensations as different as pressure, texture, and temperature simultaneously and allows them to be differentiated, it communicates to our senses that we are sensing. Classical philologist Daniel Heller-Roazen has linked this sensation, the *koine aisthesis* or common sense, to the perception of an 'inner touch', a sensory self-reference that occupies the same position in Greek thought that consciousness, as a 'more cognitivistic concept', later comes to occupy (Heller-Roazen 2007). Furthermore, the sense of touch differs from other sense perceptions insofar as the medium and organ of perception cannot be clearly distinguished in the act of touching. While the visual can be seen 'through' the transparent (*diaphanes*) 'with' the eye, and the audible 'reaches' the ear 'through' a movement of air – that is, the medium affects the organ and the organ suffers from the medium – this is not quite as clear with the sense of touch. What is felt touches the skin immediately, but the organ does not suffer from the medium. Rather, we are affected *'along with* the medium; it is as if a man were struck through his shield' (Aristotle 1986, p. 42).

The sense of touch is thus also the sense that makes the perceiving creature especially vulnerable. This premise leads Aristotle to understand the flesh, including the skin, not as an organ, but as a medium of the sense of touch, while the sense organ of touch is located somewhere on the inside. What is touched through the medium of the skin and the flesh is the soul itself. The body, by contrast, is the 'medium for the faculty of touch, naturally attached to us' (Aristotle 1986, p. 41). Skin and flesh are the intermediaries to the soul as organ; the organic substrate itself *is* the medium (and not the organ). The sense of touch therefore is *koine aisthesis*, the common sense, in two regards: by mixing and separating sense perceptions, it renders sense perceptions differentiable in the first place, and it guarantees self-awareness through the inner touch, the soul. As a singular sense, the sense of touch operates simultaneously with many other senses, and is at the same time the 'central organ' (*Zentralorgan*) of (self)perception. In this way, the sense of touch is similar to a 'point' since 'being at once one and two', it can 'properly be said to be divisible' (Aristotle 1986, p. 48). Aristotle uses the point as a model of the dual character of the sense of touch. The point is both a point of departure and a limit-phenomenon, at once the centre of a circle and an (always further divisible) transit point for a line. The sense of touch is a liminal phenomenon in two regards: as a mediator between inner and outer in the medium of skin, and as the sense that enables demarcations and differentiations.

Teletactility

The unusual character of the sense of touch has subsequently preoccupied philosophy and aesthetics in a variety of ways. Even experimental physiology has been haunted by the problems already observed by Aristotle. The psycho-physics of the nineteenth century came across grave problems investigating the sense of touch. The extent to which sense perceptions could be objecti-vized was in itself a complicated issue, and this was all the more so for the sense of touch, given its dubious relation to the sense of self and the external world, its multiple manifestations, and the myriad of organs it involves (skin, muscular system, nerves).[1] Two books from the middle of the nineteenth century offer a vivid account of this epistemological dilemma: Ernst Heinrich Weber's *Tastsinn und Gemeingefühl* (The sense of touch and the common sen-sibility, 1846/1905) and Rudolf Hermann Lotze's *Mikrokosmus* (Microcosmus) (3 volumes, 1856–1864/1923). Both works were enthusiastically received by contemporaries. Lotze was a bestseller in his time. For both authors, common sense (*Gemeingefühl*) does not above all imply something social, but rather something subjective: perceptions of pain and other sensations that are not distinctly localizable.

The teacher (Weber) and his student (Lotze) were interested in similar phenomena, namely in remote touching (*Ferntasten*) and synesthetic phenomena, but they explored these phenomena with different methods. In comparison to Weber, the younger Lotze's arguments are based less on measurability and experimental objectivity. Instead, they attempt to integrate physiology into philosophy and anthropology. His arguments are both more speculative and closer to everyday life. In contrast to quantitative physiology, which aims to probe universal laws of nature, Lotze's concern is the philoso-phical formulation of anthropological laws. As modest as the title *Mikrokosmus* (Microcosmus) might sound in comparison to Humboldt's *Kosmos* (Cosmos), the subtitle of Lotze's book, *Ideen zur Naturgeschichte und Geschichte der Menschheit. Versuch einer Anthropologie* (Ideas on natural history and the history of humanity. An attempt at anthropology), clearly signals a claim to a general explanation with regard to the anthropos.[2]

Yet, why is Lotze significant at all, and why does he count as more than a footnote in the history of psychology? His thought experiments resonated and were taken up in the field of psychology in the twentieth century, especially in Gestalt psychology, in phenomenology, and in philosophical anthropology. *Mikrokosmus* was influential for intellectuals as diverse as Sigmund Freud (whose library contained some of Lotze's books), William James, Maurice Merleau-Ponty, Helmuth Plessner, and Arnold Gehlen. Lotze was a central point of reference in psychological prosthetic research as well. The passages that became especially influential deal with two subjects: the self-perception of a subject as related to his environment and the issue of tel-etactility, or extra-bodily tactile perception. Lotze developed a new approach and nomenclature that would be definitive for both subjects. With regard to spatial self-perception, Lotze took a path that neither adhered to an emphasis on the independence of the formation of spatiotemporal categories from experience, to the Kantian 'a priori', nor did he favour a theory of mere acqui-sition of spatial and temporal intuition, that is, a form of cultural constructi-vism. Instead, Lotze propagated a unique approach to bodily reflexivity that we would refer to today as 'praxeological' or pragmatic. Lotze addressed the question of how categories, orders and systems of knowledge crystallize by emphasizing the to-and-fro of experience and memory, the sensual differ-entiation of inside from outside, and how relations to the outer world are gradually built up by playful and intervening actions. Categories, orders, and systems of knowledge are for Lotze a result of experiences and modes of knowledge that are shaped at the periphery of the body. For this kind of experience he coins the term 'local signs' (1888, pp. 309, 586), signs that will later be known as 'engrams' in psychology.

Lotze is interested in the cognitive and sensory expansion of the actual body beyond its physical boundaries. This is why he deals with the human capacity for 'projection' into and empathy with nonhuman worlds of experi-ence. By this capacity, humans can, for example, project themselves into a bird's flight or into the close quarters of a mussel's existence, 'into the slender proportions of the tree whose twigs are animated by the pleasure of graceful bending and waving' (Lotze 1888, p. 585). Anticipating William James' 'panpsychism',[3] Lotze conceives of knowledge and action as situated in the body and its relations. The sense of touch thus serves the 'easy linking' (*leichte Verknüpfung*), that is, the synthesization of earlier experiences with current ones. In such instances, hand-eye coordination is of notable sig-nificance. Prototypical for this kind of action is the scientific experiment: 'While the one hand is grasping the object, the other examining it and changing its position so as to examine it further, our experimental knowledge is coming into being' (Lotze 1888, p. 587). Lotze attributes hand–eye coordination to the general tendency of humans towards 'eccentric projection'. 'Eccentric pro-jection' was an area of research that encompassed many heterogeneous issues in the middle of the nineteenth century. Lotze's teacher Ernst Heinrich Weber likely would have explicitly warned of inexactitude in this regard:

THINKING MEDIA AND BEYOND

Weber (1905, p. 12) wanted to theorize the processes of 'projection' and 'anticipation' (concurrent movement, phantom sensations, the development of a sense of space, time and number, formation of abstract concepts) as strictly different. But it was precisely the vague areas between physiological 'fact' and epistemological problem that made eccentric projection such an attractive area of research.

At a central point in his study *Tastsinn und Gemeingefühl*, Ernst Heinrich Weber addresses the phenomenon, that tactile sensation extends into things that do not belong to the sensing body. Weber investigates the phenomenon with help of small sticks attached to fingers and teeth, that is, by means of, somewhat unglamorous, extensions. Lotze adds to Weber's experiments with naturalistic observations. Lotze (1888, pp. 587–588) writes about a small stick operated by the hand that, with the help of the stick, one could feel something distant as if one were touching it immediately. He (Lotze 1888, p. 592) thus establishes an arsenal of figures for '[prolonging] our personal existence into the extremities and surfaces of [a] foreign body' that is still present today in phenomenology, Gestalt theory, and media theory: the blind person with his cane, the doctor with his probe, the writer with his quill, the painter with his brush. In Lotze's (1888, p. 589) understanding, co-sensation (*Mitempfindung*, usually translated as sympathy) is not always congenial empathy, but is also the sensual basis for acts of violence: Only those that can sense how a club feels on the back of one's neighbour, will feel an impulse to beat him with that club. Accordingly, when it comes to social functions Lotze describes teletactility as a liminal phenomenon. The co-apprehension of extra-bodily realities has communicative aspects. It is real because it has an effect but nevertheless remains ontologically dubious. Remote sensation and co-sensation are equally 'beneficial illusions' (Lotze 1888, p. 588), illusions that nevertheless facilitate purposeful action and sociality. Teletactility, co-sensation and eccentric projection are therefore metarational phenomena. As impossible as it is to determine whether a sensory perception 'really' occurs, the effects of such perceptions can be just as unequivocally observed.

Sensitive prostheses

I have given a relatively extensive account of Lotze because he serves as an extremely important point of reference for psychological research on prosthesis of the 1910s and 1920s. Prosthetics psychologists drew on his work to address practical problems in the construction of prostheses: How can the prosthetic be purposefully operated? How is a prosthesis to be constructed so that it can be integrated into a system of proprioception that has already been learned by patients? How can feedback between sensation, self-perception and movement be technically coordinated? How does self-perception change when an alien part is added to the body?

One of the most influential readers of Lotze was the pedagogue and later Gestalt psychologist David Katz, who conducted experiments with prostheses on disabled war soldiers starting in 1918. The transition in Katz's publication record from applied research referring to specific cases, to basic research, and ultimately to theoretical generalizations in Gestalt theory is exemplary. He published the first results on prosthetics in 1920 (*Psychologische Versuche mit Amputierten*) followed by a synopsis and theoretical explication in 1921 (*Zur Psychologie des Amputierten und seiner Prothese*). The experiments with patients with prostheses were again referred to in his 1925 book *Der Aufbau der Tastwelt* (The world of touch), notably in a chapter on 'Touching with intermediaries' (Katz 1989).

The question that Katz raises at the outset is pragmatic: How can one achieve a better fit between the prosthesis and the amputated body part? This question thus responded to a demand by the Ministry of War and the Ministry of Welfare to use prostheses to help veterans of war become fit for work and willing to function in civil society again. Katz criticized the previous focus in prosthetics on mechanical factors and demanded a 'sensitization of prostheses' (Katz 1921, p. 2). His concern with the sensitivity of prostheses is thus triggered by a desire for efficiency. The talk of 'animating the prosthesis', which sounds so peculiar today, was meant quite practically. 'Animation' implied the activation of sensory functions that had become inactive, functions that slumbered atop the 'pillow of the prosthesis' (Katz 1921, p. 2). For Katz, there are two paths that lead to 'animation' in practice. First, a better utilization of the remaining muscular system and of the sensibilities of the stump; second, the sensitization of the prosthesis itself, for instance by constructing the end of the stump out of thin-walled leather. Katz himself was also interested in the psychology of everyday life and claimed, following Lotze, that entirely normal perception is likewise 'prosthetic'. Katz changes sides from a clinical problem to prosthetics as a model subject of general psychology:

> The well-known psychological mechanism, according to which ... the sensitization [of the prosthesis] occurs, is that through which we expand, with the help of hand tools or even simply our articles of clothing, the sensory domain of our bodily ego mastered by us; just as the doctor uses a probe ... , as the blind man feels his way around the world with his stick or as we all perceive the texture of the ground on which we walk through the soles of our shoes. (Katz 1921, p. 7)

This passage is incisive since Lotze's examples are echoed almost verbatim. Notable in addition is the levelling of the difference between deficient and 'normal' perception. An amputee, a blind person, a doctor, and in the last instance, everyone, handles prostheses in order to expand their bodily ego.

THINKING MEDIA AND BEYOND

In his book *Aufbau der Tastwelt* (The world of touch), Katz takes a further step in the direction of a psychological interpretation of the technologically expanded body:

> Somewhat tongue-in-cheek, Lotze stated what significance our articles of clothing, which act according to this principle, have for expanding the space infused by our bodily self. In the age of the automobile and airplane, it is by the same principle of external projection that the automobile driver feels the goodness of the road via the tires, and the pilot feels the elasticity of the air via the wings of the airplane. (Katz 1989, p. 121)

On the basis of Lotze's less technology-based conception, Katz advances his way to the field that 22 years later will be known as cybernetics: the theory of feed-back-systems and control circuits, particularly those in which humans and machines interact purposefully. What was begun with the work on 'sensitive prostheses', transforms via a general theory of human perception into a metatheory of 'all' systems, whether organic or mechanic, animal or human.[4]

In the standard works on Gestalt theory that he writes from the 1940s on, Katz distances himself from cybernetics and moves closer to philosophical anthropology. However, his early publications make clear how a notion of tactility emerges out of research with amputees and prostheses, and in connection with Lotze's speculative anthropology. It is a notion similar to the one that Marshall McLuhan – who, as is well known, flirted with cybernetics, Gestalt theory, *and* physiology – will use: tactility as an 'inner' faculty that enables relations to the environment, as a faculty for the reaching out of thought and feeling to remote entities, as a faculty that completes and feeds back, and as one that both facilitates orientation in the world and encourages empathy. Conceived in this way, the sense of touch is paradoxically de-incarnated and incarnated at the same time: it is a corporeal faculty for making the non-corporeal present.

Optophonetics and eccentric sensation

In 1922, as DADA Berlin was in first bloom, Raoul Hausmann wrote *Optophonetik* (1982), a manifesto that propagates, among other things, the notion of 'eccentric sensation'. If the physiological concept of 'eccentric projection' was directed at the correspondences between inside and outside, 'eccentric sensation' in Hausmanns account addressed the internal sensory economy above all. Hausmann desired, like Marshall McLuhan would later, the technological reconstruction of a synesthetic 'primal state' in which sensory qualities are in a balanced relationship. This correlates with, even already in Hausmann's work, the phantasmagoric idea of a global 'expansion of sensory emanations'. This expansion is meant to revolutionize both an individual's perceptive abilities and social life, thereby bringing forth a sixth sense, namely 'eccentric sensation'. For Hausmann, the key to this groundbreaking revolution of perception in the 1920s was *Optophonetik* (Optophonetics), that is, the translation of acoustic signals into optic ones, and vice versa.[5] Hausmann invokes the bee as an example of optophonetic perception since a bee simultaneously sees and 'hears' with its eyes and utilizes its eyes as a sort of sonar, an acoustic scanner, for building the cells of its beehive.[6] In this phase of Hausmann's work, his concern with technical modifications of sense perception seems to follow two trajectories: experimental physiology in the tradition of Hermann von Helmholtz on the one hand, and a kind of 'prosthetic anthropology' whose goal is the media-technological improvement of organic equipment on the other hand.

Around the time that he was working on *Optophonetik*, Hausmann, who was an avid and wild reader, with the help of Solomo Friedländer/Mynona came across the today relatively unknown philosopher Ernst Marcus and his theory of the 'eccentricity of sensation'. Marcus' theory attempted to emphasize the Kantian postulate of the subjectivity of sense perception, but in Hausmanns reading also contains reflections on the internal economy of sense perception. Marcus posits that numerous sense perceptions are constantly mixed with the haptic sense. The mixing serves not only to synthesize and differentiate, like the sense of touch in Aristotle, but also to enhance perception. 'Eccentric sensation' interested Hausmann as a theory of originary synesthesia. It also interested him insofar as it theorizes a physiological organizational principle for thought immediately linked to sense perceptions, that is, as a physiological theory of the mind (*Geist*). In a much later text from the 1960s (*Eccentric Sensation* (*Exzentrische Empfindung*)), Hausmann still writes 'One can assume that the eccentric optic sensation actually resides in or has its source in the brain, where, like in an electrical station, the different signals that mediate the senses are transferred about' (1994, p. 37).

Yet, how do Hausmann's theory-montages fit with his artistic work? In the 1920s he developed methods of collage and montage that I will refer to as 'prosthetic mimicry': a parodic affirmation of what is both a technological-engineering and artistic programme of bodily and social change. This can identified in his collages and sculptures, for instance, in his 1920 collage *Tatlin zu Hause* depicting the constructivist Tatlin with grotesque, monstrous machine parts that protrude from his head. 'Prosthetic mimicry' plays with strategies of erred substitutions. Its undermining of reliable systems of reference was a strategy that was central for the Dadaists more generally. Playing with false substitutions and juxtaposing heterogeneous material was aimed more at interrupting perceptual automatisms than it was at a 'synthetic' expansion of the senses (Bexte 2011). Walter Benjamin's comparison of Dadaistic art to a 'bullet' gives a sense of the calculus of a violent impact that defined the aesthetic of the Dadaists. The exhibits and publications

THINKING MEDIA AND BEYOND

were thought of as attacks on the senses and aimed to tear the veil of normalized perception to pieces. The motif of the soldier who has been mangled by war, prosthetically repaired, and whose bodily boundaries have been violently perforated serves as an icon for the desire for a more intense, and sometimes even violent, impact on the audience. The expansion of sense perception demanded first of all the destruction of perceptual automatisms and the prosthesis figured as an iconic placeholder for the destroyed unity.

As indicated above, in 1969 Raoul Hausmann wrote a further manifesto on eccentric sensation. The text was written in French and published posthumously (1994) in German. Hausmann's view towards the issue of sensory expansion was divided, as I have suggested, in the 1920s between euphoria for a physiological-technological reworking of the sensory landscape on one hand, and an experience of the destructive character of technologies on the other. To be sure, Hausmann's text from the 1960s retains a concept of eccentric sensation as a socially revolutionary force, but aims at something very different.

First, one is struck by the much stronger sympathy for tactility and resonance phenomena, while the visual appears to be a sort of narcissistic, intellectual self-deception, a 'pseudologia phantasica'. The sense of touch on the other hand now guarantees an ultimately 'non-cognitive' understanding among living creatures. The model for such a mode of responsiveness is the cell, which has defined external boundaries and even in mitosis undertakes a concentration of its 'essence', yet maintains contact with the remaining organism by osmosis and motility, through resonance and touch. The haptic eccentric sensation is, according to Hausmann, intuitive just because it empathizes with the impressionability of what is touched. Second of all, *Die exzentrische Empfindung* is, in contrast to Hausmann's earlier writings, anti-technocratic: 'Humans have invented tools, weapons in order to enhance their somatic abilities; but to rest on their prostheses, whether electronic or for husbandry, means nothing else than to sink into intellectual and moral stagnations' (1994, p. 43). Hausmann is still concerned with revolutionizing perception, but not by means of technology. On the contrary, Hausmann offers an unequivocal judgment on the media-technological permeation of society in the section entitled 'Die neue Zivilisation': ' ... since the radio, electronics and the computer have channeled world-information, one disguises oneself everywhere in the same manner; and the proliferation of nuclear weapons increases the synchronization [*Gleichschaltung*] of imagination and thought' (1994, p. 47). The apparatuses make everything uniform and facilitate the 'shifting of self-responsibility onto the gods!!!' (Hausmann 1994, p. 45).

But if the expansion of sense perception, the somatic revolution, and the decentralization of the ego cannot be achieved technologically – nor can it be achieved through lysergic acid diethylamide (LSD), by the way, as

165

Hausmann makes clear – then how can it be achieved? On one hand, eccentric sensation will be able to be cultivated if language regains its haptic qualities. Hausmann prefers spoken, sung, and lyrical language, that is, language that 'touches' through sound waves to written prose: '[O]ne must feel the weight of the word. One must bow down under the heaviness of sound' (1994, p. 57). Like Marshall McLuhan, Hausmann aligns his hopes with the acoustic as a counterweight to the dominance of the optic. Hausmann's second solution also echoes with McLuhan's catholic undertones: 'Another form of eccentric sensation is love' (1994, p. 56). The solution is love because love combines sensual pleasure and a sense of responsibility for another person. Even when corporeal love represents an act of appropriation and subjugation, love qua eccentric sensation goes beyond that. For love is the 'renunciation of one's own I for the sake of YOU' (1994, p. 57).

Both of these things – the emphasis on the sensory qualities of language and the utopia of love – are limit-cases of communication, limit-cases of the social. Rather than 'pushing its way through' skin and flesh, the sense of touch comes into its own as the sensory quality that centers around vulner-ability and the fragility of commiseration. It remains a medium in a strict sense: an intermediary, a passageway, a capacity for differentiation. When it comes to tactile mediality it is rather not intensity or quality of the concrete touch that counts, but the ability to become eccentric, to allow oneself to be touched by something other/foreign. The self and the other do not col-lapse into one; they remain necessarily separated and differentiated. *Koine aisthesis* is not the common sense of an undifferentiated 'we', of an organic community; it can be understood as a twofold ability to differentiate: percep-tion that knows it is perceiving, differentiation that knows that it is differen-tiating, a commonality that knows that it (processually, via resonating) produces itself (Translated by Nathan Taylor).

Notes

1. Researchers grappled with this difficulty through, among other things, self-experimentation and a veritable training of their own sensory capacities and introspective competence. See Solhdju (2011).
2. Translators note: The subtitle of the English translation reads: 'An essay concern-ing man and his relation to the world.'
3. James draws on Lotze's work numerous times, in particular on the latter's concept of local signs and his reflections on synesthesia. See James (1950).
4. On the relationship between Gestalt theory and cybernetics, see Rieger (2003, p. 349f) and Bühler (2004, p. 86).
5. The idea is inspired by, among other things, Emil du Dubois-Reymond's exper-iments with transectioning and transposing nerve fibres to bring about the redirection of sensory impulses to incorrect processing centers (see Bexte 2011).
6. Later, Hausmann, with the help of an engineer, technologically thinks through optophonetics and puts it into practice. Though it is not quite clear how far

this practical engagement went, Hausmann was engaged in research on the conversion of light waves into acoustic waves with the help of selenium cells. These efforts resulted in an application for a patent that Daniel Broido, the brother of Hausmann's model at the time, Vera Broido, submitted in England. The patent was based not on an acoustic transducer but on a switch mechanism that uses selenium cells (see Borck 2010).

Disclosure statement

No potential conflict of interest was reported by the author.

Notes on contributor

Karin Harrasser is professor for cultural studies (Kulturwissenschaft) at the University of Art and Design Linz, Germany.

ORCID

Karin Harrasser ⓘ http://orcid.org/0000-0001-5591-9995

References

Aristotle, 1986. *De anima*. W.D. Ross, trans. Oxford: Oxford University Press.

Bexte, P., 2011. Mit den Augen hören/mit den Ohren Sehen. Raoul Hausmanns opto-phonetische Schnittmengen. *In*: H. Schramm, L. Schwarte, and J. Lazardzig, eds. *Spuren der Avantgarde: Theatrum anatomicum. Frühe Neuzeit und Moderne im Vergleich*. Berlin: de Gruyter, 426–441.

Borck, C., 2010. Sinnesmontagen: Die Sehprothese zwischen Ersatzapparat und Technovison. *In*: S. Flach and M. Vöhringer, eds. *Ultravision: Zum Wissenschaftsverständnis der Avantgarden*. Munich: Fink, 149–164.

Bühler, B., 2004. *Lebende Körper: Biologisches und anthropologisches Wissen bei Rilke, Döblin und Jünger*. Würzburg: Königshausen & Neumann.

Hausmann, R., 1982. Optophonetik. *In*: M. Erlhoff, ed. *Sieg Triumf Tabak mit Bohnen: Texte bis 1933*. vol. 2. Munich: Edition Text & Kritik, 41–45.

Hausmann, R., 1982/1994. *Die exzentrische Empfindung: La Sensorialité excentrique, mit Illustration von Raoul Hausmann*. Graz: Droschl.

Heller-Roazen, D., 2007. *The inner touch. Archaeology of a sensation*. New York: Zone Books.

James, W., 1890/1950. *The principles of psychology. vol. 1*. New York: Henry Holt & Co. (1890). (1950 unabridged reprint [vols 1 and 2 together], Mineola, New York: Dover Publications Inc.)

Katz, D., 1920. Psychologische Versuche mit Amputierten. *Zeitschrift für Psychologie und Physiologie der Sinnesorgane*, 85, 83–117.

Katz, D., 1921. *Zur Psychologie des Aputierten und seiner Prosthese*. Leipzig: J. A. Barth.

Katz, D., 1989. *The world of touch*. L.E. Krueger, trans. Hillsdale: Erlbaum.

Lotze, H., 1923. *Mikrokosmus: Ideen zur Naturgeschichte und Geschichte der Menscheit. Versuch einer Anthropologie (1853)*, 3 Vols. Leipzig: Meiner.

Lotze, H., 1888. *Microcosmus: an essay concerning man and his relation to the world*. Vol. 2. E. Hamilton and E.E.C. Jones, trans. Edinburgh: T&T Clark.

Rieger, S., 2003. *Kybernetische Anthropolgie. Eine Geschichte der Virtualität*. Frankfurt/Main: Suhrkamp.

Solhdju, K., 2011. *Selbstexperimente: Die Suche nach der Innenperspektive und ihre epistemologischen Folgen*. Munich: Fink.

Weber, E.H., 1846/1905. *Tastsinn und Gemeingefühl*. Leipzig: Engelmann.

Index

a priori 69
abgewinnen 35
Ablauf 33
actus purus 69–70
Adorno, Theodor W. 104–105
affective operations 46–47
affective powers 46–47
affective/affecting agents 46
Affizierung 74
Aletheia 112
alienation-effect 56
amalgamation of causes with effects 53–54
Amherst Typewriter & Computer 2–6, 14
anachoresis 63
Angerer, Marie Luise 60n1
Anima, De 92
Anordnungen 33
Anthropology, digitology 7
anthropomediality 59–60
Apocalyse-Cinema: 2012 and Other Ends of the World 27n21
Apollo 8 televised mission 17
Apollo 17 mission 17
Archaeology of Knowledge, The 136–138
Arendt, Hannah 33, 42n9
Aristotle 10, 83, 85, 92, 120, 156, 158
atmospheres 53
Aufbau der Tastwelt 163
Aufriss 123–124
Aufschreibesystem 16, 142
auslösend 34
Austin, John 120

Bach, Carl Phillip Emanuel 1
Bachelard, Gaston 98n7
Balke, Peder 72
becoming media 17–21
Begriff 102

Begriff 97n2
Begriffsgeschichte 97n2
belatedness 148–149; media studies 149–151
Benjamin, Walter 25n1, 102–105, 151, 152n5
Benveniste, Émile 114
bestimmten 32
Bexte, Peter 98n20
Bilderstatus 128n41
Binczek, Natalie 99n21
Birth of the Clinic, The 12
Blue Marble, The 17–19
Blumenberg, Hans 67
Böhme, Hartmut 42n15
Boscovich, Roger Joseph 90
Bourbaki, Nicolas 114
Brecht, Bertolt 56

Cage, John 8
Canguilhem, Georges 82
Carnap, Rudolf 79n2
Cassirer, Ernst 103
causa efficiens 85
causa finalis 85
causa formalis 85
causa materialis 85
chains of continuity 85–87
Chomsky, Noam 115
Civilization and its discontents 107
Clarke, Samuel 98n10
Claudel, Paul 64–65
clicks and leaps 143–146
Clock, The 30–42, 45–55; reflexive medium of affect-transformation 55–60
combining or separating by strengthening or weakening 47
communicating sticks 87–93
communication 82–83

INDEX

conditio humana 103
condition postmoderne, Le 64
conditiones sine quibus non 109–110
conditions of actuality 21–25
contagious aspect of the affective access 54
critical philosophies 21
Critique 109
cybernetic-amalgamating aspect of the affective access 54

Damisch, Hubert 98n11
Darstellung 32, 42n4
Das Medium ist die Botschaft. Anmerkungen zu Marshall McLuhan 113
De Anima 156–158
Deleuze, Gilles 34, 72, 77
'Der Körper des Denkens' 62, 79n5
Derrida, Jacques 84–85, 103, 106, 127n30, 148; *Writing and difference* 114–117
Descartes, René 48, 62, 82; versus Baruch Spinoza 73–75; communicating sticks 87–93; evidence of instant contact 93–95; exclusion of body and dislocation of thought 63–73; *Meditations on first philosophy* 64, 85; *Principia Philosophia* 85–86
de-tailer 4
deus malignus 85
dia versus meta 117–120
différance principle 114–117
Diogenes 126n6
Dioptrique 88–89, 92, 93
Discours de la Methode 89
discourse, locating medium in 102–105
Discourses on Salt and Iron 26n12
discreteness of time 143–144
discursive 14
dispositifs 20
Döring, Sabine 60n2
Draculas Vermächtnis 112
Dreyfus, Richard 71
dualistic theories 48
Dubois-Reymond, Emil du 166n5

Earthrise 17–18
eccentric sensation 163–166
economic critique 140–141
Eigensinnigkeit 39
Einstein, Carl 4
Engell, Lorenz 62, 79n5
environment 82

Enzensbergers, Hans Magnus 127n23
Epicurus 68
esotericism of knowledge 12
Ethics 74
evaluative-presentative aspect of the affective access and perception 54
evidence of instant contact 93–95
exclusion of body and dislocation of thought 63–65; radicalization 65–73
exemlary parts 4

feedback theory of affects 47–54
flache Formalismen (flat formalisms) 114
Flusser, Vilem 128n41
Foucault, Michel 11–13, 72, 138–140, 142, 152n4; *Archaeology of Knowledge, The* 136–138
Freud, Sigmund 107, 142, 147, 160
future event of the greatest possible threat 78

Gadamer, Hans-Georg 102
Galileo Galilei 18
Gegebenheitsweisen 72
Gehlen, Arnold 107, 160
Gemeingefühl 159
German media theory 16–17, 22–25, 26n15, 82, 132
Gestalt 74, 156
Görling, Lars 149–151
Grammophone, Film, Typewriter 112
Gramophone, Film, Typewriter 14
Guattari, Félix 77, 78
Guilbaud, Georges-Théodule 114
Guillory, John 97n1, 98n4

Hagner, Donald A. 98n15
Handlung 39
Hansen, Mark 60n1
haptic-tactile aspect of affective access 54
hard core of modern communication 6
Hartmann, Frank 62, 79n5
Haussman, Raoul 157, 164–166, 166n6
hedonistic colouring 51–52
Hegel, Georg Wilhelm Freidrich 103
Heidegger, Martin 1, 7, 9, 14, 19, 22, 25n7, 42n14, 103, 106, 111, 118
Heißenbüttel, Helmut 113
Heller, Agnes 60n2
Heller-Roazen, Daniel 158
Herder, Johann Gottfried 107
Hinüber- Setzen 116
Hinüber-Tragen 116

INDEX

Hoffman, E.T.A 142
Husserl, Edmund 68

*Ideen zur Naturgeschichte und Geschichte
der Menschheit* 159
Idhe, Don 128n43
indispensible conditions 109–110
information theory 111–114

James, William 160, 166n3
James, William, feedback theory of affects
47–54
Jensen, Theo 16
Jung, Carl 147

Kant, Immanuel 21, 57, 71, 109, 136, 151n1
Kapp, Hegelian Ernst 107
Katz, David 162–163
Keppler, Johannes 18
Kittler, Friedrich 14, 42n2, 108, 109, 112,
113, 126n11, 135, 142, 142–143
known invisibility of media 14
koine aisthesis 158
Köselitz, Heinrich 108–109
Koselleck, Reinhart 83
Kuleschow-experiment 54–55

Lacan, Jacques 14, 74, 75, 113
Latour, Bruno 33, 37, 42n9
Law, John 42n8
leaps and clicks 143–146
legitimacy of the modern age, The 67
Leibniz, Gottfried Wilhelm 98n10
locality of medial 105–108
Lotze, Hermann 159, 160–162
Lucan 64–65
Luhmann, Niklas 33, 39, 40
Lyotard, Jean-Francois 62, 63–64, 77–78;
technological wager 65–73

machina 77
machinic agencements 78
Machinic pleasures and interpellations
42n8
Mandelbrot, Benoit 112
Marclay, Christian, *Clock,
The* 30–42, 45–60
Marcus, Ernst 157
Marx, Karl 140–141
Massumi, Brian 60n1
mathemtical theory of communication, A 112
matière subtile 88–90, 90
McLuahn, Marshall 157

McLuhan, Marshall 8, 85, 98n18, 105, 107,
116, 123, 156, 163
media; becoming 17–21; conditions
of actuality 21–25; objects of
knowledge 134
media of immediacy 96–97
media theory, implicit theory of time
135–136
medial, performativity 120–122
medial a priori, passageways to 146–148
Meditationes 94
meditations of physics 83–85
Meditations on first philosophy 64, 85
medium 82; locating in cultural discourse
102–105
Mendelsohn, Moses 151n1
Merleau-Ponty, Maurice 160
meta versus dia 117–120
metapherein 116
metaxy 85
Mikrokosmus 160
milieu 82
Mission: Impossible 35–36
Mitarbeit 109
Molcan, Ted 26n20
moon landing 20
Music and language: a fragment 104

Nachträglichkeit 148
*Narrative Emotionen. Möglichkeiten
und Grenzen philosophischer
Emotionstheorien* 60n3
necessary mediatedness 105
Negative dialectics 104
Newton, Isaac 88, 98n10
Nietzsche, Friedrich 1, 7, 14, 107–111,
123–125
non-fulfilment of human relations 105

Öffentlichkeit 42n14
ontology, versus pragmatics 15
optophonetics 163–166
Optophonetik 164
Origin of the German tragedy 103–104
originären Ursprung 84
Other Night Sky, The 26n20

Paglen, Trevor 26n20
paradox of programmable hardware
142–143
pars pro toto 4
Paulo, Eustachius a Sancto 98n9
performativity of the medial 120–122

INDEX

Phaedrus 85
Philosophical investigations 106–107
Philosophie der Gefühle 60n2
physics, meditations 83–85
Plato 48, 85
Plessner, Helmuth 160
Poetry, language, thought 106
pragmatics, versus ontology 15
price of programmability 141–146
Principia Philosophia 85, 86, 98n5
principium contradictionis 114
programmable hardware, paradox 142–143
prosthesis 161–163
Psychoanalysis and cybernetics 113–114

question concerning technology, The 111

Regulae ad directionem ingenii 93
Rembrandt 13
res cogitans 65–66, 76, 79, 88
res extensa 67
Rheinberger, Josef 78
Rules for the Direction of the Mind 93

Schreber, Daniel Paul 142
Searle, John 120
sensations 52
Serres, Michel 8, 42n12
Shannon, Claude 8, 112
Siegert, Bernhard 25n8, 27n22
sinnförmig 31
spectrum of affectual phenomena 51–54
Spinoza, Baruch 62, 79n6, 105; versus René Descartes 73–75
Spitzer, Leo 82, 98n9
Strandbeests 16
Strawson, P. F. 109
structuralism 111–114
'sturcture of intersubjectivity' 20
sub specie aeternitatis 73
Szendy, Peter 27n21

Taktzeit 39
Tastsinn und Gemeingefühl 160–161
technological a priori 141–146
technological wager 65–73
teletactility 159–161

Theorie der Gefühle 60n2
third form 60
Tholen, Georg Christoph 108, 115–116, 127n25
threreness 6
transfer–transmission–transformation relationship 116
trauma 148–149
tubula rosa 64
Tulp, Nicolaes 13
Turing, Alan 143–146

Über- Setzung 118
Über-Setzung 116
Über-Tragung 103, 116
Umschlag 32
Umwelt 23–24
Understanding media 105, 113
Unter-Schiede 103
ursprüngliche (primordial) 103

Vermitteltheit 102
Ver-Wendungen 123–124
Vogl, Peter 97n2
Vom Take Off der Operatoren 112
von Berlichingen, Götz 157
Voss, Christiane 30, 32, 62, 79n5

Warburg, Aby 4
Was Mensch heißt, bestimmen keine Attribute 112
Weber, Ernst Heinrich 159–161, 160–161
Weber, Max 152n4
Weigel, Sigrid 42n9
weiter- oder zurückspielen 37
Wieder-Holung 115
Wilke, Tobias 98n20
Winthrop-Young, Geoffrey 25n8
Wittgenstein, Ludwig 106–107, 107, 108, 115, 126n9
Wohlers, Christian 98n12
Writing and difference 114–117

Zeitmesspunkte 40
Zittel, Claus 98n14
Žižek, Slavoj 58
Zurückholung 115